Ngũgĩ wa Thiong'o

Twayne's World Authors Series

African Literature

Bernth Lindfors, Editor

University of Texas at Austin

TWAS 890

NGŨGĨ WA THIONG'O

Photograph by Carrie Craig, courtesy of Heinemann's African Writers Series.

Ngũgĩ wa Thiong'o

Oliver Lovesey

Okanagan University College

Twayne Publishers
New York

Twayne's World Authors Series No. 890

Ngũgĩ wa Thiong'o
Oliver Lovesey

Twayne Publishers
1633 Broadway
New York, NY 10019

Library of Congress Cataloging-in-Publication Data

Lovesey, Oliver.
 Ngũgĩ wa Thiong'o / Oliver Lovesey.
  p. cm. — (Twayne's world authors series ; TWAS 890. African literature)
  Includes bibliographical references (p.) and index.
  ISBN 0-8057-1695-5 (alk. paper)
  1. Ngũgĩ wa Thiong'o, 1938—Criticism and interpretation. 2. Kenya—In literature. I. Title. II. Twayne's world authors series ; TWAS 890. III. Twayne's world authors series. African literature.

PR9381.9.N45 Z76 2000
823—dc21
                                                                99-050023

This paper meets the requirements of ANSI/NISO Z3948-1992 (Permanence of Paper).

10 9 8 7 6 5 4 3 2 1

Printed in the United States of America

For Marie Helena

Contents

Acknowledgment

Acknowledgment is made to Heinemann's African Writers Series for permission to use the photograph of Ngũgĩ wa Thiong'o by Carrie Craig.

Chronology

1961–1964   Writes articles for the *Sunday Post,* the *Daily Nation,* and the *Sunday Nation.*

1963   Kenyan independence, December 12.

1964   Enters Leeds University, England, on British Council scholarship, and begins dissertation on Caribbean literature. Publication of *Weep Not, Child.*

1965   Publishes *The River Between.*

1967   Publishes *A Grain of Wheat.* Begins teaching at University College, Nairobi.

1968   Debate in the English department about its future and its teaching and research focus.

1970   Publishes *This Time Tomorrow.*

1970–1971   Teaches in United States at Northwestern University as visiting associate professor.

1972   Publishes *Homecoming,* partly based on his unfinished Leeds University M.A. dissertation.

1973   Acting head, Department of Literature, University of Nairobi.

1975   Publishes *Secret Lives.*

1976   Begins work with the Kamīrīīthū Community Educational and Cultural Centre. *The Trial of Dedan Kimathi* performed at Kenya National Theatre, Nairobi.

1977   Changes name legally from "James Ngugi" to Ngūgī wa Thiong'o. *The Trial of Dedan Kimathi* performed at the Second World African and Black Festival of Arts and Culture (FESTAC 1977) in Lagos, Nigeria. Publishes *Petals of Blood. Ngaahika Ndeenda (I Will Marry When I Want)* performed at Kamīrīīthū, until on November 16, the performance license is withdrawn. Arrested on December 31 and detained.

1978   Writes *Caitaani Mūtharaba-inī (Devil on the Cross)* in prison. Released from detention on December 12 but denied resumption of work at the university.

1979   Victimized by political harassment but continues work to regain his position at the university.

1980   Publishes *Ngaahika Ndeenda* (trans. *I Will Marry When I Want*) and *Caitaani Mūtharaba-inī* (trans. *Devil on the Cross*).

1981   Publishes *Detained: A Writer's Prison Diary* and *Writers in Politics*.

1982   Performances of *Maitū Njugīra (Mother, Sing for Me)*. Total destruction of Kamīrīīthū's theater. *I Will Marry When I Want* and *Njamba Nene na Mbaathi ī Mathagu (Njamba Nene and the Flying Bus)* published. Learns of threatened imprisonment in Kenya. Exile begins.

1983   Publishes *Barrel of a Pen*.

1985–1986   Involved in filmmaking.

1986   Publishes *Matigari ma Njirūūngi (Matigari)* and *Decolonising the Mind*.

1987   Chairs Umoja, umbrella organization of Kenyan dissident groups.

1992   After years of teaching at Yale, Smith, and Amherst, becomes professor of performance studies and Erich Maria Remarque Professor of Comparative Literature at New York University.

1993   Publishes *Moving the Centre*. With Manthia Diawara, directs *Sembene: The Making of African Cinema*.

1994   Edits *Mūtiiri*, New York University–based Gīkūyū journal. A large international conference on his work is convened by Charles Cantalupo.

1996   Delivers Clarendon lectures at Oxford University.

1997   Publishes "revised and enlarged" edition of *Writers in Politics*.

1998   Publishes *Penpoints, Gunpoints, and Dreams*.

1999   Completing English translation of new Gīkūyū novel, tentatively titled *Murogi wa Kagoogo*.

Chapter One

Introduction: Kenyan History, Ngũgĩ's Life and Career, Ngũgĩ and Postcolonial Studies

With Chinua Achebe and Wole Soyinka, Ngũgĩ wa Thiong'o is one of the best-known African writers who emerged in Africa's independence and postindependence climate of the late 1950s and early 1960s. Much of Ngũgĩ's work conveys a sense of both the transcendent hope of independence and freedom, *uhuru,* and also the absolute despair that followed when this hope was compromised. Although he has not written an acknowledged masterpiece, a staple of college and university syllabi like Achebe's *Things Fall Apart,* or, like Soyinka, won the Nobel Prize for Literature, Ngũgĩ has inspired a generation of writers and is celebrated for his stand on political and linguistic issues. It has taken some years for postcolonial and cultural studies to catch up with his position in areas such as curriculum reform and the importance of African languages and orature. Whereas Ngũgĩ's popular reputation rests on his six novels, the first three written in a realistic mode and the last three in an allegorical mode, his place in the academic community rests increasingly on his six books of polemical essays. A close relationship exists between his theoretical and his novelistic work, and his novels often work out problems expounded in the essays. A highly versatile artist, Ngũgĩ is also a writer of plays, short stories, and children's stories, and he has published a diary. Some of his most evocative and powerful writing is autobiographical. Most recently he has been involved in film and video, and in performance studies, attracted by these media's ability to reach a wide African audience.

Ngũgĩ is passionate about the need for African writing to speak to Africans in African languages and in readily accessible forms. While in many respects his position is close to that expounded by Achebe in "The Novelist as Teacher,"[1] Ngũgĩ has always been alert to the ease with which the African teacher and intellectual may become assimilated into a Westernized elite and in turn be compromised in his or her relationship to the general public. Intellectuals and educators in Ngũgĩ's novels are often ambivalently portrayed: on the one hand, they extend the prospect of technological advancement and freedom from poverty, but on the other, they mimic non-African values, act on selfish motives, hesitate at moments demanding decisive action, and even passively support those who exploit the common people. This ambivalence about the intellectual's role is central to Ngũgĩ's work, and he has argued that the intellectual's position is not at the head but rather within the ranks of the "anti-imperialist cultural army."[2] Ngũgĩ's conflicted intellectuals indicate a persistent questioning of the role of the artist and a long-standing uneasiness with Western narrative forms such as the novel and of Westernized education in African society. Since the early 1970s, Ngũgĩ has been a vocal advocate of African languages and African narrative forms. He has put his commitment into practice by publishing novels in Gĩkũyũ, his mother tongue; by exploring the possibility of collective authorship in some of his plays; and by incorporating diverse narrative techniques in his novels to make them accessible to a largely illiterate peasantry that can experience his writing only by hearing it read aloud. He has also been forthright in presenting his political views and in criticizing his nation's government, at considerable personal cost. Just six months before his arrest in December 1977, he was asked by a Nairobi journalist if he feared repression for his writing, and he responded, "I have no such fears because I do believe that criticism of our social institutions and structure is a very healthy thing."[3] Being a social critic, he asserted, is the writer's "duty."

Ngũgĩ's work is anchored in a concern for common people, especially the Gĩkũyũ people of Kenya, and for the land, which holds profound spiritual importance. In a memoir of a visit to Tanzania to research a film, Ngũgĩ writes movingly of the geography of East Africa, which for him bears the imprint of a human form:

> A line drawing of a map of the physical features of Kenya, Uganda and Tanzania looks to me like a sketch of a bust of a human head wearing a slightly flat muslim cap whose slightly flattened top is the long border with Ethiopia. The neck rests on the Ruvuma river to the south. The back is formed by the tiny folds of the coastline on the Indian Ocean. The face is the line of lakes to the west from Malawi to Albert with Lake Tanganyika and Kivu making the outline of the chin and mouth. Lakes Edward and Albert form a retreating forehead. This strong human shaped head is facing into the heart and belly of the continent.[4]

This spectacular natural beauty, Ngũgĩ continues, "dominates the East African literary imagination" (*Moving*, 163).

It is outside Kenya, however, that most of Ngũgĩ's novels have been written. Ngũgĩ is one of those writers who reenvision their homeland when they go abroad. *The River Between* and *Weep Not, Child* were composed in Uganda; *A Grain of Wheat* was written in England, and *Petals of Blood* in England, America, the Soviet Union, and Kenya. *Matigari ma Njirũũngi (Matigari)* was written in England. *Caitaani Mũtharaba-inĩ (Devil on the Cross)* was produced in Ngũgĩ's homeland, but within the walls of a maximum-security prison. The location of the act of writing may account in part for the fondness for home, and the anguish of exile and return, so prevalent in his fiction. Ngũgĩ's home area, Kenya's Gĩkũyũ highlands, is one of the most beautiful in the world, and his appreciation of this landscape was heightened just before his detention by a long drive he took through the region. Poised on the edge of the Great Rift Valley, this area, with its dry, warm climate and fertile soil, though subject to sudden drought, was immediately attractive to potential European settlers in the early twentieth century. When Ngũgĩ was a child, Kenya had become a settler colony of England, and the ancestral lands of his people had been taken over. In 1967 Ngũgĩ signed a contract with Heinemann for a book on settler life in colonial Kenya, to be entitled "A Colonial Affair," but he could not complete the project, finding himself unable to locate the correct tone, suspecting that his subject lacked any genuine "culture," and angered that this historical colonial aberration was still very much alive in postindependence Kenya. Ngũgĩ does address settler culture in a number of his essays, and most extensively in *Detained*,[5] and he has an intense loathing for the racist portrayal of Africans in the work of colonial writers such as Isak Dinesen (Karen Blixen), exceeded only by his animosity toward the tacit endorsement of such portrayals by the cultural policies of the postindependence authorities in Kenya.

In the West, popular images of the geography of Ngũgĩ's novels, reproduced in movies and television programs, display an achingly beautiful never-never land, remote from the anxiety and chaos of European cities, where the Western individual may arrive at self-realization. This sensual landscape sometimes provides the backdrop for the melodrama and lurid sexual excess in the lives of bored, rich settlers in the 1930s and 1940s—members of the Happy Valley set. This geography also surrounds pious missionaries, even from the world of basketball, who scout and train malleable Africans in the wonders of hoop magic and six-figure contracts, and who even, in their spare time, solve local "tribal" squabbles. Other stereotypical images of Ngūgī's homeland glorify an Eden of teeming, myriad wildlife, including monstrous, demonic, man-eating lions—mythic recastings of the historical Tsavo incident. In these images, Kenya is a setting for the performance of the Westerner's angst or awakening self-awareness, and Africa is the "dark continent,"[6] a site of human prehistory, or a geographic tabula rasa devoid of recognizably human culture. In such representations, Africans are as much background as Mount Kenya. They become invisible, or merely part of an exotic "human zoo." They are inscrutable and demonic, or merely child-like and easily manipulated. In his novels, Ngūgī writes against such Western stereotypes.

Kenyan History

The story that lies behind much of Ngūgī's writing is one of dispossession and the struggle for justice and restitution. The theft of Kenyan land by the British, particularly after World War II, and the attempt to reclaim it in the 1950s, which led indirectly to Kenyan independence and then to the later disillusionment with the results of this independence, belong to Ngūgī's story. Although, unlike Achebe in *Things Fall Apart*, Ngūgī has not attempted a fictional re-creation of Gīkūyū life before first contact with outsiders, his work's historical grounding, which may have been influenced by Achebe,[7] lies in the destructiveness of contact with the British. Narratives of European contact begin with long-standing links along the coast of present-day Kenya between Arab and Portuguese sailors. Until the nineteenth century, however, most of Kenya was a blank space on the map of English exploration,[8] the uncharted land between Mombasa and Lake Victoria. By the end of Queen Victoria's reign, what we know as Kenya was being "transformed from a footpath 1,000 km (600 miles) long into a colonial administration."[9]

Britain's colonization of Kenya was an outgrowth of imperial expansion in the area in the later nineteenth century, often referred to as the Scramble for Africa, the attempt to forestall German expansion in the district, and the search for the sources of the Nile. British missionary and antislavery sentiments and commercial enthusiasm for ready access to the promised riches of Uganda led to discussions about East African free-trade zones and the military establishment of political influence. There was even widespread media fascination. For example, Henry Morton Stanley's famous mission to "find" the explorer Dr. Livingstone (who was never really lost) was funded by the *New York Herald*. The *Herald* and London's *Daily Telegraph* financed later expeditions, and Stanley's carefully crafted dispatches in the popular press and his extravagant "multimedia" books of exploration made him an international celebrity.[10] With the appetite for carving out spheres of interest in the area and the subsequent territorial acquisition of vast tracts of land at the Berlin Conference of 1884 to 1885 came a mania to define boundaries and create maps. In this climate, the British East African Association was created, emphasizing the first part of Livingstone's rallying cry, "Commerce and Christianity." The British kept the cost-effectiveness of empire ever in mind, initially allowing a chartered company, the Imperial British East Africa Company, to rule the region. A protectorate was proclaimed only in 1895 after the balance of potential costs and revenues of other suggested private schemes had been weighed. Before this period, the fertile agricultural lands of the Gĩkũyũ had been largely protected from European influence by the power of the sultan of Zanzibar, the hostility of local populations as a result of the historic threat of slave raiders, and the dread of the military prowess of the Gĩkũyũ's pastoral neighbors, the Masai. With the Masai's military stature declining at the turn of the century owing to the effects of civil war, the devastation of smallpox and rinderpest (Lonsdale, 22–23, 51), and the growing appetite for global imperial expansion, even this barrier to foreign incursion began to collapse.

Accounts of travelers, adventurers, and explorers in the region at this time invoke the dread of dangerous, warring tribesmen in the interior. Joseph Thomson, exploring the region in 1883 for the Royal Geographic Society, wrote in *Through Masailand* that the Gĩkũyũ were "murderous and thievish."[11] The self-proclaimed "king of the Kikuyu," John Boyes, labeled the Gĩkũyũ "fickle and treacherous."[12] Thomson and Boyes recount similar tales of using Eno, a bubbling antacid drink, to amaze the locals, who the authors claim saw it as a medicine to produce white children or as magically boiling water that only the powerful white medicine man could consume without harm. Such tales rapidly became a type of white mythology confirming the naïveté and innocence of indigenous peoples and affirming the coolness of the European facing the hazards of deepest, darkest Africa. John Boyes, however, was a highly suspect figure even to the British authorities and was nicknamed "Who eats beans" by some of his Gĩkũyũ "subjects," a possible reference to his facility at producing verbal as well as intestinal gas (Boyes, 126).

The prospect of an ascent of Mount Kenya, the sacred mountain of the Gīkūyū,[13] lured to Gīkūyūland the geographer Halford John Mackinder, whose access to the interior was greatly aided by the building of the new Mombasa to Lake Victoria railway. In his diary of 1899, the publication of which may have been suppressed to cover up the extrajudicial "execution," or murder, of eight porters during his expedition,[14] Mackinder repeatedly notes parallels between the territory of the Gīkūyū and England's green and pleasant land, though he also compares the Gīkūyū themselves to animals. Gīkūyū country, with its fertile red soil, is for him an Edenic "rough apple orchard" (Mackinder, 116), though at the time of his expedition, the land was in the grip of a drought that caused widespread famine. The latter is referred to by Ngūgī in *Petals of Blood* as "the famine of England."[15] Mackinder is happy he has had the foresight to have porters carry a large assortment of British canned food, justified by his maxim: "On safari it is all-important to provide cheerful encouragement in times of discouragement" (Mackinder, 33); he wards off morbid thoughts when facing possible starvation or a "native" attack by reading Charles Dickens's *The Old Curiosity Shop*. Dealing with his porters, however, he placed greater reliance on "the moral suasion of my Mauser" rifle (159). Mackinder's successful ascent of Mount Kenya contributed to the vogue for adventure tourism in British East Africa and the perception of the region, referred to since 1920 as Kenya, as a boundless European playground. In his account, we can perceive an untroubled myopia regarding the history and culture of a people and a place, a conscienceless willingness to appropriate land, and a ready resort to violence.

Some of those who came to East Africa for adventure returned after the turn of the century to settle in the highlands of Kenya for the life of a self-fashioned landed gentry. Theodore Roosevelt was one of those fired with enthusiasm at the prospect of transforming this area, seemingly so geographically similar to Europe, into white man's country. Cecil Rhodes had dreamed of a continuous sphere of British influence extending from the Cape to the Nile, believing that raw, young Englishmen would readily carve out such a corridor of power, lured by the promise of "gunpowder and glory." Certainly the prospect of vast tracts of fertile land, with a railway to the coast, assurances of a passive African population who would provide cheap labor, and land deals made particularly generous to offset the competition from Canada, Australia, and New Zealand swelled the approximately 12 European farms in Gīkūyū territory at the turn of the century to a total European population of about 3,000 in Kenya by 1914, and 9,000 by 1919.[16] Although the government of Kenya Colony, created in 1920, was mandated to protect the interests of the indigenous population, the settlers were anxious to assert their own exclusive rights as landowners and taxpayers. They also wanted to maintain the large reserve of cheap African labor for their increasingly lucrative plantation crops, from European vegetables to coffee and tea, and by 1930 pyrethrum, a type of chrysanthemum.

Partly to impel Africans to labor on European farms (located on land appropriated from Africans), a hut tax was introduced at the turn of the century, and paramount chiefs were installed in disregard of traditional familial and clan social structures to collect it. Grievances over taxes, labor, and land led to the formation of African associations that evolved into nationalist associations. The Gīkūyū, for example, had a system of agriculture that entailed land rotation, and they had different notions of land tenure and ownership from those of the Europeans. For the Gīkūyū, land was a common inheritance and could not be bought or sold, as Ngūgī explains in *A Grain of Wheat*.[17] Instead of being temporary tenants, as the Gīkūyū regarded them, the Europeans believed that they had absolute rights over the land, and the settlers soon banded together even against the colonial government for what they saw as protection of their interests, which meant dominance over the African population. The settler response to Gīkūyū grievances was a denial that their lands had ever been farmed by the Gīkūyū, though even early European visitors had noted how intensively the Gīkūyū cultivated their land. The settlers also had recourse to the old rhetoric of the European's "civilizing" mission in the area. Different perceptions of land tenure and ownership had contributed to the influx of white settlers, as had the decimation of the Gīkūyū by smallpox, drought, and famine, which had also afflicted the Masai. Furthermore, the historic animosities between rival national groups, such as the Gīkūyū and the Masai, and the Gīkūyū's own internal rivalries between various groups on different ridges, examined by Ngūgī in *The River Between*, were fully exploited by the Europeans. For some settlers, the solution to the "native problem" was clear. At the turn of the century, Frank Hall, who would later be a district commissioner, wrote of the difficulty of an attempt to "exterminate" the Masai and conducted a number of punitive expeditions against the Gīkūyū, wiping out whole villages.[18]

The Mau Mau insurrection during which Ngūgī was raised and which provides in many ways the starting point of his fiction was the final explosion of many decades of accumulated grievances. Expropriation of

land, virtually enforced labor, and the levying of taxes without representation were causes of bitterness, exacerbated by prohibitions against raising certain lucrative cash crops such as coffee, the enforcement of
apartheid-like laws entailing the carrying of pass cards, wage discrimina-
tion based on race, and the at best patronizing and paternalistic attitude
of some Europeans. Kenyans who had served the British as carriers in
World War I and as soldiers in World War II returned home with a developing sense of national identity, with a sharper understanding of their
overlords' vulnerable humanity, and after 1945 with skills in modern
warfare. To the weight of lost land, taxation, and general dissatisfaction,
moreover, was added the burden of unemployment, especially among the
increasing numbers migrating from impoverished rural areas to the city
of Nairobi, the new center for the poor and dispossessed, as the unemployed ex-soldier Boro does in *Weep Not, Child*. A rapidly growing population further exacerbated the effects of unemployment, even among
those educated in mission schools and later in independent schools. To
the unemployed's bitterness and frustration was added a further source of
injury. Those who had sacrificed so much for their colonial masters and
bristled under an unfulfilled sense of entitlement were outraged when,
after the wars, they saw waves of European settlers taking the lands of
African families. For the unemployed, this insult reconfirmed a growing
impatience with the glacial pace of ameliorative change. At this time,
aware of the climate of political dissatisfaction in his homeland, Jomo
Kenyatta, who would be the first prime minister of independent Kenya,
returned from study at London University, where he had written an
anthropological study of the Gĩkũyũ, *Facing Mount Kenya*. Formerly
active in the Kikuyu Central Association (KCA) and the Independent
Schools Association, in 1946 Kenyatta became president of the Kenya
African National Union and principal of Githunguri Training College.
For Kenyatta, as for the young Ngũgĩ, national political aspirations were
tied directly to the importance of formal education. Although by 1948
there were four African members in the colonial governor's legislative
council, references to Mau Mau were already appearing.

The term "Mau Mau," by which the movement is now generally
known, is of questionable and bewildering origin.[19] A film documentary
entitled *Mau Mau,* including interviews with former Mau Mau fighters
such as Karari Njama, argues that the movement was largely a creation
of hostile settler forces, and that armed resistance was organized only
after the settlers created the myth of an African secret society and this
myth was given official support by the British government.[20] The more

formal name for the movement's military wing was the Kenya Land and Freedom Army (KLFA), and the KLFA and Dedan Kimathi, one of its main leaders, in his 1953 Mau Mau Charter, disdained the term "Mau Mau."[21] J. M. Kariuki, in *"Mau Mau" Detainee,* identifies "Mau Mau" as a term of abuse, a children's phrase, though possibly also an anagram of warning.[22] Donald L. Barnett and Karari Njama, in *Mau Mau from Within,* support these possible interpretations, though further suggesting that the term may refer to the practice of oathing or even to greed in overeating.[23] In his foreword to Robert Buijtenhuijs's *Mau Mau: Twenty Years After, the Myth and the Survivors,* the historian Ali A. Mazrui adds to these suggestions the idea that the initials of "Mau Mau," when reversed, spell out "Underground African Movement," and that the sound of the phrase echoes that made by a black cat at night, or even that it may be a corruption of Mao Tse-tung.[24] The clearest conclusion to be drawn from such a bewilderment of differing interpretations is that the term's origin is obscure, and that, although the leadership disliked it, "Mau Mau" has stuck and is now employed by former members of the movement.

The Mau Mau period in Kenya is still hotly contested. Controversial aspects include the movement's composition, its leaders' ideological grounding and cohesion, its reliance on spiritual ritual and guidance, its similarity to other popular historic uprisings, and most importantly its role in bringing about independence. Interpretation of the movement and the strategic use of such interpretation as a weapon of war began well before the movement ended. The potent legacy of the struggle between Mau Mau and colonialism continues to be fought over by various camps of historians, politicians, and cultural intellectuals. Even Ngũgĩ's own position has undergone a dramatic shift.[25] A pro-colonial interpretation of Mau Mau had dominated in Kenya's school history texts, at least until the mid-1970s,[26] and this is an interpretation Ngũgĩ has contested in his *Njamba Nene* series of children's stories. Research on the period, however, is hampered by the covert nature of the movement, the illiteracy of many participants, the pervasiveness of colonial propaganda, and the fact that in Kenya today Mau Mau historiography remains highly politically sensitive. Wunyabari O. Maloba, in a generally thorough and balanced study that concludes with a plea for further analysis, argues that while Mau Mau was a "nationalist, anticolonial, peasant movement,"[27] motivated by economic distress, it lacked a unified political ideology or an "intellectual revolutionary cadre" (Maloba, 16).[28] Although Barnett and Njama stress the predominance of illiterate peasants in the active forces and trace a critical internal schism between Stanley Mathenge and Dedan Kimathi to the clash between illiterates and literates, Kimathi himself was clearly a rebel intellectual, maintaining an archive (sealed until 2013) and forging international links, though he has never been afforded the status of a Che Guevara, Mao Tse-tung, or Amílcar Cabral.

Ngũgĩ has sought to garner recognition for Kimathi's heroic role, to downplay the significance of Kenyatta, and to emphasize the importance of the oral history of Mau Mau and of oathing. Maloba criticizes Ngũgĩ for interpreting Kimathi and the KLFA as socialist (Maloba, 173–74).[29] *The Trial of Dedan Kimathi,* Maloba argues, lacks "any historical evidence" (174). He overlooks, however, the similarities between the play's handling of Kimathi's trial of his brother and its treatment in Barnett and Njama's *Mau Mau from Within* (379–80). Maloba, moreover, clearly discounts references in the play's preface to the gathering of the oral record, something he admits is lacking in his own study, which demonstrates a general distrust of oral sources, of such importance in establishing the history of a popular movement composed largely of illiterate peasants. Maloba offers a detailed account of the sexual and spiritual elements of various oathing ceremonies, unleashing the power of violated taboos (98–113), though he admits his evidence is based partly on material elicited through torture by colonial authorities, a factor that understandably leads J. M. Kariuki to discount the existence of so-called "advanced oaths" (Kariuki, 52–73). In *Weep Not, Child,* Ngũgĩ acknowledges certain elders' discomfort about the inappropriate use of traditional ritual and especially oathing by the young. Elsewhere, however, writing of oathing's justification, he echoes Chairman Mao's famous dictum: a revolution is not a dinner party.[30] Colonial and neocolonial historians seized on the oathing rituals to confirm the nature of an organization that they regarded as a criminal, culturally atavistic, demonic, communist secret society that had no legitimate grievance but sought Gĩkũyũ supremacy and might even be a manifestation of mass hysteria (see Rosberg and Nottingham, 320–47).

The Mau Mau movement began as an organized drive for land and freedom, as its formal name indicates, advocating the necessity of violence as the only effective means to achieve its goals. By 1952, it became an underground organization, and on October 20, 1952, the new colonial governor of Kenya, Sir Evelyn Baring, declared a state of emergency, allowing detention without trial and an increased number of capital offenses, one being for the administration of oaths. Jomo Kenyatta was detained, tried, and convicted of managing the movement, though the prosecution witnesses were well rewarded for their testimony, and the principal witness later recanted (Trench, 235–37). The armed struggle moved to the Aberdares and Mount Kenya, where the movement was organized in cells, a more effective strategy for a flexible guerrilla war, the last resort of the downtrodden and dispossessed. To cut off support for the fighters in the forests, the colonial authorities inaugurated a scorched-earth policy at the forest edge and initiated "villagization," whereby Gĩkũyũ were placed in fenced and moated compounds (217–67). Following the capture and confession of the Mount Kenya military leader "General China" (Itote, 161–99; Odinga, 118), in 1954 Operation Anvil rounded up tens of thousands of supposed Mau Mau members and sympathizers in Nairobi, one of the main bases of support. The prisoners were detained in camps, in brutal conditions that attracted attention in the British press. Colonial troops were rewarded in cash for each Mau Mau suspect killed, and corpses were put on public display. There was some Gĩkũyũ resistance to Mau Mau among Christian groups and the educated, and among elderly Gĩkũyũ who were suspicious of false traditionalism. The active military operation of the movement largely ended in 1956 with the capture, trial, and execution of Field Marshal Dedan Kimathi. Statistics of the precise number of Europeans and Africans killed in the conflict vary enormously; however, probably fewer than 100 Europeans (who made up only about 1 percent of the population), but more than 10,000 Africans, lost their lives. The state of emergency ended in February 1960.

The late 1950s and early 1960s saw some redistribution and consolidation of tiny parcels of Gĩkũyũ land—collectively known as the Million-Acre Settlement Scheme—and other colonial efforts to settle African grievances. These measures may have been contrived to placate the new African middle class and may have succeeded in dividing Kenyans at independence more sharply along class lines.[31] The road to a new Kenya was cleared by the declaration of independence in Ghana in 1957, and after the Lancaster House conference in 1962, Kenya became independent on December 12, 1963. A year later, the country was declared a republic, with Jomo Kenyatta the president of a virtual one-party state. Kenyatta reiterated his presumed desire to work for reconciliation between the previously warring groups. After independence, Kenyatta was visited by Sir Evelyn Baring, governor of Kenya during the Mau Mau period, and Baring mentioned signing the order for Kenyatta's detention on the president's table. Kenyatta replied: "In your shoes, at that time, I'd have done exactly the same. And I've signed a good few Detention Orders on it myself" (Trench, 236). Kenyatta's response has a resonance for Ngũgĩ's career, because it was Kenyatta's successor as president, Daniel arap Moi, who signed Ngũgĩ's own detention order in 1977 when Moi was minister for home affairs, though that was a number of years after the first flowering of the promise of independence. In the years just after 1963, many settler farms were bought by Kenyans, often government ministers or individuals who had been loyal to the colonial authorities, and a new elite was rapidly being created. In 1978 Kenyatta died, and Ngũgĩ, who had protested against the social disintegration Kenyatta fostered, was released. Kenyatta's successor has become Ngũgĩ's nemesis, and his regime has so threatened Ngũgĩ that he has lived in exile for nearly two decades. Ngũgĩ was released in a group of 16 political detainees that included three former members of Parliament, one of whom, Wasonga Sijeyo, had been in detention since 1969. President Moi announced the "amnesty" on the 15th anniversary of Kenyan independence, though the detention legislation, the Preservation of Public Security Act, remained in force; and in a speech marking the occasion, Moi reiterated his willingness to enact the law to preserve "peace, unity and stability."[32]

Ngũgĩ has witnessed many of the tumultuous events in his nation's history, and his writing reflects the despair of the colonial years and the brutal attempt to crush the Mau Mau resistance movement, the enormous promise at the dawn of independence, and the growing disillusionment as it seemed that little was changing in the succeeding years and that domestic corruption and exploitation were replacing colonial oppression. This period, which for Ngũgĩ still continues (save that it is increasingly characterized by the aggressive involvement of multinational corporations), is neocolonial: colonial structures remain in place though the operators have changed. Such a historical trajectory could not have been anticipated at the time of Ngũgĩ's birth.

Ngũgĩ's Life and Career

Ngũgĩ was born on January 5, 1938, in Kamĩrĩĩthũ, Limuru. His mother was the third of his father's four wives, and Ngũgĩ was one of 27 brothers and sisters.[33] He attended both independent Gĩkũyũ and Christian mission primary schools. During the Mau Mau struggle, his stepbrother was shot and killed, and in 1954 his elder brother joined the Mau Mau fighters in the forest. Owing to her son's participation in the struggle, Ngũgĩ's mother was tortured at a Home Guard post. Amid this turmoil, Ngũgĩ entered Alliance High School in 1955, one of the best mission schools in the country, where he was warned by the headmaster not to become a political agitator. For a brief period, Ngũgĩ became a devout Christian. A sense of guilt about his enjoyment of comfortable school life in this time of familial and national crisis informs some of Ngũgĩ's early fiction. His brother wrote from the forest, however, encouraging Ngũgĩ to focus on his education. His interest in politics and Christianity developed further, and he began writing fiction and reading widely, especially the novels of Charles Dickens, Robert Louis Stevenson, and Leo Tolstoy, in addition to popular thrillers. Ngũgĩ returned from school to find his home and village wiped out and his family relocated, part of the colonial government's "villagization" policy. This alienating homecoming was one of the landmark experiences of Ngũgĩ's life.

After a brief stint as a primary school teacher, Ngũgĩ entered Makerere University College in Uganda, and he began to read extensively in African and Caribbean literature, though his special subject for his B.A. was Joseph Conrad, with a focus on *Nostromo*. He continued to write short stories and plays. It was an exciting and fertile period for Ngũgĩ, though as Peter Nazareth, Ngũgĩ's near contemporary at Makerere, recalled: "There was a heavy colonial pall over the place."[34] In 1961 he wrote "The Black Messiah," which was revised and published as *The River Between* four years later. He began to write columns for a variety of Nairobi newspapers.[35] In 1962 he wrote *Weep Not, Child,* and his play *The Black Hermit* was performed in Kampala in the Ugandan independence celebrations and published by Makerere University Press. He entered Leeds University in England, researching Caribbean literature and especially the writing of George Lamming. As he explains in the preface to *Secret Lives,* Ngũgĩ found himself unable to grapple in fiction with the Brontë landscape around Leeds. Peter Nazareth, who was also studying at the university during the same period, recalls the Leeds experience for African students as intellectually challenging, due in part to a shared interest in the work of Frantz Fanon, but personally demoralizing. Nazareth's own personal situation was different from Ngũgĩ's, but his response to Leeds may give some indication of Ngũgĩ's experience there:

> Deep disillusionment. The first big shock was when I got to Leeds. I had never really imagined an industrial city like that. I'd read about it in

Lawrence and Dickens but could not imagine an England as nasty as that. Colonialism had persuaded us that England was a perfect place, a developed country where everybody was happy, had perfect knowledge, had good houses. . . . Otherwise, how were they ruling us? When I got there, it was a real shock to see Leeds. The buildings looked like giant cockroach shells. People used to say that Leeds was a place where you woke up to the sound of birds coughing. The city hall was completely blackened with soot. Before I left, they were cleaning it up so there was this very black building guarded by white lions. Symbolic, perhaps. (Nazareth, 88)

Whatever his personal feelings about his residence within the former colonial power, Ngūgī was very productive. Although his Leeds University project on Caribbean literature was never completed, he did publish some essays from it in his collection *Homecoming*. He also wrote *A Grain of Wheat*, though he was already becoming somewhat disenchanted with writing novels in English, a language that few of his fellow Kenyans would be able to read. He began to be deeply influenced by the writings of Frantz Fanon, Karl Marx, and Friedrich Engels. Engels had deplored the squalor of industrial Manchester in the 1840s in *The Condition of the Working Class in England*, published when he was just 24. The similarly youthful and resourceful Ngūgī published *Weep Not, Child* in 1964, *The River Between* in 1965, and *A Grain of Wheat* in 1967.

In 1967 Ngūgī joined the English Department of University College, Nairobi, its first African faculty member, and in 1973 he became its first African head of department. During his years at Nairobi, the department structure and curriculum were revised to focus on African languages and literatures. In these years, Ngūgī gave a variety of lectures throughout Africa and around the world, some of them included in *Homecoming*, published in 1972. In 1970, *This Time Tomorrow*, a collection of plays, was published, his last book to appear under the name "James Ngugi," though he did not change his name legally until 1977. In 1976 he completed *Petals of Blood*, his longest novel, at the Yalta guest house of the Soviet Writers Union and began work with the Kamīrīīthū Community Educational and Cultural Centre, where parts of his play, *The Trial of Dedan Kimathi*, cowritten by Mīcere Gīthae Mūgo, were performed. With Ngūgī wa Mīrii, and based on the lived experience of the Centre's participants, he wrote *Ngaahika Ndeenda (I Will Marry When I Want)*, which was a great success. In December 1977, Daniel arap Moi, Kenyan vice president and minister for home affairs, signed Ngūgī's detention order, and he was imprisoned without charge or trial in Kamītī Maximum Security Prison.

Detention was a devastating and also a transforming experience for Ngũgĩ, who began writing *Caitaani Mũtharaba-inĩ (Devil on the Cross)* in Gĩkũyũ on the prison's rough toilet paper; but upon his release, he was denied further employment at the University of Nairobi, and he was briefly imprisoned again in 1981 and also in 1982, the year now-president Moi declared Kenya a one-party state. In 1980 *Ngaahika Ndeenda* and *Caitaani Mũtharaba-inĩ* were published; *Detained,* an account of his prison experience including a diary, and *Writers in Politics* were also published. The Nairobi production of Ngũgĩ's collectively authored play *Maitũ Njugĩra (Mother, Sing for Me)* was suppressed by the government. This period of intense creativity and repression culminated in the 1983 publication of *Barrel of a Pen,* a collection of essays focused on the increasingly hostile political atmosphere in the country.

Living in exile in London since 1982, Ngũgĩ has worked for the release of political prisoners in Kenya. In 1986 rumors circulated in Kenya about Ngũgĩ's involvement with the radical political group Mwakenya. *Matigari ma Njirũũngi (Matigari)* and *Decolonising the Mind* were published. In 1987 Ngũgĩ chaired Umoja, an umbrella group of radical Kenyan organizations. *The African Communist* reported in the following year the formation of Umoja Wa Kupigania Democrasia Kenya (United Movement for Democracy in Kenya) at a meeting in London on October 20, 1987. The report included excerpts from a statement read by Ngũgĩ: "Umoja, which now brings together the resistance abroad under one umbrella, is an anti-imperialist organisation wholly committed to the restoration of our national sovereignty, the building of a truly democratic Kenya and the restructuring of the economy for the social progress of the Kenyan people. Umoja is not a new party but a support movement for the struggle at home."[36] Ngũgĩ continued to unite his political and literary commitments.

Although Ngũgĩ has not published any fiction since *Matigari,* he has issued revised editions of some of his earlier work, and he continues to lecture and to publish collections of essays. In 1993 *Moving the Centre* and in 1998 *Penpoints, Gunpoints, and Dreams* appeared, the latter a series of lectures delivered at Oxford University in 1996. His interest in film, begun in the mid-eighties, has developed, and with Manthia Diawara he has directed *Sembene: The Making of African Cinema.* Ngũgĩ's exile has led him from Kenya to Britain and America, where he has taught at Yale, Smith, and Amherst. Since 1992 he has been professor of performance studies and Erich Maria Remarque Professor of Comparative Literature at New York University, having declined an offer of tenure at Yale. He has also been guest artist at the Tisch School of the Arts. Beginning in 1994, he has edited *Mũtiiri,* a New York University–based Gĩkũyũ language journal of literature and culture, cofounded by Ngũgĩ and his wife Njeeri. In April 1994, Ngũgĩ was the subject of "the largest conference on an African writer ever held in the United States or anywhere, for that matter, including Africa itself," in the words of the conference convenor and Ngũgĩ scholar Charles Cantalupo.[37]

Ngũgĩ and Postcolonial Studies

In addition to being a novelist and playwright, Ngũgĩ has been a journalist and a teacher, and a postcolonial theorist. "Postcolonial" is a problematic and much-debated term[38] because it seems to give undue influence to the colonial experience in the formerly colonized nation's history and to make this traumatic past the genesis of all future developments. The term also lumps together a diverse collection of global historical and political experiences and national literatures, such as those of Kenya, Canada, Jamaica, India, and New Zealand, and might appear to homogenize important differences while ostensibly celebrating difference and diversity. The discipline of postcolonial studies is sometimes criticized as the creation of the Western academic establishment, which has defined and delimited the field in a kind of intellectual colonization, a process mimicking the historical actions of the imperialists.[39] Such a colonization is thus regarded as being in some ways even more insidious because it still more skillfully disguises its actions behind a smoke screen of benevolent intentions and appears to speak often in highfalutin terms for the oppressed of the postcolonial world. The postcolonial project, however, openly acknowledges the inevitably contested terrain in which it works. It stresses the deep cultural roots of Western imperialism, the historical trauma of colonialism and the difficulty of the transfer from colonialism to independence, the importance of history generally, and by implication the complications of moving beyond a colonized mentality. Both the writing in postcolonial countries and the critical practice that engages with it, moreover, are, as writers such as Chris Tiffin and Stephen Slemon point out, explicitly political.[40] Postcolonial literary and critical practices are enmeshed in the realities of the postcolonial condition, and they aim to facilitate the process of decolonization.

Ngũgĩ's polemical essays obviously advance the postcolonial project. They also frequently elaborate positions that form the basis for his fiction, and his essays have often been used somewhat uncritically to interpret his fiction. Ngũgĩ has long been an important figure in postcolonial studies. His essays consider the special position of the African writer in relationship to tradition, language, audience, history, and the state. He is best known in this connection for his advocacy of African languages and the political commitment of the African writer. He has declared categorically that for him to write fiction in English is to foster a neocolonial mentality. For Ngũgĩ, a language is the repository of cultural memory, allowing its speakers to possess their world and providing them with a voice to address both ancestors and the generations yet unborn. English was the language of the colonizer, and linguistic imperialism was one of the aims of the Philological Society of London, which initiated the *Oxford English Dictionary* in Victorian England.[41] Ngũgĩ advocates linguistic decolonization. Although he has not abandoned English entirely and continues to lecture and to publish critical work in English, Ngũgĩ is an enthusiastic supporter of African language developments, such as the Gĩkũyũ journal *Mũtiiri,* and much of his writing and public speaking has attacked linguistic colonization. Writing in African languages for Ngũgĩ is a blow against oppression, a political act, especially in a continent with a colonial legacy in which the postcolonial writer has so often been regarded as an enemy of the state.[42] Ngũgĩ, moreover, has focused attention on the linguistic and material plight of his own country and of Africa generally, and in his last collection of essays, he reaffirms the power of artistic freedom in the struggle against oppression.

A concern for his readers motivates Ngũgĩ's linguistic preoccupations. In his novelistic practice since 1977, he has written primarily for a mass African audience, and he responds to critics who protest that writing in Gĩkũyũ reaches only a portion of even a Kenyan audience[43] by explaining that he intends his writing to be translated from Gĩkũyũ into Swahili and other African languages. He has been somewhat less candid in acknowledging the difficulties faced by writers who do not have his international stature in finding a market for their work and in having it translated.[44] The question of whether to write in African languages is a serious one for the African writer, as Albert S. Gérard has noted: "This is the dilemma of the African writer today: either he may use a European language and thus gain recognition (and financial reward) from a worldwide audience, but at the risk of cutting himself off from the very roots of all but the most esoteric creative flowering, the common experience of his own society; or he may use his own mother tongue, stoically shun the appeal of the world market, remain one of the inglorious Miltons of the present age, but help his own people's advance into the age of mass

literacy, and pave the way for future achievements and renown."[45]
While somewhat sheltered by his international stature, Ngũgĩ has made
his position clear and has supported other writers. He gave editorial
assistance in the late 1960s to a number of journals, including *Zuka,*
which encouraged submissions in East African languages, though
accompanied by English translation;[46] and he has encouraged writers in
other ways, though sometimes, because of his notoriety, with disastrous
consequences.[47] Ngũgĩ has also worked collaboratively and has welcomed the informal public reading of his work to illiterates. He has chosen both the language of his last novels and their narrative form—transformed tales from the Bible, for example—to make his fiction readily
comprehensible by a mass Kenyan audience. More recently, he has been
magnetized by the potential of popular theater and video to attract a
mass, often illiterate, audience. In 1983 he wrote in *Barrel of a Pen* that
"modern technology (e.g. video, cinema, television, radio) should make
it possible to actually reclaim the positive aspects of tradition and peasant cultures which are withering away under the pressures of the economic exploitation" (*Barrel,* 78). Ngũgĩ today celebrates cyberspace as a
medium for performative orature (*Penpoints,* 118).

Ngũgĩ must be regarded as one of the most significant interpreters of
Frantz Fanon, whose work is so important for the influential postcolonial theorists Edward Said and Homi Bhabha. Fanon, a psychotherapist
and theorist, counseled victims of torture and developed a view of colonialism that stressed that one of its most insidious and lasting consequences was the devastation of the psyche of its victims. He suggested
that a deeply implanted sense of degradation and inferiority stunted the
colonized individual. For Ngũgĩ, healing the trauma of colonialism is
one of the functions of art. In *Decolonising the Mind,* he writes of the consequences of years of racism, legalized bigotry, and dispossession on the
national consciousness. Although Ngũgĩ's interests have moved beyond
Fanon, his continuing advocacy of African languages and their use in
aiding the process of decolonization has roots in Fanon's thinking.
Ngũgĩ remains sincerely committed to the ideals of Karl Marx and
Friedrich Engels. Ngũgĩ's essays cite these great nineteenth-century
political theorists extensively, and some of his characters, especially in
his plays, sometimes appear to be merely mouthing communist slogans.
After the demise of the Soviet Union, such zeal may seem at best dated
and even fondly nostalgic, and Ngũgĩ has acknowledged, in *Moving the
Centre,* his own exasperation that the merely 70-year-old term "socialism" should seem "old-fashioned" (*Moving,* 34). Readers of Ngũgĩ's work

must keep in mind Kenya's recent history, and that a number of liberation movements in Africa have had Marxist roots; the Cold War was often fought not directly by the superpowers but by proxy, and sometimes by client states in Africa, with devastating consequences. Ngũgĩ celebrates the "African socialism" of Julius Nyerere, a socialism with a distinctively regional face.

Ngũgĩ embodies the ambivalent position of the postcolonial intellectual. The difficulty of this figure's position derives on the one hand from an association, through education and career, with Europe and the colonizers, and on the other hand from a newly acquired linguistic and cultural distance from the majority of the people. Writers such as Kwame Anthony Appiah suggest that the African intellectual's association with Europe is inevitable and necessarily involves him or her in a conflicted ideological relationship; moreover, he regards the attempt to deny or escape from such an identification as ineffective and dishonest, the recourse of Fanon's shortsighted "native intellectual."[48] African philosopher Tsenay Serequeberhan would agree: "To be a Westernized African in today's post-colonial Africa means ultimately to be marked/branded—in one way or another—by the historical experience of European colonialism. We should not try to 'hide' from this all pervasive element of our modern African historicity. Rather, our efforts to surmount it must begin by facing up to and confronting this enigmatic actuality. This then is the hermeneutic task of this study, for ultimately the antidote is always located in the poison!"[49] Writers from Achebe to Gayatri Chakravorty Spivak have loudly deplored the postcolonial intellectual's divorce from the people. Achebe has written that art separated from the reality of African society is "deodorised dog-shit,"[50] and Spivak demands that intellectuals "learn to speak in such a way that the masses will not regard as bullshit."[51]

Ngũgĩ writes similarly in *Devil on the Cross* of the allure of intellectual food and the intellectual's ability to mystify, to the extent that "a child . . . [may mistake] foreign shit for a delicious national dish."[52] Ngũgĩ frequently enjoins the African intellectual to interrogate the position of power from which writing and cultural expression originate. He recommends, in his latest collection of essays, tapping into the wisdom of intellectual ancestors such as Leo Africanus and Olaudah Equiano, and the "oral intellectual[s]" of the national past (*Penpoints*, 96). Ngũgĩ is always suspicious and even contemptuous, however, of attempts by "state intellectuals" (*Decolonising*, 102)—that is, those who blindly parrot the ideology of the neocolonial state—to appropriate cultural traditions and place them in antiseptic tourist-friendly cultural centers or museums. He demands that, as in the past, intellectual and artistic achievement be regarded as "communal property" (*Writers,* 2d ed., 143–44). Ngũgĩ's African cultural intellectual, who resembles Antonio Gramsci's "'organic' intellectual,"[53] must write in the language and idiom of the masses and must lead, but lead from within the cultural army (*Writers,* 1st ed., 31). Part of Ngũgĩ's project in his various writings is to elevate revolutionary national intellectuals such as Dedan Kimathi into a position of spiritual leadership.

The postcolonial condition is characterized by hybridity, migration, and exile, and Ngũgĩ has lived in exile since 1982, first in England and then in the United States. While his exile has been productive, his separation from his homeland has left him feeling severed from his core audience, and uninterested in creating new fiction. In his exile, Ngũgĩ has become, like Salman Rushdie and Nuruddin Farah,[54] a hybrid cultural intellectual, living between countries and cultures. The condition of hybridity, as postcolonial theorist Homi Bhabha explains,[55] may be stimulating, in that it intensifies the individual's awareness of difference, but it is also dislocating in personal terms, rendering the familiar strange, and dividing the self. In his exile, Ngũgĩ has continued to focus on his homeland despite his geographic distance. This concern with the nation and its story, the national narrative,[56] is of central importance in postcolonial theory and in Ngũgĩ's work.

His novels taken together form a people's history of Kenya,[57] even in his last novel *Matigari* projecting into the future. His novels' history differs, however, from colonial or neocolonial versions of events, and his view of the Emergency, for example, has landed him in trouble with official historians. His novels offer a counterhistory, an alternative view that is in creative conflict with the official version. For instance, he has always stressed women's participation in Mau Mau, and in *Devil on the Cross* he emphasizes women's potential for revolutionary action. In 1986 Ngũgĩ participated in "The Challenge of Third World Culture," a conference at Duke University; and in the same year, Duke's Fredric Jameson published "Third-World Literature in the Era of Multinational Capitalism."[58] Although Jameson's formulation and especially its catholic application of the monolithic phrase "third world" has attracted criticism,[59] his notion of "national allegory" has proved remarkably buoyant. In his provocative and influential essay, which refers to Ngũgĩ's work, Jameson suggests that "third-world literature" tells the story of the nation from which it emerges, and forms a national allegory, embodying or paralleling the development of the nation, and melding the private and the public. The national allegory, Jameson elaborates, ends with uncertainty regarding the future, a "crisis of closure." Although Ngũgĩ's narratives, especially his early ones, often end with such a crisis, their protagonists torn between rival responsibilities and obligations, they do suggest a conclusion. The protagonist's dilemma must be experienced by, and resolved within, the reader. In his last novels, Ngũgĩ attempts to inspire the reader into taking responsibility for a collective homecoming to a newly liberated nation.

Ngũgĩ is an important theorist of postcolonial and African literature, but his last, most difficult narratives, with their ambitious closure, have not had the same enthusiastic response from some Western readers as have his earlier novels, which display more obviously the influence of writers like Joseph Conrad and D. H. Lawrence. In the last novels, Ngũgĩ has moved beyond realism and a focus on the private angst of troubled individuals to employ broad "type" characters who clearly represent portions of the public, common aspirations, or ideologies. The use of allegory clearly imbues these novels with a postcolonial—but also a postmodern—sensibility, self-consciously celebrating their own artificial, constructed nature, mimicking other (especially biblical) plots and phrases, and displaying an unwillingness to accept the "master narratives" of state-sanctioned historians.

Chapter Two

(Re)writing History: Early Fiction

Ngũgĩ's narrative powers are immediately apparent in his often-auto-biographical apprentice novels drafted while he was a student at Makerere University College. The stories in *Secret Lives,* collected and published in 1975, have a loosely chronological organization beginning with Gĩkũyũ myths and moving to the Emergency in the 1950s, and on to the post-Emergency, independence, and postindependence periods. After his early short stories, some of which explore themes developed in the novels, Ngũgĩ's first-written, though second-published, novel was *The River Between,* an earlier version of which won the East African Literature Bureau competition.[1] *Weep Not, Child,* also written when the precocious Ngũgĩ was in his early twenties, is still considered by some to be his masterpiece. These relatively short, tightly organized apprentice novels are somewhat formulaic and diagrammatic, only hinting at the sustained and multifaceted brilliance of *A Grain of Wheat,* a novel that completes and concludes his first stage as a novelist. The liberal, ameliorative political stance of most of Ngũgĩ's writing in this first part of his career is striking given the radical shift in his later work.

Early Short Stories in *Secret Lives*

It might appear from Ngũgĩ's earliest writings that he is primarily a religious writer. One of his first written stories, "Mugumo" in *Secret Lives,* takes as its starting point the sacred tree of the Gĩkũyũ people, which is also the site at which Ngũgĩ's last novel, *Matigari,* ends. *The River Between,* Ngũgĩ's first-written novel, originally had the working title "The Black Messiah." Like all of his writing, however, these works' references to religion, both Gĩkũyũ and Christian, indicate the central role of the spiritual in the lifeways of all Kenyans, a role that the Mau Mau fighters and Ngũgĩ himself in his last novels attempted to use to convey political messages. Ngũgĩ said after writing *A Grain of Wheat* that he employs Christian and African mythology in his writing "as a frame of reference, as the only body of assumptions I can take for granted, especially in the area I come from" (Sander and Munro, 54). Ngũgĩ's early fictions are deeply colored, moreover, by a powerful moral consciousness; their heroes are divided men. Facing a terrible dilemma, caught between rival claims, these characters are buffeted by the realities of Kenya's history.

Ngũgĩ writes in the preface to *Secret Lives* that the stories partly "form my creative autobiography over the last twelve years and touch on ideas and moods affecting me over the same period. My writing is really an attempt to understand myself and my situation in society and in history."[2] Although he has confessed modestly to being not "particularly good" at writing short fiction (Sander and Munro, 54), Ngũgĩ was raised in an oral culture in which storytelling was woven into the pattern of daily life. His short stories, however, with their careful handling of plot reversals and climaxes, in some ways more closely resemble the literary tales of Edgar Allan Poe, though with a modernist and in some cases a postmodernist bent. David Cook and Michael Okenimkpe persuasively demonstrate Ngũgĩ's skillful, intuitive grasp of the genre,[3] and Kimani Njogu points out that one of the most distinctively postcolonial features of Ngũgĩ's novels is that they are a fabric of embedded tales and stories like those in *Secret Lives,*[4] a contention that is especially true of *Petals of Blood.*

The first story in *Secret Lives,* "Mugumo," published earlier in *Origin East Africa* as "The Fig Tree,"[5] is about a woman who, motivated by passion, has married, against the advice of her family and friends, a man who already has three wives. She has left him after he beats her savagely when she fails to become pregnant. When first published, the story had an epigraph taken from two of D. H. Lawrence's poems, "Figs" and "Bare Fig-Trees," the latter slightly misquoted. The two poetic fragments conjure the "nude fig-tree" with its inward-folding flowers and fruit.[6] The womblike fruit indicates the fig tree's role as an aid to fertility in Ngũgĩ's story. "Mugumo" evokes a sensuous engagement with nature, focusing on a woman who has stolen her mate's soul and must recognize her own fault and humbly return to her abuser. Ngũgĩ supersedes Lawrence's perverse Freudian fantasy of the relations of the sexes by introducing the Gĩkũyũ genesis story, the myth of the founding couple Gĩkũyũ and Mumbi, Mount Kenya, and the sacred fig tree. Ngũgĩ leaves some Gĩkũyũ words untranslated and does not explain the context of Gĩkũyũ myth, as if he is already writing for an audience at least partly familiar with Kenya, even if reading in English. In the *Secret Lives* edition of the story, he changes some references to the "tribe" into the "nation" or the "people," perhaps reflecting his growing disenchantment with the colonial propensity to dismiss all social problems as products of "tribalism" (Cook, 76; *Secret Lives,* 7).

While Ngũgĩ's portrait of the central character, Mukami, balances a critical perception of traditional polygamy with a type of biological determinism (her destiny is motherhood), there is a strong sense that her developing child will have a role in creating the future of the nation. Ngũgĩ's respect for traditions and customs is clear, as is his interest in female experience, though this story (like "And the Rain Came Down!") ends with a barren woman seemingly rewarded with pregnancy for her humble acceptance of village customs, biological destiny, and male authority. Here, Ngũgĩ, writing in the early 1960s, is decidedly more conservative in his account of gender relations than writers like the Nigerian Buchi Emecheta will be in the 1970s in the powerful, tragic, and ironically titled *The Joys of Motherhood,* or than Ngũgĩ himself will be in his assertions of female agency in his later novels. In this early story, Ngũgĩ's interest is clearly in the fate of the nation, unborn at the time of writing, and also in the tension between individual aspiration, and familial and communal obligation. Furthermore, "Mugumo" suggests Ngũgĩ's fiction's early obsession with the notion of a savior or messiah who will liberate his people from all forms of oppression.

Other early stories by Ngũgĩ deal with a common theme in much African writing from this period, the confrontation between tradition and modernity. In "The Village Priest," Joshua, a failed priest, feels trapped between the white missionaries, settlers, and colonial officers on the one side and the traditional rainmakers, medicine men, and prophets on the other. Joshua's reaction to the traditional challenge to his Christian faith leads to an action that has the potential for reconciliation but causes despair, self-loathing, and shame—the same emotional and intellectual hiatus at which Ngũgĩ's first two novels conclude. Joshua has embarked on a journey, as do the protagonists of *The River Between* and *Weep Not, Child,* eventually leading indirectly to self-discovery. Before this final momentary epiphany—experienced as a humble, contrite response to the white missionary Livingstone's sympathy for Joshua's moment of doubt at the *mugumo* tree—he desperately contemplates running away. He has sacrificed himself for the "condescending sympathy" of a living stone (*Secret Lives,* 27).

"The Black Bird" is another story about a man driven to desperation over his ideological crisis, in this case a split between his commitment to modern science and his belief in the necessity of making a sacrifice to cleanse his grandfather's violation of an old prophet's ritual objects. As in "The Village Priest," the setting here is named as Limuru; the ridges surrounding it, of such importance in *The River Between,* represent ideological conflict. The story's ending, the fated Mangara's committing suicide to assuage the curse of his family, is more detached than that of *The River Between* because the events are relayed through the perspective of an observing narrator, who presents the tale, resembling a ghost story, from an unconvincing stance of objective disbelief that changes to final anxiety.

"The Martyr" also laments divided loyalties, both personal and societal, and it is Ngũgĩ's first story to address the Emergency. The Garstones, white settlers, have just been murdered, and the old settler widow, Mrs. Hill, liberal if patronizing in her view of Africans, is warned to be on guard by her friends. The second part of the story examines the sense of historical grievance felt by Mrs. Hill's houseboy, Njoroge, whose ancestral lands have been appropriated by his condescending employer. He is party to a plan to murder her in the evening, but recalling her simple acts of humanity, Njoroge resolves to warn her of the danger and then enter the forest to join the Mau Mau forces. At the very moment of his kindly assessment, she is thinking of how she too has previously overlooked the harsh realities of his life, but ironically, hearing a knock at the door, her resolution to change her attitude buckles into raw, instinctive fear, and she opens the door, simultaneously firing her gun and murdering her would-be savior. Ngũgĩ presents the tension of the Mau Mau period and its historical antecedents as a tragic muddle of mixed perceptions, limited points of view, and missed opportunities for mutual cultural understanding. He shows how the settlers appropriated Gĩkũyũ land, regarding it as unoccupied, when the Gĩkũyũ had only left it temporarily because of a famine; Njoroge knows the land is rightfully his. Each character views the other across the "rift" of racial and cultural difference, seeing no more than a stereotypical embodiment of the settler or the houseboy. The coming conflagration is merely the result of a tragic failure of communication, that the story implies might have been patched over. The liberalism of the story and its "balanced" presentation of highly sensitive issues, a quality often admired in Ngũgĩ's fiction before *Petals of Blood,* contrasts sharply with the strident, utterly uncompromising political stance of the later fiction.

A similar reduction of historical injustice to a lapse in communication lies at the heart of "Goodbye Africa," an account of a white couple, during Africanization, remembering and bidding farewell to the climactic events of their 15 years in Africa. The couple's moments of solitary confession, his of a murder, hers of a love affair, collide. The man feels tormented by the memory of a once-beloved African laborer whom he drove himself to torture and murder for being a Mau Mau suspect. He writes out this agonized recollection, but after his wife's confession of a love affair with the same man, he burns his account. He now knows he has murdered his wife's lover. Both characters, we assume, will bury the wreck of their past lives in Kenya. "Goodbye Africa" again takes a liberal, evenhanded position, showing the dire effects of oppression on both the oppressed and the oppressor. The Emergency has destroyed human relationships, families, and noble aims. The story suggests, nevertheless, that the legacy of sexual betrayal, especially across ethnic lines, is more devastating than the memory of murder and the campaign of terror of which it was a part.

Past and present injustice in "The Return" leads the protagonist to bitter stasis. In many respects, the story is a companion piece to "Goodbye Africa," demonstrating the dire consequences that everyone, innocent and guilty, endured as a result of the disruptions of the Emergency. Kamau has fought against the colonial authorities, has been detained without trial and subjected to hard labor and beatings, and has now returned to find that his village has been wiped out and that his wife has run off with his old rival Karanja (here Ngũgĩ employs an anti–romance plot convention anticipating *A Grain of Wheat*). Tricked out of his land in the past, Kamau now feels betrayed by his family and community, who have believed lies circulated about him and watched his wife depart. His despair at this legacy of deceit and misfortune, equally enacted by the colonial powers and by his neighbors and friends, leads him to thoughts of suicide, until he accepts his position and realizes that his past has been lost forever. He stands brutalized and disillusioned but also relieved on the brink of the future. The conclusion here is more ambivalent than in the version of the story published in *Origin East Africa*, in which, as at the end of *Weep Not, Child*, Kamau's mother arrives to forestall his possible suicide (Cook, 58–59).

"A Meeting in the Dark" again features an internally conflicted protagonist, John, but the story is more complex in its handling of cultural contexts. John is about to depart for study at Makerere University College, but his lover Wamuhu is pregnant, and his father is a strict Calvinist preacher who will not permit the marriage, a change in his son's status that might also make him ineligible for a bursary. John feels tortured by guilt but paralyzed by indecision. He refuses to accept responsibility for his dilemma, and ultimately, when goaded beyond endurance into action, he murders Wamuhu. Ngũgĩ's early fiction frequently portrays individuals imprisoned in the special hell of indecision reserved for the timid, dreading the day of trial and madly scheming to escape it, then failing miserably when put to the final test.

John in "A Meeting in the Dark" is torn between the law of the church (which becomes the law of his father, forbidding him to marry a circumcised girl); the law of traditional marriage that dictates he should marry a virgin, though he may previously have slept with her; the law of his own sexual desires; and finally his ambition for education and social status. He envies the poor illiterates of the town who he thinks identify fully and effortlessly with traditional aspirations, though clearly even his father is "a product of the disintegration of the tribe due to the new influences" (68). John's dilemma is that of the Gĩkũyũ, many of whom are now "coated with the white clay of the whiteman's ways"; "the tribe had nowhere to go to. And it could not be what it was before" (62). In this temporal interregnum between past and future—and between the competing laws of church and father, tradition, desire, and personal ambition—John arrives at an irritated, frustrating indecision. Like Njoroge in *Weep Not, Child,* John is troubled before the catastrophe at the story's end by dreams of angels wrestling, and he feels that the gods of both the Calvinistic missionary Carstone and his own people are powerless to help him. He blames Wamuhu for seducing him, just as his father, Stanley, blames his wife for their premarital sexual relationship; and in the final confrontation with Wamuhu, his father's rage, pulsing in John's blood, causes him to murder his lover and their own unborn child. The tragic, melodramatic deus ex machina results from his fateful indecision and his emotional inheritance. Even here he relinquishes responsibility, a sign of bad faith, as if the murder were an accident and not the destructive result of his compromises. John's angst and alienation, however, are more personal than political or ideological. The story's seemingly pat closed ending merely synthesizes its unresolved ideological conflicts.

The River Between

In *The River Between,* Ngũgĩ's first novel (though it was not published until 1965, after *Weep Not, Child*), he develops a number of the themes of "A Meeting in the Dark." This short novel has the economical structure of a short story, and its terse, understated prose style delivers the full impact of sometimes fantastical incidents. As in "A Meeting in the

Dark," the novel has a decisive and climactic closure, but it is ideologically conflicted and leaves a number of the novel's themes unresolved. As in a number of Ngũgĩ's early short stories, the novel introduces opposing forces, such as tradition and modernity, and the two ridges representing conflicting belief systems. This somewhat formulaic program suggests that in the novel, Ngũgĩ is working out ideas,[7] and its inconclusiveness shows an unwillingness to pose simplistic solutions to complex problems with deep historical roots. The novel focuses on a young man, full of fire and promise, who aspires to be his people's savior, but whose career falters in moral compromise, frustration, and fatal indecision.

The River Between is concise and compact and, unlike Achebe's *Things Fall Apart* (another deftly organized first novel that Ngũgĩ greatly admired, which voices indigenous perspectives on African culture and introduced generations of readers to the worlds of African literature), provides only spare details about the society's economy and customs, the appearance of the village, and the telling commonplaces of daily life regarding dress and food. Ngũgĩ's focus is on conflict, within and between individuals. Cultural context is imparted through brief descriptions of Gĩkũyũ ceremonies, like the second birth and circumcision, and the routine of the Christian week. The spirit of place is conveyed through nearly allegorical description of the two ridges, the site near the river where circumcision takes place, and the sacred ground near the *mugumo* tree. Like the river that both unites and separates the two ridges, Waiyaki (the novel's protagonist) may be, as Charles Nnolim suggests, "the human 'River Between.' "[8]

In many ways a coming-of-age novel, a scaled-down bildungsroman, the novel has a sharply delineated narrative structure. The first of two main narratives is a social and political story, Waiyaki's quest to develop educational opportunities in the district and his conflict with Kabonyi about the identity of the savior foretold in Gĩkũyũ prophecy. The second major narrative is a type of *Romeo and Juliet* beside the Great Rift Valley. It tells of Waiyaki's love for Nyambura, who comes from a family starkly different from his, representing an opposing faction on a separate ridge. Unlike Wamuhu in "A Meeting in the Dark," whose being circumcised makes her in John's father's opinion an unfit bride, Nyambura is not circumcised, and this renders her unsuitable for Waiyaki in the opinion of his supporters. *The River Between*'s story lines follow the life cycle of Waiyaki from his school days and his circumcision, to his failure to graduate and his initial career steps, to his final desire to marry. He must find his identity and his place in society amid conflicting community forces and differing interpretations of the wishes of ancestors and prophets, and of the role of history itself.

The novel begins with an almost ritualistic retelling of Gĩkũyũ history, present in one form or another in many of Ngũgĩ's novels, and of the prophecy that inspires and torments Waiyaki. We learn of the ancestor of the tribe who cleared the forests "at the beginning of time,"[9] of the period when women were the sole owners and rulers of everything and the men rebelled against them, and of Gĩkũyũ and Mumbi, the father and mother of the Gĩkũyũ. Mingled with this mythical oral history of the Gĩkũyũ in chapter 1, though not conveyed in a style that conjures the richness of orature,[10] is the account of the seer Mugo wa Kibiro, who prophesied the arrival of "a people with clothes like butterflies" (*River,* 2); that is, the invasion of the colonizers, who do not actually appear in the novel. The people of the ridges are introduced as proud guardians of secrets, rituals, and magic powers. Waiyaki's father, Chege, takes him to the sacred grove by the *mugumo* tree from which they survey the land and Waiyaki learns that he is the offspring of Mugo wa Kibiro, and the last of his line. The seer prophesies that Waiyaki's descendants will study the ways of the white men to use their own methods to defeat them and thereby save the people. Waiyaki, Chege declares, is the savior.

The River Between is the story of the intersection of this mythic past with colonial history. The latter is indicated by the missionary Livingstone's school, Siriana, and by references to taxes and a government post. Livingstone, unlike the older missionaries who fought against Gĩkũyũ customs, but to some degree like Waiyaki himself, advocates accommodation with tradition and gradual change. The confrontations of the past, however, are carried into the present in the rivalry between the convert Kabonyi and his son Kamau, representing one ridge, and Chege and Waiyaki, representing the other. This rivalry, which heats up after Kabonyi renounces Christianity and becomes a zealous promoter of Gĩkũyũ traditions, concerns the designation of either Kabonyi's son or Waiyaki as the true savior. Both young men also compete for the affection of Nyambura. The prophecy's ultimate outcome and the fate of Waiyaki are, however, to some extent anticipated in Chege's complaint that the words of the true prophet, like Mugo wa Kibiro, are always ignored and disdained by the people. The novel complicates its handling of Gĩkũyũ prophecy and colonial history by drawing parallels between these narratives and biblical stories, such as when it equates the colonial dispossession of the Gĩkũyũ's land with the Israelites' slavery and bondage in Egypt, and their pilgrimage to the New Jerusalem. Mugo wa Kibiro's second prophecy, about the coming of a Gĩkũyũ savior, is linked to Isaiah's foretelling the coming of Christ. Most significantly, Waiyaki is the African messiah for Joshua's daughters Muthoni and Nyambura, and he is even finally betrayed by a character resembling Peter, his friend Kinuthia. This identification of Waiyaki and Christ, an incomplete biblical allegory, is obscured somewhat by Muthoni's terrible death, an indirect consequence of her attempt to unite the people of the two ridges, the believers in tradition and the Christian converts. Both sides exploit her death for their own purposes; each justifies its cause on the site of Muthoni's dead body.

Waiyaki is thrown into the dilemma that consumes him by a variety of conflicting forces: his respect for his father and tradition, his love for Nyambura, and his appreciation of the power of Gĩkũyũ and biblical prophecy. He feels he must be the savior his father intended and bridge the gap between the Kameno and Makuyu ridges, and between tradition and modernity, but he is thrown off balance by his father's death and his father's rival Kabonyi's breaking with the church and becoming an advocate for tradition and a vocal contender for Waiyaki's authority in the community. He is caught in a series of binary oppositions: the two ridges, the colonial school Siriana and the independent school Marioshoni, a duty to the community and personal desire, and even the gap between himself and Nyambura that is "as big as the one dividing Kameno and Makuyu" (*River,* 78). Waiyaki feels he is the savior, the sent one, the promised one, and the black messiah, as the figure is variously identified, but his passion is muffled by indecision. He is as often confused and equivocal as he is inflated by messianic aspirations.

Waiyaki's colonial education, the weapon that Mugo wa Kibiro predicted the savior would wield against the colonial forces, leads Waiyaki away from his prophesied destiny and exacerbates his internal division. In fact, he even forgets about the experience at the *mugumo* tree. Because of the number of years he has spent at the mission school, he has not learned to dance and has not participated in the rituals that would have bound him to his people. His education in the ways of his people has given way to his Westernized schooling. With the increased Christian zeal in the community resulting from the reaction to Muthoni's death, Waiyaki must leave Siriana. He desires more strongly than ever now to fulfill the prophecy to unite the ridges and reconcile old antagonisms, but "he did not know himself" (*River,* 86). He vacillates and second-guesses his every thought and action. For example, after he takes the oath of allegiance to preserve the purity and togetherness of the tribe, he blames himself for failing to seize the opportunity the oathing provided to speak of reconciliation. He resigns from the traditional council, the Kiama, and then regrets resigning. Feeling guilty at another missed opportunity to preach tolerance and unity, and resolving to speak his mind at the following year's parents' conference, he wonders for what purpose he will ask the parents to unite. He even dreams fondly of his beloved Nyambura, who wants a religion of unity, but his dream includes tearing her to pieces. He speculates about speaking to the people whom she wants to bring together, but he doesn't know what to say. He knows a new political awareness is needed, but he is too mystified and frightened by forces in the country to realize it. Waiyaki comes closest to a really coherent resolution with his notion that while all foreign things are not innately evil, their truth must be reconciled to the people's traditions.

The ultimate failure of Waiyaki's reforming mission of reconciliation may stem from the historic ineffectiveness of prophets, which Chege laments. Ironically, Waiyaki is the name of a nineteenth-century Gīkūyū leader who fought against the British incursion into Gīkūyū country. In the novel, Waiyaki's appetite for compromise, however, entices him to promote a political movement of liberation from colonialism that will respect both tradition and Western education while also allowing him to marry Nyambura, a proposal that a broad cross section of the people categorically refuses to accept because she is uncircumcised. Furthermore, he restrains the people's anger against Kabonyi, who is probably behind the rumors about Waiyaki's ritual contamination through involvement in Muthoni's death after her circumcision. His desires are paradoxical, and he will not make vital compromises to achieve his principal ends. Finally, in a kind of reversal of the story of Pilate's judgment, Waiyaki is given over to the justice of the Kiama and likely ritually executed. Waiyaki embodies the contradictions and conflicts of his people at this moment in history to such an extent that he cannot make vital decisions and sacrifice either his enemy or his beloved, and he is fashioned as a kind of sacrificial Christ.

The novel's closure is ambivalent. The much-vaunted unity and reconciliation are impossible with a weak leader who is as internally divided as Waiyaki, pulled by both a commitment to traditional values and a devotion to Western education and individual freedom. The novel's account of Waiyaki's existential crisis of identity at the critical moment of his campaign is befuddled by the complication of his relationship to

his beloved and by portentous biblical parallels. *The River Between* examines powerful historical forces focused in a single individual, but
Waiyaki's personal problems obscure the novel's handling of these forces
and their cultural contexts. Waiyaki is a figure clearly designed to
embody the people's historic aspirations, but he is also a very modern,
even Westernized intellectual tortured by personal angst and middle-
class choices. He even speculates on eloping to Nairobi with Nyambura
in an escape that would resolve nothing, so common in D. H. Lawrence's
novels. In this respect, the novel is ideologically conflicted, its political
implications muddled. It is unclear whether Waiyaki's somewhat unrealistic agenda of overthrowing the colonial forces through the spread
of Westernized education is being criticized, or whether his utopian
scheme of achieving a Gĩkũyũ cultural renaissance and at the same time
marrying the despised Nyambura is being undermined. Is Waiyaki's
program, as far as it is ever elucidated, too radical or not radical enough,
and what is the alternative? Is his story a cautionary tale about the danger of investing unrealistic hopes in any savior?[11] Various implications
are suggested in the novel, and Waiyaki's final, vague demand for mili-
tant action is closest to the program of Ngũgĩ's final novels, in which
the individual's private torment is submerged in the progress of an
entire community. *The River Between*'s conflicts are resolved, however, in
a somewhat contrived, destructive final confrontation. The longed-for
savior will be martyred by his uncomprehending people ostensibly
because of his inability to separate public duty and private affection.[12]
Finally, the novel subsumes the political in the personal.

    The River Between notably contains two powerful female characters,
who generate Waiyaki's most coherent solutions to the area's problems.
They embody Gĩkũyũ history and a vision of the future.[13] Muthoni
clearly strives for reconciliation between Gĩkũyũ ritual and Christian
practice, and her horrible death renders her a martyr for her cause, a
Christlike sacrifice prefiguring Waiyaki's own probable death. Similarly,
Muthoni's sister Nyambura wants a religion of unity and recognizes
Waiyaki as a messiah. Waiyaki may be inspired and motivated by witnessing the female rebellion, undertaken by Muthoni, and emboldened
by Nyambura's virtual worship. The crux of his fall from power, however, also relates to these women, particularly to their position regarding
circumcision. He faces accusations of being ritually unclean for aiding
Muthoni after her botched circumcision and later for wishing to marry
the uncircumcised Nyambura. Although male and female circumcision
is not described in the novel, the ceremony is of central significance.

Female circumcision, or genital mutilation as it is often called in the West, is the operation of cutting away a woman's clitoris, and sometimes also the inner and outer lips of the vagina. Traditionally, female circumcision is equated with male circumcision, and with a ritual initiation into the adult life of the community. The Gĩkũyũ believed that the uncircumcised woman would have difficulty in conception, and that uncircumcised girls' uncontrolled sexual desire would create social chaos. Concerns relating to hygiene and even odor were used to justify the practice, though perhaps the strongest force behind it was the weight of tradition itself. In *A Grain of Wheat,* for example, the missionaries' criticism of female circumcision is considered an attack on "the roots and the stem of the Gikuyu society" (*Grain,* 83); the astute Kihika in that novel realizes that Europeans, and not the Bible, oppose the practice on cultural grounds, though claiming it violates Christian beliefs. Western outrage against the practice continues to grow, and much has been written on the subject.[14] Jomo Kenyatta, in *Facing Mount Kenya,* his anthropological study of the Gĩkũyũ (a book that influenced Ngũgĩ), does not oppose the practice.[15] Clitoridectomy, however, is not exclusively Kenyan or even African and was advocated, for example, by some radical doctors, such as Isaac Baker Brown, in Victorian England as a "cure" for masturbation.[16] Missionaries in Kenya opposed the practice, as we see in *The River Between,* and historically the banning of circumcised girls from mission schools provided a critical impetus behind the formation of the Gĩkũyũ Independent Schools Association. Theodore Natsoulas explains that the Gĩkũyũ "wished to maintain deeply held customs such as female circumcision and at the same time send their children to western-style schools which they saw as the only road to advancement in colonial society."[17] The maintenance of a practice still common in large parts of Africa that seems cruel, unnecessary, and dangerous to many must be considered in terms of its connection with notions of traditional cultural identity, and even as an act of resistance to perhaps well-meaning but also condescending criticism from abroad.

The River Between appears to take an ameliorative approach to the problem, though in a newspaper article from 1962, Ngũgĩ referred to female circumcision as a "brutal" practice (Lindfors 1981, 28). The novel seems to recognize that the practice should and will end, but that it will happen gradually. Waiyaki acknowledges just before the novel's catastrophe that "circumcision of women was not important as a physical operation. It was what it did inside a person. It could not be stopped overnight" (*River,* 142). This passage implies that female circumcision will be stopped, but it still stresses the value of initiation. A modified ritual, in which a pinprick and the loss of a few drops of blood are substituted for radical excision, has been suggested, and in some parts of Africa there has been a grassroots movement to abandon the practice.[18] In *The River Between*, Ngũgĩ takes a radical position on circumcision for a novel published in 1965. The novel represents the tragedy of a woman's death as a result of the practice, the scandal that taints Waiyaki when he assists the dying victim, and the consequences for him and his mission when he declares his intention to marry an uncircumcised woman.

Weep Not, Child

The River Between's abrupt, perplexing ending anticipates what may be read as its sequel, *Weep Not, Child,* written after the first novel (composition began around January 1962),[19] but published in 1964, the year before *The River Between. Weep Not, Child,* which follows the earlier novel in terms of historical chronology and develops many of the same themes, is a historical novel but also, like its predecessor, a tightly controlled, largely autobiographical coming-of-age novel with a mythic dimension. The narrative continues Ngũgĩ's project of exploring Kenya's historical consciousness, by anatomizing its effect on one representative family group. Njoroge's story of the destruction of educational promise and national optimism, and the shattering of a family, unfolds on the eve of the darkest days of the Emergency, which is presented here primarily as a conflict wreaking destruction on inter-African relations, and not as an anticolonial revolutionary struggle. The Mau Mau struggle in the novel is, as Ngũgĩ characterized it a few years later, a "civil war" (Sander and Munro, 52). In another interview, Ngũgĩ said that he attempted in *Weep Not, Child* "to show the effect of the Mau Mau war on the ordinary man and woman who were left in the villages. I think the terrible thing about the Mau Mau war was the destruction of family life, the destruction of personal relationships. You found a friend betraying a friend, father suspicious of the son, a brother doubting the sincerity or the good intentions of a brother, and above all these things the terrible fear under which all these people lived" (Pieterse and Duerden, 121).

Weep Not, Child mixes different histories: personal, national, and mythic. Much of the narrative traces Njoroge's educational career, beginning with his delight at the prospect of entering primary school and wearing a school uniform. We follow his progress from Standard

One at Kamae Primary School, to Kamahou Intermediate School, and finally to high school, the elite Siriana that, as in *The River Between,* resembles Ngũgĩ's own Alliance. Njoroge is already a member of an exclusive minority, "the only boy in all that area who would go to High School."[20] Amid the increasingly bewildering turmoil and danger of the Emergency, Siriana is a place of shelter and escape, a "little paradise, a paradise where children from all walks of life and of different religious faiths could work together" (*Weep Not,* 115). The school seems distant from the troubles, even able to ignore a letter, presumably from Mau Mau leaders, demanding its closure. Siriana appears to lead a charmed life, antiseptically separated from the national trauma. The school's headmaster is strict though evenhanded, but his racial bias is clear. Just after the school is described as a paradise, we discover that it is relentlessly Eurocentric and denigrates African cultural values. As in *The River Between,* the colonial education Siriana offers is represented as a potential unifying force, but one carrying a heavy load of barely disguised ideological baggage. The headmaster "believed that the best, the really excellent could only come from the white man. He brought up his boys to copy and cherish the white man's civilization as the only hope of mankind and especially of the black races. He was automatically against all black politicians who in any way made people to be discontented with the white man's rule and civilizing mission" (*Weep Not,* 115).

Immediately after this explanation of the scholastic "paradise," the headmaster calls Njoroge out of class and delivers him to police officers who take him to the Home Guard post, the house of pain, where he is tortured to ascertain his knowledge about the murder of Jacobo, who supported and profited from the colonial presence. At the house of pain, the white settler Mr. Howlands holds "Njoroge's private parts with a pair of pincers and [starts] to press tentatively" (*Weep Not,* 118) and then threatens him with castration. With the breaking of his body, Njoroge's paradise is almost instantly lost, and the pace of the novel's denouement accelerates. Realizing he is living in "a different world from that he had believed himself living in" (120), Njoroge descends into nihilistic despair, worsened by the indignity of having to do meaningless, low-status work. Ejected from school, with his family torn apart, Njoroge directs his rage toward Jacobo's family. In a kind of trance, he walks through the night to Jacobo's house to avenge his family through the destruction of Jacobo's home, though this would mean the murder of Njoroge's beloved Mwihaki, Jacobo's daughter. Like Waiyaki, Njoroge harbors a barely suppressed murderous rage against his beloved. He abhors the very thing he loves. This misdirected desire to lash out and wound eventually initiates his own suicide attempt.

Kenya's colonial history is presented in *Weep Not, Child* against the backdrop of African involvement in World War I and World War II. The novel appears to begin in 1945, just at the close of the second war, and 15 years after *The River Between* ends (Cook and Okenimkpe, 49). Haunting memories of wartime horror and loss are shared by Howlands and Njoroge's father, Ngotho, who acted as a porter in the first war, clearing bush and making roads. Both men also endured the death of a son in World War II. These common losses might have drawn them together, and before the Emergency, they do share a brittle, unspoken respect; but this tentative bridge to communication is never crossed. The novel, like some of Ngũgĩ's short stories dealing with the Emergency, suggests that the roots of colonial oppression and political discord lie in miscommunication and misunderstanding, as well as in fundamentals such as land. Njoroge is briefly a friend of the son of his torturer, and the beloved of the daughter of the man his brother murdered. Ngotho's son Mwangi dies in the war, provoking the enduring resentment of Mwangi's brother, Boro, who seeks revenge against all Europeans. Boro's desire for vengeance is quickened by his bitterness at the loss of ancestral lands and his unemployment after the war, at a time when land is being given for the settlement of white soldiers.[21] Boro has returned from the war schooled in the arts of violence, and this expertise, coupled with his personal animosity, fuels the developing conflict. His departure for Nairobi signals an acknowledgment of the capital as Mau Mau's base, one severely affected by the colonial Operation Anvil in April 1954. The background for the crisis is related to the appropriation of land and to the privileges given white settlers and their supporters like Jacobo, such as permission to grow valuable cash crops like coffee and pyrethrum. The swiftness of the conflict's escalation appears in the rapid-fire references in the course of a few pages to the chief's assassination, Jomo Kenyatta's arrest, the mysterious sightings of Dedan Kimathi, Mau Mau oathing, the color-bar, Home Guards, forest battles, the colonial policy of "divide and conquer," curfews, Home Guard posts, and detention camps. After this deft sketching of the quickening national conflagration, the novel's focus returns to the personal and mythic plots.

As in *The River Between,* mythic history in *Weep Not, Child* includes the retelling of the founding myth of the Gĩkũyũ. The patriarch Ngotho, and not a professional storyteller, recounts the story of Murungu, the

creator, and of the sacred *mukuyu* tree at the base of Kerinyaga, Mount
Kenya, and the first man and woman, Gĩkũyũ and Mumbi, the children
of the great one. Ngotho then tells of a catastrophic drought sent by evil
forces as a punishment to Mumbi's children, who neglected to offer ritual sacrifices. Ngotho repeats Mugo wa Kibiro's prophecy about the
coming of the whites and the potential savior's being killed by the
wicked. Later, these Gĩkũyũ myths are supplanted by references to biblical myth, and particularly to the story that has such resonance in
Africa and the African diaspora, that of the prophet Moses leading the
people of Israel out of bondage to the Egyptian pharaoh. Jomo Kenyatta, the charismatic leader of Gĩkũyũ and nationalist forces, is the
black Moses. There are also references to the Second Coming of Christ,
and implied references later to the parable of the prodigal son. With his
belief in universal justice and his willingness to merge the essence of
Gĩkũyũ and Christian myth, Njoroge awaits the coming of a hybrid
prophet who can satisfy both political and spiritual longings. His search
for this prophet, savior, or messiah intensifies during the time of
national crisis that wrecks Njoroge's family life and his personal dreams
and aspirations. Jomo Kenyatta is the most obvious candidate, but
another is the elliptical Dedan Kimathi, whose exploits circulate in fantastical rumors.

Conscious, however, of his own "vital role in the country" and "his
task of comforting people," Njoroge too feels a sense of election: "He
felt a bit awed to imagine that God may have chosen him to be the
instrument of His Divine Service" (*Weep Not*, 94, 95). He begins to identify with his biblical heroes Jesus and David, who defeats the giant
Goliath. Njoroge is ever aware of the "responsibility for which he had
prepared himself since childhood" to take care of his family and to realize his potential in the country (136). As a revolutionary agent of
change, however, Njoroge is deeply flawed. He is a limited, fallible center of consciousness. He "dithers" (Cook and Okenimkpe, 50), and at
best his messianic crusade simply expresses his "callow," "adolescent
romanticism" (Killam 1980, 48, 49). Njoroge's perception of his own
messianic sanctification, unlike Waiyaki's, is clearly both narcissistic and
deluded. He resembles the tarmac road that promises unlimited opportunity and breathtaking vistas but leads nowhere.[22]

Another powerful prophetic force lies in Walt Whitman's poem "On
the Beach at Night," from which the novel derives its title. The poem's
dramatic situation has a father and daughter observing the clouds in the
night sky from the vantage point of a beach. At line 14, the poem shifts

from third person, the point of view in which the land- and sky-scapes are described, to first person, just after the first reference to the Pleiades, the seven daughters of Atlas in Greek mythology. In this myth, these seven sisters flee from the pursuit of Orion, until Zeus, the lord of the gods, takes pity and places them in the heavens as stars, though the lovesick Orion continues his tireless pursuit even in the night sky. In Whitman's poem, the young girl watches the swirling, dark clouds and weeps at the seeming obliteration of the constellations. At line 14, the father directly addresses his daughter, a passage from which the novel's epigraph and its title are taken. The father advises that the god Zeus, or the planet Jupiter, and the Pleiades shall emerge from the clouds and be victorious eternally though they have temporarily disappeared. In addition, Whitman's speaker evokes a force or power that will endure even longer than the stars. In *Weep Not, Child,* this reassuring exchange between father and daughter is replayed silently in the final meeting of Njoroge and his mother. Njoroge, commanded by Ngotho on his deathbed to care for his mother, is about to commit suicide. In the novel, unconditional maternal love conquers despair over the worsening political situation, or the cloudy night that obscures the stars of hope for a brighter tomorrow. This theme is reinforced in the titles of the novel's two parts: "The Waning Light" and "Darkness Falls." Even in the darkest hour, the novel suggests, there is hope, though it may be obscured. More effectively than in *The River Between, Weep Not, Child* not only submerges but actively blends the personal and family plot with the communal and national story.

Njoroge has a messiah complex but also paradoxically a deep sense of guilt (Cook and Okenimkpe, 54). He knows he has betrayed his father's trust and fears he has compromised family and community loyalty by loving Mwihaki, and especially by visiting her home, and indirectly by regarding Siriana as paradise and not actively fighting Jacobo. Njoroge's relationship with Mwihaki links the novel's personal and political concerns. The peasant son loves the daughter of his father's enemy, a colonial sympathizer. In *Weep Not, Child,* the tension between fathers and sons complicates the *Romeo and Juliet* plot of *The River Between.* Ngotho's son Boro blames his father personally for the loss of their ancestral land, and for what Boro regards as Ngotho's cowardice in not defending his family. Boro also condemns Ngotho for refusing to take the Mau Mau oath, to which Ngotho objects because it seems to abrogate traditional ritual (and not because he is reluctant to face danger or assert his people's political rights).

Partly as an act of love for his son, Ngotho accepts responsibility for Boro's murder of Jacobo, and Boro returns to seek his father's forgiveness. The suddenly childlike Boro becomes the prodigal son of the biblical parable, and Njoroge the faithful son who stayed home. After blessing Boro, Ngotho asks Njoroge to care for his mother, and then, weakened by his torture at the hands of Mr. Howlands, Ngotho dies. Ngotho's torture has involved his castration, a symbolic end to his family line. At the close of the novel, Ngotho's sons are all either dead (Mwangi) or awaiting execution (Boro) or in prison for life (Kamau) or in detention (Kori) or in a state of suicidal despair (Njoroge). Njoroge's attempt to take his own life, at the sacred tree, represents the near annihilation of a people. At the end, Njoroge has lost faith in everything: education, Christianity, prophets, love, and himself. At this moment of utter hopelessness, a nuclear bomb of emotional desolation, his mother appears, recalling the novel's title and its optimistic beginning, a faint glimmer of hope in the darkest moment of the nation's history.[23] Therein lies the seed of Kenya's future.

A Grain of Wheat

Ngũgĩ's 1967 novel *A Grain of Wheat* is a great, mournful song of freedom. It deals with Kenyan independence and has a wide epic sweep, bringing together individual and communal aspirations and despair. In terms of structure and handling of historical context, the novel is a far more complex work than either of its predecessors. Like those novels, at the core of *A Grain of Wheat* lies the story of a troubled love affair. Here it is that of Mumbi, an idealistic, Christianized woman who identifies with the biblical Esther and Ruth; she is the sister of the revolutionary martyr Kihika and the wife of the morally compromised but repentant Gikonyo. We follow their developing love affair, the promise of their early marriage, and their separation during the Emergency when Gikonyo is detained for six years. His despair in detention leads him to confess secrets to the colonial authorities to obtain his release, upon which he is devastated to discover that during his imprisonment, Mumbi has given birth to the child of his rival, Karanja. At the end of the novel, a physically and morally chastened Gikonyo prepares to labor toward a reconciliation with his estranged wife. This story focuses the novel's account of the conflicting blend of heroism and idealism, on the one hand, and opportunism and even treachery, on the other, lying behind the people's actions in the struggle leading to national independence. This sacred day, paid for by tremendous sacrifice and suffering, seems somehow compromised by the advantages gained by traitors to the cause, and cheapened by profit-motivated association with business ventures.

Mugo is another central pillar in the novel's construction, and frequently this image of the architecture of the house is used to conjure the reconstruction of the home of the family, community, and nation. Like many characters in the novel, such as General R. and Gikonyo, Mugo is a man who has been psychologically damaged by a ruptured family life. He is a motherless, fatherless child, whose very manhood was mocked by the aunt who raised him. He is one of the legion of the walking wounded. During the Emergency he betrayed Kihika to the all-powerful district officer, an action motivated by a desire to be spared a symbolic father figure's wrath. Ironically, Mugo is regarded by everyone in Thabai village and its surrounding ridge communities as a great, morally upstanding hero and leader. While striving to live independently, he has entertained grand illusions of founding and leading a mission. Like the protagonists of *The River Between* and *Weep Not, Child*, he has at least for a time regarded himself as a member of God's elect, as a Moses, though later he identifies more closely with Judas. By sheer accident or as a result of a deeply bruised respect for justice, Mugo has performed selfless and heroic acts, now well known, but he has also consciously betrayed Kihika, and the secret memory of his betrayal haunts Mugo's days and provokes terrifying hallucinations, making the awed respect of the community seem hollow. He finally pays for his crime at a people's trial presided over by General R. and Lieutenant Koina.[24]

Structurally, unlike *The River Between* and *Weep Not, Child*, this novel is a series of intertwined snapshots or interrelated autobiographical narratives. In this respect it resembles the slowly developing portraits in George Lamming's masterpiece *In the Castle of My Skin*, which Ngūgī greatly admired. Its form also resembles that of Joseph Conrad's *Under Western Eyes*, a correspondence noted by a number of critics.[25] *A Grain of Wheat* recounts personal stories as memories triggered, as in stream-of-consciousness fiction, by incidental and accidental occurrences, or as confessions told to a seemingly sympathetic listener. The novel's use of flashbacks underlies its psychological realism and emphasizes its theme of the omnipresence of historical memory. The novel employs the role of storytelling as a means of re-creating history and also as a method for obtaining psychological comfort and release (Nazareth 1974, 131; Pieterse and Duerden, 128). Frequently, as in the case of Gikonyo's confession to Mugo (who is unwittingly the receiver of many personal confessions), the act of speaking reinforces the fundamental isolation and detachment of the penitent, despite the temporary relief speaking brings. These characters are haunted by their own traumatic histories and governed by them as by fixed stars, and they seem to be blinkered by a limited, solipsistic view of the world. This is especially true of Mugo, Karanja, and Gikonyo, who share a deeply ingrained sense of guilt, and the possibly mad Githua, the injured driver who invents a phantom heroic history for himself. As Mugo explains, "He invents a meaning for this life. . . . Don't we all do that?" (*Grain,* 152). These characters can't see beyond their own childhood traumas, or their painful guilt about a sudden cruel action, an unperformed gesture of comfort, or an outright act of treachery. They seek a type of self-forgiveness that is one of the Christian themes of the novel. Their obsessive private memories and confessions, however, do lead to a final public conflagration, a scene resembling the violent public accounting at the close of *The River Between.* The novel has two endings, the first dealing with the fate of Mugo, and the second with the future of Gikonyo and Mumbi. In the first ending, the private court of judgment gives way to the public trial of truth and justice. In the second ending, there is a recourse to the trial of private conscience and the desire for peace, forgiveness, reconstruction, and reconciliation. Just before the meeting on Independence Day, at which Mugo courageously confesses and after which he is taken away to face the punishment of his crime (a death that may well foster regeneration),[26] the people of the community, in song, re-create their shared history, a history that opens and closes the novel and provides the lens through which the stories of individual anguish are viewed.

The novel concerns three historical periods, separated by approximately 13 years: the time before the Emergency, the time of the Emergency and detention and villagization, and the eve of independence. There are also references, as in Ngũgĩ's first novels, to Gĩkũyũ and Mumbi (a symbolic reenactment of their union closes the novel) (Jan-Mohamed, 219), the seer Mugo wa Kibiro, and the time when women ruled the land, and also to early heroes of the Gĩkũyũ liberation movement and would-be national saviors such as Harry Thuku and Jomo Kenyatta. Harry Thuku gets the lion's share of attention, perhaps because his story of initial idealism followed by a crushing seven-year imprisonment, release, and a conservative change of heart echoes the experience of Gikonyo. While the novel relates historical incidents such as the 1923 procession to Nairobi to free Harry Thuku and the resulting massacre, the 1950 Bata Shoe Factory strike, the daring Mau Mau assault on the police garrison, and the hunger strike at Rira detention camp leading to the beating death of 11 prisoners (the historic Hola massacre), it makes clear that these are only isolated fragments from the larger mosaic of the collective experience of oppression and resistance.

The quest for a hero, of such importance in *The River Between* and *Weep Not, Child,* is here undermined with bitter irony by the community's elevating the sad and lonely traitor Mugo to the stature of great leader and even conscience of the people. This quest also finds a distorted reflection in the white district officer John Thompson, who sees Englishness as a state of mind and presumably pictures himself as the hero of his unwritten book, "Prospero in Africa." Like his predecessor Thomas Robson, Thompson is corrupted by his position and brutalizes those in his power, ranting, in words echoing those of the megalomaniac Kurtz in Conrad's *Heart of Darkness,* "Eliminate the vermin" (*Grain,* 134).[27] Another would-be hero, Gatu, commits suicide in detention. Furthermore, the new member of Parliament for the area is cynical and corrupt, lives comfortably in Nairobi, not his home district, and cheats Gikonyo and a collective of five in their attempt to buy Green Hill Farm from a departing white settler. Hope for a brighter future cannot be ensured by the redress of past grievances, and even the traitor Karanja escapes justice, though the failure of his suicide attempt may indicate his future in a purgatory of unrelieved remorse. He may have annihilated his identity along with his self-worth by wearing the hood under which he identified Mau Mau participants. Wambui, a woman who carried guns for the freedom fighters, even has second thoughts about the trial and punishment of Mugo. Amid the disillusionment with the past and the questioning of the promise of independence, shared by the freedom fighter Koina and the elder Warui, and shown in the equally pathetic and unrealistic aspirations of the peasants (*Grain,* 216), the only uncompromised hero is Jomo Kenyatta, the burning spear, though he is a remote figure. More obviously, the novel's hero is the grain of its title, the very notion of hope itself, which must die to bring forth new life. This grain is the legacy of the passionate freedom fighter Kihika, whose vision of a new Kenya is colored by his daily reading and revolutionary interpretation of the Bible.

The novel's title, its epigraph, and its many chapter epigraphs are taken from the Bible. In addition, the characters' speech contains biblical echoes. The novel's epigraph, from 1 Corinthians 15:36, about the necessity of death for regeneration, and one of the last chapter's epigraphs, from John 12:24, on the same theme, emphasize the notion that the sacrifice of men and women during the Emergency, and especially the martyrdom of people like Kihika, nourished the fruit of independence. A number of biblical references are indicated in the text as being underlined in Kihika's Bible. Kihika, though opposing Christian meekness and the missionaries' betrayal, is clearly inspired by liberation theology's social gospel, the biblical fight against oppression and injustice interpreted especially in the life of Jesus and the Old Testament. The Old Testament story most frequently referred to here is that of Moses leading the children of Israel out of bondage in Egypt. These biblical stories maintain a type of intertextual relationship with the events in the lives of Gikonyo, Mumbi, and Mugo, stressing the ethical importance of their decisions and actions, and the mythical resonance of the struggle in which they have been involved. Links between biblical stories and Gĩkũyũ myth are also mentioned by Kihika, who identifies personally with Christ and relates the Mau Mau oath to baptism, and deaths in the struggle to the promise of eternal life contained in the Crucifixion. During the Mau Mau struggle, Christian hymns and Gĩkũyũ initiation chants and choruses similarly merged into Mau Mau liberation songs. Ngũgĩ does not draw on the merging of these two sources to inspire the transformative structure of *A Grain of Wheat* as he will do in his later, more obviously revolutionary novels, employing his Mau Mau aesthetics, but he does recount that the practice was common. Some scholars have found this novel's seemingly sympathetic treatment of Christian themes incompatible with a strictly revolutionary purpose.[28]

The use of Christian references is only one of the novel's stylistic features that tie it to the tradition of the European novel. For example, unlike *The River Between* and *Weep Not, Child, A Grain of Wheat* (originally titled "Wrestling with God") is full of recurring motifs and images. The central image is of sowing, cultivation, and harvest, significant in a novel dealing with the consequences of unjust land tenure and dispossession, but also clearly suggesting a positive, hopeful conclusion. The novel also makes many references to weather, particularly the cycles of rainfall and near drought. It contains the most extensive and poetically charged descriptions of landscape in any of Ngũgĩ's novels, and a similarly heightened discourse is employed only to describe sexual encounters. Frequently, an elevated sensual awareness of nature is associated with an intense physical longing, and in Gikonyo's case with religious rebirth or "a covenant with God" (*Grain,* 99), a feature of the work of D. H. Lawrence, which Ngũgĩ admired when he was contemplating the novel (Pieterse and Duerden, 123–24). The mythopoeic merging of personal emotion and landscape, however, is never allowed to run into a romantic personification, or anthropomorphization of nature. The novel instead balances poetic flights with wry, naturalistic detail about bodily functions and the odor of vomit, feces, and urine.

The novel's imagery is grounded in social and political concerns. For example, the Mau Mau fighters refer to bullets as "maize grains" (*Grain,* 151). Agricultural imagery evokes the importance of land and the peasantry, just as the imagery of carpentry celebrates the importance of the working class. Gikonyo is a carpenter proud of his craft and his service to his community, who often undersells his labor to assist the needy. He renders a beautiful and functional knife for Mumbi's mother and in detention meditates on carving a love gift for his wife. This gift is a traditional stool, but one based on a design he settles on in hospital, each of the stool's three legs being sculpted in one of the following shapes: a father, a child, a pregnant woman. This design acknowledges his acceptance of his wife's child with his treacherous rival Karanja, and Gikonyo's renewed affection for Mumbi. The three figures support a platform on which he will tool the design of a river. Beside the river, he places an agricultural implement, rather than his first choice, a panga, or machete, indicating his renunciation of a desire for revenge and his willingness to work for personal, familial, and national reconciliation.

The landscape of the novel, like the stool's design, bears the scars of a bloody history. Gikonyo's final design is an artistic compromise, just as he has accepted a compromise in his personal life in forgiving Mumbi and acknowledging her child. The novel ends with a rejection of comfortable illusions, even those about the absolute purity of the movement that brought about liberation. Psychologically wounded characters like Gikonyo have moved beyond the sweet bitterness of isolation, selfishness, and disillusionment, a nursing of their sense of personal grievance, and a refusal to take responsibility for their thoughts and actions. In addition, given the many references to violent and contemptuous behavior of husbands to wives, Gikonyo significantly recognizes the rights of his wife to independent thought and action. He will not perpetuate exploitative master-slave relations in his marriage. This final acceptance of personal responsibility succeeds confession and a readiness for reconciliation, which was the official postindependence government line on the history of national grievances. As Mumbi and her parents agree, everyone must now embrace life, build the village and the market, cultivate the fields, and tend the children. This commitment to collective endeavor is indicated in the title of the final chapter, "Harambee." Despite its seemingly harmonious, closed double ending, in which revolutionary aspirations are merged with Christian forgiveness, the novel is somewhat politically ambivalent[29] and leaves unresolved questions about the fairness of a justice system that allows the Home Guard and colonial chief Karanja to escape while Mugo is tried. The novel also links traitors and collaborators with those "who ran to the shelter of schools and universities" as profiteers from the sacrifice of the peasantry (*Grain,* 68). The specter of the cheating, grasping, amoral member of Parliament on the horizon, his acts of plunder and hypocrisy unchecked and unpunished, further undercuts the satisfaction and resolve of the harmonious pull-together spirit that ends the novel, anticipating the social disillusionment of Ngũgĩ's next phase.

Chapter Three
Mau Mau Aesthetics: Later Fiction

Ngũgĩ's last three novels and his children's stories, ushered in by his three short stories composed between 1971 and 1975, represent a second phase in his writing. His last three novels are marked by an abandonment of the techniques of the classic realist novel with its focus on an angst-ridden individual's attempts to fit into the social mainstream, and its underpinnings of romance. Ngũgĩ abandons realistic reportage and poetic description in favor of allegory, using transformed biblical stories to transmit his radical message, just as the Mau Mau freedom fighters did in their songs. He embraces what he regards as a distinctively African aesthetics or poetics of fiction, a view of African art, the African artist, and the African state outlined in his essays. His characters are less individualized and instead resemble representative social types, standing for social groups or ideas. Some critics have noted a tendency in this direction in his early novels (Killam 1980, 41; Cook and Oken-imkpe, 63). The later novels, furthermore, lose the political and ideological ambivalence of *The River Between* and *Weep Not, Child,* for example, and the sense of evenhanded, liberal balance (Nazareth 1974, 146–47) and stridently advance a committed, engaged political position and a revolutionary program. Similarly, his children's stories, the *Njamba Nene* series, present a radical counterhistory of Kenya to tackle the slant of neocolonial history promoted in Kenyan schools.

Ngũgĩ's narrative practice in these years was deeply marked by three events of enormous significance. The first was the inspiration he gained from his work in communal theater, from writing to production, at Kamĩrĩĩthũ. The second was his yearlong detention without trial or sentence. The third was the total destruction of the Kamĩrĩĩthũ theater, which convinced him of the correctness of his view of a repressive state apparatus and hardened his attitudes regarding the means of liberation. These were deeply disillusioning experiences that grimly reaffirmed his perception of his artistic work as belonging to the history of political struggle in his country and confirmed his worst fears about the appropriation of the fruits of independence. Significantly, the last two novels Ngũgĩ has written, *Devil on the Cross* and *Matigari* (as they are titled in

English), were first written and published in Gĩkũyũ. This use of Gĩkũyũ as a linguistic medium indicates Ngũgĩ's commitment to addressing a rural audience in his homeland in a direct and comprehensible fashion. In addition, *Matigari* speaks not just to readers but to listeners, to the large audience of illiterate farmers whom Ngũgĩ engaged in his collaboratively written Gĩkũyũ plays. In *Matigari,* Ngũgĩ was thinking of video technique, as if he were "standing behind a camera," in his words,[1] a direction he felt would render his work still more accessible to a mass audience, following the practice of Sembene Ousmane, but in part would herald his movement away from fiction.

Late Short Stories in *Secret Lives*

In the preface to *Secret Lives,* a collection that includes three stories forming a bridge between *A Grain of Wheat* and *Petals of Blood,* Ngũgĩ writes of the disillusionment that afflicted him upon his return to Kenya in 1971, witnessing the collapse of the promise of independence. Earlier he wrote in an editorial for the journal *Zuka* that writers must be social explorers, "for we need not be afraid to look at ourselves: we must continue to search for the truth that lies behind the empty phrase, penetrate the mask of our public faces, go for a drink in the condemned parts of our cities and write about what we see there—the hopes, the aspirations, the despair. Let us go into the offices and houses of our new men of power: what do we find there? This is a writer's task."[2] Ngũgĩ himself had clearly accepted this task and was overwhelmed by the results of his social investigations. After his return to Kenya in 1971, he heard a story that inspired "Minutes of Glory," "Wedding at the Cross," and "A Mercedes Funeral." The story he heard, as he writes in the preface to *Secret Lives,* was of "a barmaid [who] had been arrested for stealing money from an aged trader, her one-night lover. The friend who told the story was condemning the rather petty and amateurish theft. But I was intrigued by the fact that the girl had returned to the same bar and for a whole day lived in an ostentatious display of wealth and well-being" ([12]). This account of a fleeting moment of reckless bravado, following a self-destructive act, committed out of despair over a rootless, meaningless existence, indicates the pathos behind Ngũgĩ's seemingly flamboyant, exuberant stories. Each one concerns the brokenhearted, disappointed, shiftless poor, those untouched by the prosperity of the elite following independence. Especially "Wedding at the Cross" and "A Mercedes Funeral" are written in a fantastical comic mode, with a grimly satirical underpinning, resembling what Bakhtin termed "grotesque real-ism."[3] Their intoxicated hilarity and madcap exaggeration imperfectly mask the melancholy cynicism of their pathological clownishness. They focus on spectacle, often a perversion of traditional marriage or funeral ritual. Such ceremonies become travesties mimicking foreign practices or the extravagant follies of newly wealthy Kenyans. The teller of Wahinya's story in "A Mercedes Funeral" points out that in a riotous, chaotic time, such scandalous, outrageous acts are commonplace. Under-lying these accounts is a concern for traditional cultural values and prac-tices, forgotten or corrupted during the Emergency, and an attack on slavish cultural imitation growing out of the psychological debasement of colonialism.

These three stories, like Ngũgĩ's last two novels, share an absurd humor with an underlying pathos and a focus on spectacle and charade. They also contain frequent references to modern consumer commodities and brand names. This concentration on commodity culture reflects Kenya's changing economic climate in the early 1970s and gestures to what is sometimes called "coca-colaization," or the globalization of dis-posable consumer culture. The arrival of a foreign material culture imperceptibly brings with it foreign values and belief systems. This process is indirectly related to the shrinking of the economic global vil-lage and its homogenization along the lines of the dominant culture, and also to cultural imperialism, an attack on entertainment and plea-sure industries as the soft spots of other cultures most vulnerable to eco-nomic and political intervention. The stories and novels also share a less self-consciously "literary," "writerly," or metaphorically embellished writ-ing style such as that used in *A Grain of Wheat,* or the very different, unadorned, journalistic style of *A River Between.* In fact, these stories, and especially "A Mercedes Funeral," have a striking oral quality. They are tales told, and the telling is an integral part of the narrative. They acknowledge their audience, even providing gaps for readers' reactions, and they have an informal, conversational tone. These three qualities— the emphasis on spectacle and charade, repeated reference to consumer culture, and oral techniques—all belong to postmodern fiction, which self-consciously acknowledges the very artificiality of art while reflect-ing a fragmented, media-saturated, morally relative or value-neutral, consumption-driven, and increasingly homogeneous global culture.

"Minutes of Glory," the most conventional of the three stories of cul-tural alienation, tells of a barmaid and sometime prostitute, Wanjiru, who takes an English name and tries to overcome her "black self-hatred" with the skin-lightening cream Ambi: "She was part of a generation which would never again be one with the soil, the crops, the wind and the moon" (*Secret Lives,* 84, 86). She entertains romantic notions about the past and wildly idealistic delusions about grasping happiness through material prosperity. One night she unfolds her dreams to a somnolent client, robs him, acquires the fashion accessories of success, and returns to the scene of the crime to celebrate frantically her few minutes of fame. Only her rival Nyagūthiĩ, another who has lost her cultural identity, weeps for Wanjiru. The two characters in "Wedding at the Cross" are similarly adrift from traditional anchors. Wariuki weds Miriamu in a traditional marriage, but he cannot tolerate her parents' disdain for their poverty. Her parents' Christian rhetoric disguises raw financial opportunism, and Wariuki imitates their mad, stylish dash for success in its religious guise. He profits from the Emergency and after it from the survivors' fatigue, which allows collaborators to escape vengeance. Like Wanjiru in "Minutes of Glory," Wariuki takes an English name, Livingstone, and mimics Western ways, deciding to satisfy his in-laws' earlier request that their daughter have a church wedding. Miriamu, in the meantime, has grown to lament the transformation of her husband and has been influenced by a religious sect that stresses Christ's commitment to the poor. Having attempted to wipe out his past, to obliterate all cultural markers, and to re-create himself, Wariuki is dumbfounded by his wife's metamorphosis into an admirer of the workers and her refusal to consent to a second marriage. She can't marry Livingstone, she explains archly, because she's already married to Wariuki. Her evolving sense of solidarity with her cultural roots and with the workers, and her surprising, decisive act, anticipate the pattern of *Devil on the Cross,* and Ngũgĩ's attempt to create a Kenyan feminist ideal in Warĩĩnga.

"A Mercedes Funeral" also clearly anticipates *Devil on the Cross* in the story's use of type characters representing particular social classes and its focus on an outrageous competition. It begins with a direct, imperative appeal to the reader: "If you ever find yourself in Ilmorog, don't fail to visit Ilmorog Bar & Restaurant" (*Secret Lives,* 113). The story has a clearly delineated narrative frame, and it is mostly related by a rich Nairobi banker, who is slowly corrupted through the course of his narrative. He tells of a rural electoral race that degenerates into a zany competition for the most ostentatious display of wealth, thinly masked behind a pretended philanthropic action. The competition is generated by the circumstances of the poor man Wahinya and the statement

"These days the poor die and don't even have a hole in which to be put, leave alone a burial in a decent coffin" (117). The seemingly modest proposal generated by this declaration requires the various candidates to display how they would each demonstrate their concern for the poor by lavishly burying the poor man. Their far-fetched, monstrous schemes, which represent the "plastic tears" of the candidates (118)—with the exception of the idealism of the student or "intellectual worker" candidate (115)—indicate the torn fabric of society and an absence of propriety regarding death and its rites. Embedded in this tale of ego-driven political shenanigans is the narrator's personal story of meeting Wahinya, the man who has died, at different stages in his descent into poverty and abjection. As the narrator says, Wahinya's story is "the story of our troubled times" (120). Wahinya has been a man fired with an interest in national history by an inspired teacher who was killed during the Emergency. Full of dreams that are increasingly tinged by a longing for material prosperity, Wahinya descends from being a carpenter and then a bus conductor to being a servant in a bar and finally a drunken member of the unemployed.

The most poignant part of "A Mercedes Funeral" is the buried story of the narrator, once a desperately poor student, who was separated from Wahinya even in their first meetings by his self-perception as a member of a European-influenced elite at Siriana school, anticipating flamboyant rewards after independence. The intoxicating excitement of the period on the eve of independence, so closely following the rule of "guns, concentration camps and broken homes," was "a kind of collective madness" (*Secret Lives*, 126). The mad rush for status and wealth is exemplified by the bus race in the story, similar to that in Ngũgĩ's first children's story, *Njamba Nene and the Flying Bus*. In "A Mercedes Funeral," the narrator survives the near-suicidal race of the two buses to witness the race of the different candidates to provide Wahinya's coffin. The businessman candidate's coffin appears in the shape of the Hilton hotel, symbol of ostentatious luxury in central Nairobi, and the former politician produces a Mercedes Benz–shaped coffin, ostensibly to satisfy the wishes of the deceased. Everyone witnessing the competition is suddenly overwhelmed with the indecency of the sordid display, and Wahinya is buried simply. The story's aftermath is significant. The former politician, with the most exaggerated display, wins the election, and by the end, the narrator, apparently sobered and humbled by the tragedy of the tale, is eyeing his own chances in the next election. Finally, even the student, the intellectual worker, who has been a vocal supporter of workers and labor, becomes a wealthy banker, presumably corrupted—if he was in fact ever genuine in his principled objections—by his schooling and the prevailing climate of greed and corruption. In this story, so different from the muted, idealistic hope present in Ngũgĩ's first three novels, the carnival of independence has become a sad, sick joke, and from its insidious effects, no one is immune.

Petals of Blood

The title of Ngũgĩ's 1977 novel, *Petals of Blood,* is taken from the Caribbean poet and Nobel Prize winner Derek Walcott's poem "The Swamp," from his 1965 collection *The Castaway.* The collection's theme derives in part from Daniel Defoe's early-eighteenth-century novel *Robinson Crusoe,* a myth of capitalist individualism and a paradigm of colonial conquest. "The Swamp" is a descriptive, abstract poem about a bog beside a highway, and the poem conflates images of evil, travel, and sexuality in its impressionistic treatment of the origins and destinations of slave ships. The poem also celebrates the deep, organic connections of history, especially apparent in the nine-line passage Ngũgĩ chose for the epigraph. In Ngũgĩ's novel, the swamp is a strange brew of past actions that ooze up and circulate through the hearts and minds of those living in the present. The novel is full of images of blood, usually relating to the sacrifices of Kenyan history but also to sexual desire, and to the longing for meaning. Like *A Grain of Wheat,* the novel spreads a dense fabric of imagery, especially of blood, fire, and organic growth, and religious and historical allusion, but it is also a significant departure from Ngũgĩ's earlier fiction and forms a transition to his last Gĩkũyũ novels.

Petals of Blood refers often to planting and cultivation, the flowering of hope, the inspiring *theng'eta* plant, and the blood or labor of the masses and the sacrifices of the Emergency. The novel's imagery explicitly links the work of Kenya's cultivators with the work of its pastoralists. The phrase "petals of blood" is used first when Munira is on a school field trip. He is disturbed by questions about the laws of biology, survival, and God when a student finds a worm-eaten flower. Munira presumably misses a golden opportunity for expanding his natural science lesson to include the history of struggle and resistance, or the law of history. The students' spontaneous queries nudge him uncomfortably toward "an area of darkness" (*Petals,* 24),[4] a consideration of the hierarchy of laws at work in the world. Shortly afterward, governed now himself by the law of desire, he thinks of Wanja's "beautiful petals" (41), though he later considers that "by deflowering her by force" he could cause his own "flowering in blood" (76). He hopes that violent sexual conquest or possibly rape will restore his ego and his sense of agency. Finally, the phrase "petals of blood" refers to the fire that engulfs Wanja's brothel (45, 333). For Munira, this fiery conflagration is the flowering of the law of God. The phrase "petals of blood" stands for the power of different laws to direct people's lives, and the way willful blindness of such laws obstructs social awareness.

Petals of Blood is Ngũgĩ's longest and densest novel, a sprawling epic of postindependence Kenya and a veritable encyclopedia of Kenyan folktales, oral history, mythology, song, proverbial wisdom, and traditional lore. It is an archive of collective memory. It contains a vast sweep of characters but, like *A Grain of Wheat,* focuses on four individuals: Munira, Karega, Abdulla, and Wanja. These four characters are haunted by memory, wounded by disappointment and hypocrisy, yet ever resilient. Together they form an irregular family, often supporting but also disappointing, abandoning, and even exploiting each other. They are connected by an intricate and ever more fully revealed web of interrelations. Munira's sister Mukami was Karega's doomed lover, and Karega was Munira's student. Munira's father, Ezekieli, attempted unsuccessfully to seduce Karega's hardworking mother, Mariamu. Karega's brother Nding'uri was a freedom fighter betrayed at the same time as Abdulla. He may have been responsible for cutting off Munira's father's ear, a warning from the fighters in the forest for him to stop preaching against Mau Mau. Wanja was seduced and perhaps raped by Kimeria and forced to leave home and murder her baby. She has sexual relations with Munira, Karega, and Abdulla, and Abdulla is likely the father of the baby she is pregnant with at the novel's end, though symbolically the baby's father in her idealized reproduction combines the best of all three men. Karega's brother Nding'uri loved the sister of the wicked Kimeria, who in turn betrayed Nding'uri and Abdulla. The complex ties between these four and the patterns of their union and separation, support and desertion, make them into a nontraditional family, of a type that may form the cell of a model future society. Symbolic of this new and ever-changing family structure is Abdulla's adoption of Joseph, an orphan barely surviving in a junkyard, who represents Kenya's new generation of dispossessed. As the narrator points out: "If Abdulla could choose a brother, why couldn't they all do the same? Choose brothers and sisters in sweat, in toil, in struggle, and stand by one another" (*Petals,* 303).

Munira is closest to being the central character, and he is another of Ngũgĩ's vacillating intellectuals, tormented by guilt over an early sexual indiscretion, the suicide of his younger sister, his rejection by his wealthy, hypocritical father, and an awareness of being a spectator of his own life. He fails at almost everything he tries, save for the weirdly motivated act that generates the novel. Munira is associated with T. S. Eliot's alienated Prufrock when he sees "the burnt-out cigarette-ends of his life, his illusions, his desires" (*Petals*, 269), so different from the revolutionary fire that burns in Karega, indicated in the novel's reference to another modernist classic, W. B. Yeats's apocalyptic "The Second Coming," in the title of part 2. Karega was once Munira's student at Manguo, and he also once attended Siriana. Munira was expelled from school for passive involvement in a strike, and Karega was also expelled, but because of active participation. Karega's role develops in the novel's second half, when he becomes a priestlike teacher of history as resistance to oppression, an activist labor union organizer, and a political visionary who anticipates a new Kenya. Abdulla lost his leg during the Emergency when he was a brave fighter in the forest, but he feels guilty that he has not avenged the death of his comrade Nding'uri. By the end of the novel, Abdulla stands ready to murder Kimeria, who has betrayed both Nding'uri and Abdulla and has reaped the rewards of independence, becoming rich and powerful. Wanja was seduced and perhaps raped by the same Kimeria and ran away pregnant from her hypocritical Christian parents to become a bar girl and sometime prostitute. She threw her newborn into a latrine and is haunted by guilt and a dread that she will never conceive again. She has gone to Ilmorog to consult her powerful grandmother Nyakinyua, and the local medicine man Mwathi wa Mugo, and does become pregnant at the end of the novel, when she has resolved to stop perpetuating the ruthless capitalist economy by running a house of prostitution for the wealthy.

In terms of genre, *Petals of Blood* is a hybrid, combining elements of the realist novel and, like Ngũgĩ's last two novels, elements of parable and allegory. There is a focus on particularized characters' inner lives, and we see them interacting with an environment dotted with Kenyan place names. Coincidence, a structural mainstay of the Victorian novel, links the characters and their histories. Elements of parable are found in the explicit way that the characters' lives represent the lapses and fears of all Kenyans, and in the use of type names, such as Fraudsham for the English headmaster, and the once-mentioned Sir Swallow Bloodall, as well as the representation of Ilmorog as a city standing for all Kenya.

The novel has the breadth and inclusiveness of Victorian triple-decker novels, and of French[5] and African socialist novels, such as Sembene Ousmane's *God's Bits of Wood,*[6] which Abdulla and Joseph are reading at the novel's close. *Petals of Blood* is also a type of prose workers' hymn, increasingly strident and didactic in the political solutions it poses for national problems.

Petals of Blood has had a divided critical reception, and the main point of contention has been how successfully the novel handles this very didacticism. Critics such as G. D. Killam and Eustace Palmer note the novel's continuity with Ngũgĩ's earlier fiction,[7] but others have regretted the newfound didacticism, which they regard as excessive, counterproductive, and inartistic.[8] While applauding the novel's "ambitiousness," more sympathetic readers have not failed to note its "uneven[ness]."[9] Simon Gikandi, writing in 1987, had questioned the excessive "authorial intrusiveness" in *Petals of Blood,* but just five years later, he referred to Ngũgĩ's longest text as "Ngũgĩ's masterpiece."[10] Bernth Lindfors, asserting the novel's robust durability, has summarized this prevailing critical bifurcation over *Petals of Blood:* "Ngugi may have his heart in the right place, but the critical consensus seems to be that he does not always have his art where it should be."[11] In fact, the critical reception of the novel may be a valuable touchstone for the state of African literary criticism in general, as Joseph McLaren has recently suggested.[12]

The genesis of *Petals of Blood,* however, is a murder, though a potentially political one, and the novel has the suspense of a thriller, the whodunit detective novel, while also being a loosely structured series of multilayered personal narratives. We are given Munira's report of an episode, and then following it and sometimes much later the accounts of the other three characters, always supplying one more detail in the narrative jigsaw puzzle. These details partly function to supply each of the four characters with a clear motive for murder. While this technique adds suspense, it also necessitates a good deal of repetition and some turgid passages of reflective summary. The novel has a dual temporal structure, beginning in the present, immediately after the murder of Mzigo, Chui, and Kimeria, with Munira's police interrogation, and proceeding until his admission on day 12 that he set the deadly fire. The parallel time structure covers the 12 years leading up to the night of the murder. The novel's structure indicates the past's interconnections with the present, and by extension history's usefulness as a tool for understanding the present.

A relationship between a single reader and writer lies at the heart of *Petals of Blood.* Much of the narrative may be understood as Munira's extensive written confession that step by step retraces the events of the 12 years leading up to the murder. Munira is reflecting on, and trying to comprehend, his past, and into his narrative he weaves the stories of others with their gaps and uncertainties. The reader of Munira's confession is police inspector Godfrey, significantly a man who shares Munira's given name, and who may be his double, alter ego, or conscience. Like a careful reader of the novel, Godfrey is ever "sifting words, storing phrases and looks and gestures, also looking for a line, a key, a thread, a connection, an image that would help tie everything together" (*Petals,* 299). Inspector Godfrey staunchly upholds the law of the state, though he is aware of the abusers of power and position, whom these laws protect. He knows, for example, that Kimeria, one of the murdered men, was probably involved in organizing Kenyan participation in the international sex trade, but Godfrey maintains his silence. He is aware of, but largely untroubled by, the contradictions of his position as both an upholder and would-be investigator of corruption. He questions Munira's morality and also that of the other suspects, Karega, Abdulla, and Wanja, while his own moral authority is fatally undermined by his hypocrisy and willingness to torture detainees. In addition to his police confession, Munira is engaged in an angry dialogue with himself, itself an expression of his sense of being an outsider, a spectator of his own life. He reflects on his 12 wasted years of oscillation, indecision, and compromise, which commenced with his unconfessed guilt about having sex with a prostitute and end with his commitment to a charismatic cult, led by a former casual lover. While Munira's uncertainty reflects the difficulty of correctly perceiving the social and political nature of postindependence Kenya—an uncertainty shared by Karega, Abdulla, and Wanja—Munira's predicament is far more debilitating, and he escapes from it only through a crazy attempt to seize personal comfort in religious fanaticism. Karega's final commitment to a political cause, however, although hastily and somewhat unconvincingly drawn, contrasts starkly with Munira's vacillation, and Karega is one of Ngũgĩ's first largely perfect heroes.

Karega is the novel's interpreter, not of confessions, but of history. History, for him, is a discipline, a method for understanding oneself and the world, and a tool for transforming the present. Siriana has taught European history to African students, and the student strikes in which Munira and later Karega participate were organized to support curriculum revision, allowing the teaching of African history. At the time of the murder, another strike is being planned, this time against an African headmaster, Chui, who upholds the Eurocentric curriculum of the earlier English headmasters, Ironmonger and Fraudsham. Chui is one of the novel's neocolonial sham Africans, "the black zombies, black animated cartoons dancing the master's dance to the master's voice," who as teachers help create more black zombies (*Petals,* 163, 166). The strike's organizers want a history that does not present a colonial perspective on guns, money, and trains in Kenya, but a history of the Kenyan people's resistance for hundreds of years to external oppression and internal feudalism. This history of resistance is an advance on Karega's teaching program at Ilmorog school, a program that celebrates great African empires of the past and great heroes (including the Indo-Kenyan Makhan Singh) and arose from Karega's perception of his students' lack of a national consciousness. Despite its hesitations about merely historicizing great empires and heroes of the past, characteristic of African historiography of the 1950s and 1960s, the novel's own idealization of a lineage of Kenyan heroes does exemplify this type of history and by extension tends to idealize and glorify the precontact period. As one of Karega's students points out, the stories of these empires and heroes end in dust or defeat, and he wonders how they relate to the present. Karega recognizes the fatal divorce of theory and praxis, and the gap it creates between the past and present, but he cannot bridge it until after his education in trade unionism, just as the radical lawyer in Nairobi, like Trumper in Lamming's *In the Castle of My Skin,* must witness racial oppression in America before he can see the contemporary Kenyan situation clearly. Through direct experience, Karega's previous notion of history as "romantic adventures" acquires "flesh and blood" (*Petals,* 228).

Wanja, Munira, Abdulla, and even Karega seem stymied by their understanding of their personal histories and their experiences' relationship to the national narrative. For Wanja, the past is a wound that drives her to seek revenge against all men or makes her crave sweet amnesia. Munira wants to re-create the past in his confession to "show the operation of God's law" (*Petals,* 45) and to resurrect and restore his own personal "usurped history" (227), which he too has tried to escape. Abdulla must settle the scores of the past, a personal betrayal with national consequences, to move on to create a life for his new family at the novel's end. For Abdulla, correctly reading the past is a type of initiation, like circumcision, into full adulthood. Abdulla considers that the day he grasped the value of collective ownership of the means of production "was the day of his true circumcision into a man" (136), and later he feels the same about his resolution to murder Kimeria. Karega explains that "to understand the present . . . you must understand the past. To know where you are, you must know where you came from" (128). In isolation and together, the characters explore and reevaluate their own histories to heal the wounds of the past. Incorrectly understood, the past can be simply a repository of guilt and grief, hampering present decision and action. Therefore, in official neocolonial histories, the past merely justifies and sanctions contemporary injustice. The Kenyan history in the books loaned to Karega by the Nairobi lawyer deplores traditional tribal warfare and laments "undercivilisation," in effect suggesting, as Karega thinks, that the African "deserved the brutality of the coloniser to boot him into our civilisation" (199). Just as Karega rejects officially sanctioned histories, so he also questions the value of formal schooling.

The best medium for conveying historical truth that has an economic, political basis is the oral history of elders such as Nyakinyua, whose songs make the people "relive" events (*Petals*, 124, 210). Munira asserts to the inspector that his "true" confessional history is, like all personal narratives, to some extent fictional (191). By extension, the vehicle of the popular novel (Lindfors 1991, 79–86), such as *Petals of Blood*, including a variety of personal narratives, is valorized as a most effective historical medium. The novel's history is the story of developing historical consciousness. Thus Karega comes to see that history begins with present struggles against political, economic, and social oppression, and that a history of resistance works toward the creation of a new world. He begins to look favorably on the examples of the People's Republic of China and the Soviet Union as models for Kenya. Karega makes a clear statement of belief:

> The true lesson of history was this: that the so-called victims, the poor, the downtrodden, the masses, had always struggled with spears and arrows, with their hands and songs of courage and hope, to end their oppression and exploitation: that they would continue struggling until a human kingdom came: a world in which goodness and beauty and strength and courage would be seen not in how cunning one can be, not in how much power to oppress one possessed, but only in one's contribution in creating a more humane world in which the inherited inventive genius of man in culture and science from all ages and climes would be not the monopoly of a few, but for the use of all, so that all flowers in all their different colours would ripen and bear fruits and seeds. And the seeds would be put into the ground and they would once again sprout and flower in rain and sunshine. (*Petals*, 303)

Teaching historical resistance to oppression thus enables the flowering of petals of hope.

For the police inspector, this would be more "communist nonsense" (*Petals,* 299), for Munira "propaganda" (245), and perhaps for Wanja an early example of "didactic triteness" (326); but in the context of the novel as a whole, we are clearly to accept Karega's somewhat unsubtle, harping words as sincere and as the best and possibly only way out of a morass of poverty, exploitation, and vacillation. As he explains to Wanja, the past is important "but only as a living lesson to the present. I mean we must not preserve our past as a museum: rather, we must study it critically, without illusions, and see what lessons we can draw from it in today's battlefield of the future and the present. But to worship it—no. Maybe I used to do it: but I don't want to continue worshiping in the temples of a past without tarmac roads, without electric cookers, a world dominated by slavery to nature" (323). Karega does not recommend an uncritical, utopian re-creation of the past and a disregard for modern advances in technology. He values history as a weapon in the information war, a weapon to be used on the battlefield of the present and future. Knowing heroes of the past is useful in identifying heroes of the present, and the novel ends with a projection of this historical understanding, a rumored sighting of the disappeared Mau Mau general Stanley Mathenge, and the possibility of a second revolutionary struggle.

The consequences of a deluded perception of history extend to the debasement and appropriation of language and naming. Contempt is shown to Kenyans who adopt Western names, but it is also extended to Africans like Nderi wa Riera, formerly David Samuel, who insidiously trade on the cachet of "cultural authenticity" by taking manufactured African names (*Petals,* 186). Significantly, the boy orphaned in the junk-yard has no name. The rhetoric of cultural revival and harmony masks the divisive repression of the Kĩama-Kamwene Cultural Organization (KCO)'s Tea Parties, which even appropriate the ritual words of oathing that were of such significance in the Mau Mau struggle: "They took a symbol from its original beautiful purpose . . . and they think they can make it serve narrow selfish ends!" (112). A still more reprehensible appropriation occurs when the traitor Nderi wa Riera, echoing a favorite phrase of Jomo Kenyatta,[13] claims blandly, "we were all freedom fighters" (153). Words used in a slippery way produce mystification, as when the headmaster Chui, "a black replica of Fraudsham," cloaks his Eurocentrism in the language of universal brotherhood and law and order

(171). Fraudsham has presumably deluded himself into believing in his noble cause in Africa and has obscured his romantic despair and his quest for a type of glorious suicide with principled phrases. In the wrong hands, "phrases like Democracy, the Free World, for instance, are used to mean their opposite" (59). The deliberate misuse of language is especially apparent among the hypocritically pious Christian characters in the novel, who use biblical justification to censure others and refuse common charity. Their unholy trinity is "the Bible, the Coin, the Gun" (88). Both the honest and the hypocritical in *Petals of Blood* refer to the Bible. For characters like Karega, as for actual Mau Mau fighters like Njama (Barnett and Njama, 184–85, 367–68), biblical allusion is a form of rhetorical enhancement, similar to the use of proverbs in Gĩkũyũ orature. The lack of orthodox theological grounding for such references, however, does not preclude their carrying a weight of righteous indignation, a striving for forgiveness or redress, or an apocalyptic foreboding.

In addition to the debasement of language, *Petals of Blood* tackles the undermining of the family in the neocolonial state. This does not mean that the novel promotes the replication of traditional family ties; on the contrary, it anticipates radically different family groupings. Wanja has come to the end of her personal journey, the series of her "false starts to nowhere" (*Petals,* 64), and her child will combine the best of the freedom fighter Abdulla and of her wise, patriotic grandmother. Wanja produces an image of her child's father combining the idealized, hermaphroditic freedom fighter sculpture at the lawyer's home in Nairobi and the likeness of Dedan Kimathi. A victim of sexual exploitation, which continues during her career as a barmaid, Wanja embodies the features of a number of female stereotypes identified in African literature.[14] She is a prostitute, but desiring to imprison men through the power of her body, she becomes a demonic, castrating woman, and finally a mother of the nation. The misogynistic and sexually conflicted Munira sees her as an amoral sexual predator, and his wish to save Karega from her motivates his arson attack on Wanja's brothel. Wanja, who by this period has resumed a relationship with Kimeria, her former exploiter, argues disingenuously to Karega that she is simply exploiting the system that has exploited her. She implies that she has gained power and agency by controlling an interpersonal relationship that by its very nature reifies and dehumanizes those it involves. Karega refuses to credit her motive and breaks with her, a rejection that inspires her plan to abandon her trade and reemploy the prostitutes under her charge in other work. At this moment, Munira enacts his plan to destroy the brothel, and presumably to murder Wanja, just when both Abdulla and Wanja separately have resolved to murder Kimeria.

Like *A Grain of Wheat*, *Petals of Blood* closes with an unusual, uncommitted pseudofamily grouping and the prospect of birth. Wanja has murdered Kimeria, and she is pregnant with Abdulla's baby. This union joins some of the most downtrodden and wretched elements of society, who have heroic ancestors or personal involvement in struggle. The announcement of Wanja's pregnancy prefaces the news that all of Ilmorog will join the strike and that a second Mau Mau struggle may erupt. Wanja and Abdulla are dedicated to a noble purpose at the end, though this purpose is a plan to murder Kimeria; but on his way to perform the act, Abdulla passes children, like Joseph years before, living in a junkyard. This encounter, combined with Joseph's revolutionary zeal, and the sense that Wanja's baby has a freedom fighter's genes, evinces the novel's concern for children, for Kenya's next generation of dispossessed. Ngũgĩ will explore this concern in his last novel, *Matigari,* which begins with the vision of children fighting in a junkyard, and in his children's stories, their hero taking the name of Nyakinyua's heroic husband, Njamba Nene.

The focus of *Petals of Blood* forever spirals backward to the fatal night of the triple murder, but it also projects forward into the future. Karega learns from the factory worker Akinyi that there has been a murder in Nairobi, there are rumors of Mathenge's return, and the Ilmorog strike called for by the dying Nyakinyua has gone beyond the brewery and united all the town's workers. Amid all of this revolutionary optimism, Munira lies in the remand prison, quietly left to his fate for setting the fire. His arson, which might appear revolutionary in this context, is the mad, jealousy-motivated action of an overzealous member of a revivalist cult, led by a woman with whom he shared sexual relations, fraught with guilt and violence. Munira's act is only by sheer accident a blow against exploitation, providing the spark to ignite a second Mau Mau war of liberation, one "to make our independence real" (*Petals,* 10). Munira seems to link the murder plot and the story of national betrayal, and his arson appears to be directed at the "black few, allied to other interests from Europe, [who] would continue the colonial game of robbing others of their sweat" (294). Munira's arson, however, is merely a gesture of self-affirmation, an escape from his prison of low self-esteem. It is murder as self-realization. Munira is a sexually troubled man, fatally separated from his father and distanced from his own existence, and he has seized on the fire as a scheme to save the saintly Karega from the demonic Wanja, an object of desire that he is denied. The novel's heroic, apocalyptic ending, with renewed revolutionary forces marshaling to demand justice,[15] poised before a coming conflagration, is undercut by the odd motivation behind Munira's action, which has generated the novel's search for answers and allowed the righteously indignant, bard-like, and prophetic voice of the narrator to answer his own question about who will sing the song of Kenyan resistance (67).

Devil on the Cross

Although *Devil on the Cross* (*Caitaani Mũtharaba-inĩ*) and *Matigari* develop some of the themes of Ngũgĩ's earlier novels, they represent a dramatic departure in his work, "a decisive break with middle-class intellectualism" (Lazarus, 207), and an ending of what Ngũgĩ has termed "self-colonization."[16] Most importantly, they were written in Gĩkũyũ, and Ngũgĩ refers to them as his first "Africa novels," as opposed to his earlier novels written within the "Afro-Saxon" tradition of the "Afro-European novel." Although not originally part of the oral tradition or orature,[17] *Devil on the Cross* bears many markings of the oral tale, including songs, traditional mythical figures, ritualized performance, repetition of phrases, and themes of transformation. In addition, the narrator is related to a traditional storyteller, the Gĩcaandĩ Player. This figure reluctantly tells his morality tale of many-mouthed phantoms and monsters as a warning to the next generation because he is admonished to do so by the people. He reluctantly agrees, because as he says, nearly repeating Karega's phrase in *Petals of Blood* (126): "The voice of the people is the voice of God" (*Devil,* 8). Much of the novel has a performative, theatrical quality, with speakers usually addressing groups of five or more and occasionally breaking into choral song. Similarly, the novel as a whole implies a reception that is collective and communal, like that of the popular Gĩkũyũ theater in which Ngũgĩ was involved. Although the novel's first readers were prison guards, when it was published, *Devil on the Cross* was read by assembled families, by workers during lunch breaks, by people in taxis and buses, and by "professional readers" in bars: "When the reader reached an interesting episode and he discovered that his glass was empty, he would put the book down. 'Give him another bottle of beer!' some of the listeners would shout to the proprietor. So our reader would resume and go on until his glass was empty" (*Decolonising,* 83). In this way, the novel was "appropriated" into the oral tradition through its reception by the group, the reading of a text being a constitutive dimension of the work itself.

Devil on the Cross was written very quickly and carries the urgency of being composed under real duress, unlike the laborious six- or seven-year process required for assembling the hybrid *Petals of Blood,* and bears the concentration and boldness of its genesis. It is perhaps impossible to separate the novel from the circumstances of its production. *Devil on the Cross* was written during Ngũgĩ's detention in cell 16 of a detention block of Kamĩtĩ Maximum Security Prison, and whereas he was never charged or put on trial, it appears his incarceration was a state response to his activities with the Kamĩrĩĩthũ Community Educational and Cultural Center, although it may have been related to the more bitter criticism of neocolonial Kenya in *Petals of Blood,* though that novel was launched with the appearance of official sanction (*Writers,* 2d ed., 83–94). In May 1978, the *New York Times* published an account of Ngũgĩ's detention, accompanied by the first chapter of *Petals of Blood,* highlighting the similarity between Ngũgĩ's and Munira's imprisonment (Rothmyer, A27). Ngũgĩ's involvement with Kamĩrĩĩthũ with its potential to spread his ideas in Gĩkũyũ at the grassroots level may have been more sensitive, however. The center staged Gĩkũyũ plays that were collectively written and that tackled local social and political problems. The plays were enormously popular. In detention, as he writes in *Detained: A Writer's Prison Diary,* Ngũgĩ came to see his writing as belonging to a tradition of Kenyan struggle against political oppression, and partly inspired by a remark by a prison guard about intellectuals writing in English, Ngũgĩ began his novel (*Detained,* 124, 126–27), though its germ had been stirring in him for some time. In prison, he read Kwame Nkrumah's account—written originally on toilet paper—of imprisonment by colonial authorities. Ngũgĩ began *Devil on the Cross* on the rough toilet paper of the prison in which he had been shut up by neocolonial authorities.

Devil on the Cross is a novel without a hero, though in *Detained,* Ngũgĩ refers to it as "the Warĩĩnga novel" (166). The novel, like *A Grain of Wheat* and *Petals of Blood,* has four central characters: the exploited woman who turns revolutionary, Warĩĩnga; the peasant and survivor of the Mau Mau struggle, Wangari; the worker and political organizer, Mũturi; and the petit bourgeois intellectual, Gatuĩria. These characters' interaction is connected to their observation of the Competition in Modern Theft and Robbery. They meet when traveling to the competition, and during the journey they narrate their life experiences while withholding certain details such as the identity of the Rich Old Man. Like Wanja in *Petals of Blood,* Wariinga has been sexually enticed by this rich older man, and later we learn that he is the father of Gatuiria, with whom she has fallen in love. The centerpiece of the novel and one of the great achievements of Ngũgĩ's fiction is the depiction of the grotesque, fantastical competition to select leaders in modern theft and robbery. It is a performance of the self-aggrandizing, cannibalistic capitalism deplored in *Petals of Blood* where characters like Karega rail against heartless businessmen as "the drinkers of human sweat, eaters of human flesh" (*Petals,* 236). The competition takes place in a cave. As if they had taken a truth drug, participants willingly and proudly boast of the ingenuity of their involvement in robbery, slavery, and murder, without any attempt at concealment, mystification, justification, or apology. The scene recalls Ngũgĩ's account of Kenyatta's boasting speech about his own material accumulation since independence (*Writers,* 2d ed., 107). The participants are gross caricatures, and they and some of the phantoms met by Gatuiria are derived from Kenyan folklore and the "human shaped rocks of Idakho" in western Kenya (*Decolonising,* 81). Ngũgĩ's use of nonrealist techniques of characterization indicates his work's proximity to a folk idiom and also his utter exasperation with the monstrosity of actual events in his homeland. Participants boast of their brand-name material possessions as qualifications for entry in the competition. Next they relate their diabolical, nightmarish schemes for gaining wealth, cheating the population, and defying the laws of morality and nature. It is an orgy of greed celebrating the glory of getting rich: "The fart of the rich man never smelled foul" (*Devil,* 142).

Some of the competitors' schemes satirize the European fixations of economically prosperous Kenyans, and others target the consequences of unregulated greed for wealth and power. In his testimony, Nditika wa Ngũũnji boasts of his own theft and robbery, and he recommends forgetting the past, always a signal of doom in Ngũgĩ's fictional catalog of values. Nditika exports endangered animal parts and smuggles essential foodstuffs, exploiting periodic famines. He favors foreign partnerships as a way of introducing advanced technology, particularly the medical technique of transplantation. He dreams of exploiting the surgery to allow the rich unlimited consumption of every imaginable pleasure, permitting the purchase of a type of immortality: "Every rich man could have two mouths, two bellies, two cocks, two hearts—and hence two lives!" (*Devil,* 181). Death would become the purview of the poor. His manic ravings are outdone only by a man whose whole body has been grotesquely distorted by overeating into that of a "fat, hairy worm with a beak" (196). During the Emergency, this man supported the British and even drove his Landrover over the bodies of men and women. Becoming rich after independence, he realizes that "the sweat and the blood of the workers are the wellsprings of wealth" (187). He also advocates a scientific program, reminiscent of the medical tortures of the Nazi concentration camps, to extract the blood, sweat, and brains of workers caged in animal pens. He would then export these products by pipeline. Workers would willingly participate in the scheme because of persistent media- and church-sanctioned ideological brainwashing convincing them that such exploitation is part of a divine master plan. Warĩĩnga is horrified by what she hears, but she must also resist the sweet and bitter words of a ghostly tempter, who compares the last scheme to the Eucharist, the sacramental—and, he implies, cannibalistic—eating of the body and blood of Christ. Her tempter suggests that she, too, can enjoy the fruits of exploitation, just as to some degree Wanja has in *Petals of Blood,* rationalizing her actions to herself by thinking that because she cannot defeat the forces of oppression, she may at least profit from them, while trying to avoid being infected by their wickedness. Warĩĩnga, however, resists temptation. She is troubled and inspired by a dream of a devil with a white skin "being crucified by people in tattered clothes . . . and after three days, when he was in the throes of death, he would be taken down from the Cross by black people in suits and ties, and, thus restored to life, he would mock Warĩĩnga" (*Devil,* 139). Later, Warĩĩnga dreams again of the devil on the cross, but this time there is a different outcome. Poor people present at the crucifixion retreat to the forest, where they presumably prepare for a full-scale assault on the devil and his many angels.

The extensive use of biblical narratives in *Devil on the Cross* and *Matigari* is related to what we may call Ngũgĩ's Mau Mau aesthetics. At the same time, *Devil on the Cross*'s drawings from the Bible also engage its moral authority, its tendency to infuse history with prophetic urgency, and its emphasis on miraculous transformation of the material world and of the heart and mind of the believer. These novels' plots are non-realistic and instead employ the device of biblical allegory, as did the imprisoned revolutionary seventeenth-century Puritan writer John Bunyan in *The Pilgrim's Progress,* well known to Kenyan readers (*Decolonising,* 69, 70).[18] Ngũgĩ draws the underlying structure of *Devil on the Cross* from the account of the crucifixion of Christ (and to a lesser degree from the parable of the five talents), but he transforms it, substituting a contemporary Kenyan setting and political theme. Elsewhere the novel transforms the Bible's beatitudes into "the Beatitudes of the rich and the imperialists," one of which is "Blessed is the man who burns down another man's house / And in the morning joins him in grief, / For he shall be called merciful" (*Devil,* 209). *Devil on the Cross* relies so heavily on the Bible partly because a general Kenyan audience, especially a rural and illiterate one, would be intimately familiar with it, and with its typological interpretation, or a ready identification of events from their own lives with the words and deeds of Christ, the apostles, and the Old Testament prophets. The biblical language, moreover, is changed into an instantly recognizable idiom (*Barrel,* 65).

Devil on the Cross draws on the cultural practices of the Mau Mau freedom fighters.[19] These fighters, like some of the forces in the later armed revolutionary struggle in Zimbabwe,[20] took Christian hymns and biblical stories and, as Ngũgĩ explains, "gave these meanings and values in harmony with the aspirations of their struggle. Christians had often sung about heaven and angels, and a spiritual journey in a spiritual intangible universe where metaphysical disembodied evil and good were locked in perpetual spiritual warfare. . . . The Mau Mau revolutionaries took up the same song and tune and turned it into a song of actual political, visible material freedom and struggle for land. The battle was no longer in heaven but here on earth, in Kenya" (*Writers,* 1st ed., 27). Planting revolutionary messages in the soil of popular religious practice was extremely effective in establishing and then disseminating a political credo far and wide. In effect, this Mau Mau aesthetic technique transforms what Ngũgĩ perceived to be one of the most insidious, because seemingly innocuous and even ameliorative, tools of the oppressor into a weapon to fight oppression. This method illustrates the marriage of creative cultural practices, armed resistance, and radical theory that Ngũgĩ admired in the work of Amílcar Cabral and in the operations of Mau Mau. This method, and more generally the novel's fusion of a variety of genres, including the magic realism of García Márquez, orature, and even cinematic techniques, is similar to the fragmented and multifaceted heteroglossia of postmodern fiction (Gikandi 1992, 139–43). *Devil on the Cross* is distinguishable from postmodern practices because it denies that all meaning is provisional or unstable. Instead, *Devil on the Cross,* perhaps too stridently for some Western readers at least,[21] declares its message about neocolonialism and the means to correct it, boldly if relentlessly, in places nearly choking on its own expression of outrage.

Although not as virulent in its attack on the neocolonial economy of blood, *Devil on the Cross,* like *Petals of Blood,* disdains the timid, vacillating intellectual. The artist-intellectual Gatuĩria is unlike the narrator, who is a people's judge, prophet, and visionary, acknowledging freely that his tale is communal property and his voice merely the clarion call for collective justice. Gatuĩria plans a national oratorio in praise of the heroic deeds of the past. He has been somehow tainted, however, by his class background, his allegiance to a father who has exploited Warĩĩnga, and his 15 years overseas. Gatuĩria resembles Munira in *Petals of Blood,* who enjoys traditional circumcision ceremonies but, perhaps because of his years at Siriana and his sense of alienation, is a wooden dancer who doesn't know the words to the songs and gets confused when he participates in the ritualized erotic cross talk. Similarly Gatuĩria has difficulty writing African music, although the reason is that its notation has yet to be sufficiently differentiated from Western forms, a problem Ngũgĩ encountered with Gĩkũyũ orthography. Gatuĩria cannot speak Gĩkũyũ without breaking into English, a sign of his colonized mentality, "the slavery of the mind" (*Devil,* 56), a particularly debilitating inadequacy for a would-be artist of the nation in a Gĩkũyũ novel. His inability to communicate in his mother tongue is especially important because hearing is a metaphor in the novel for correct understanding. Keen hearing assuages mental "deafness," debilitating self-questioning, and the dread of listening to the echo of one's own voice betraying community secrets (7). At the end of the novel, Gatuĩria hears "in his mind music that lead[s] him nowhere" (254). His directionlessness is critical in *Devil on the Cross,* and the narrative ends stressing the imperative of choice, and of choice leading to action. His commitment to the nation and his belief in his musical composition, like his love for Warĩĩnga, stops at the boundary of hatred, which must be, as Warĩĩnga says, intertwined with true love. He reaches the same impasse as Waiyaki, at the end of *The River Between,* who refuses to take revenge against his enemies such as Kabonyi and instead dies at their hands.

In some respects, Warĩĩnga appears designed to rectify the weakness in the portrayal of Wanja in *Petals of Blood.* Although her genesis is similar to Wanja's and she also raises a weapon against the male attacker who destroyed her youthful innocence, Warĩĩnga is far from being a victim. She is Ngũgĩ's attempt to write women back into the story of colonial and neocolonial struggle.[22] In fact, in *Devil on the Cross,* Warĩĩnga's personal acceptance of feminist agency allegorizes the revolutionary struggle; her sexual exploitation is a metaphor for the nation's neocolonial seduction. The novel describes capitalist greed as cannibalistic, and the dangerous game of sexual roulette played by sugar girls and their daddies resembles the predatory relationship of hunter and hunted. The corruption of traditional styles of courtship that allows such excesses, the novel suggests, is the result of the hedonism and apolitical stance fostered in Kenyan youth through the consumption of foreign novels, songs, and films. Such a debasement of women's role and a commodification of the female body ignore the history of female participation in the liberation struggle. Wariinga herself demands: "Why have people forgotten how Kenyan women used to make guns during the Mau Mau war against the British? Can't people recall the different tasks carried out by women in the villages once the men had been sent to detention camps?" (*Devil*, 245). Wariinga is, however, like Wanja, remarkably beautiful, her attractiveness described in words resembling those of the Song of Solomon, from which part 3 of *Petals of Blood* takes two epigraphs: "Her voice was as smooth as perfume oil. Her eyes shone like stars in the night. Her body was a feast for the eyes" (*Petals*, 11). Wariinga's beauty, a conventional attribute of a female protagonist, accentuates her representation as a victim, a fallen object of pity. Although throughout the course of the novel she undergoes a dramatic metamorphosis into a worker heroine, adept at engine repair, judo, karate, and marksmanship, she is still rescued from a suicide attempt by male guardian angels: twice by Mūturi and once by the student leader. She is then transformed into a kind of spicy African Emma Peel (Evans, 134), and like the leather-clad avenging angel, suggestively named by TV producers, Wariinga is always ripe for unpeeling. At the end of the novel, although she has undergone a revolution in political and feminist consciousness, she is also a somewhat conventional figure deserted by two men and forced to accept an uncertain future, trapped in the compound of the Rich Old Man, who is murdered partly because of his refusal to take her as his second wife. Despite her shortcomings, Wariinga's heroism underscores not Ngūgī's attempt to formulate a type of "feminotopia"[23] but his faith in a worker and peasant society of complete gender equality that can transform all social relations.

Matigari

Devil on the Cross was written in prison; *Matigari (Matigari ma Njirūūngi)* was written in exile. *Devil on the Cross*'s report of the competitive feasting of destructive ogres and the growing outrage of the broader community erupts in *Matigari* into a prolonged trial of abuses and a final sentence. Like *Devil on the Cross,* Ngūgī's last novel employs the structure of a journey, but here the geography of Kenya is more obviously symbolic. The protagonist of *Matigari* wishes to return home from his long years in the forest after the revolutionary struggle to reclaim his house and land. The property was appropriated in the colonial period by Settler (Howard) Williams and later sold by his son Robert Williams, the director of a number of companies; the buyer of the house and land was John Boy Junior, the son of John Boy, the settler's cook and deputy. John Boy Junior and Robert Williams, "like twins born out of the womb of the same ogre," represent parasitic neocolonial and multinational interests.[24] The novel is full of the dismay of one who fought for freedom only to discover that freedom squandered. In the novel, two destitute peasants, obeying the order from the Orwellian radio program *The Voice of Truth* to arrest all political madmen, turn in to the police the pictures of two subversives: Jesus Christ and Karl Marx. In a strange twist, in 1987, the Kenyan government sought to arrest Ngūgī's fictional creation Matigari as a troublemaker, in response to rumors that he was roaming the countryside demanding truth and justice. Realizing their mistake, the police banned the book, which, with its English translation in 1989, has joined its author in exile.

Matigari is the account of a freedom fighter during the Mau Mau struggle who, laying down his arms and returning to reclaim his lands, asks again and again, "[W]ho can tell me where a person who has girded himself with a belt of peace can find truth and justice!" (92) Everywhere, he encounters the injustice, oppression, and fear of neocolonial Kenya. He rescues the prostitute Gūthera from a brutal police attack and is transformed instantly from a wizened elder into a vital young warrior. Imprisoned, he breaks bread and is recognized as a Christlike leader by twelve prisoners, all but one of whom (Gīcerū, the informer) were arrested on false charges. The prison doors open miraculously, although all miracles are shown to have materially verifiable causes. The presence of miracles in the novel signals the notion that anecdotes about Matigari and his powers have been frequently retold and embellished until they assume a larger-than-life, mythic dimension, re-created by their retelling, and thus become the property of the community. Matigari completes a tour of the country, where he finds a people stifled by fear. He wanders and, Christlike, meditates in the wilderness—a timeless, metaphysical landscape—and then seeks representatives of different classes, questioning them about justice. In despair, he takes up arms.

In his last novel, Ngũgĩ has created a myth. Matigari is a collective, his name referring to those who survived the bullets of the Emergency. He is variously figured as a legend, as a dream, and as both male and female, young and old. He is called "Mr Seeker of Truth and Justice," "the prophet," and "a giant who could almost touch the sky above" (*Matigari*, 75, 76). Many people who meet Matigari in marketplaces, restaurants, farms, and law courts "added salt to his story" (69), embellishing his myth. He embodies the nation's spiritual and political hopes and desires. He fuses Jesus Christ, the aspirations of the Kenyan masses, and a legendary leader of the Mau Mau freedom fighters, General Stanley Mathenge, referred to reverently at the end of *Petals of Blood*. The historical Mathenge, one of the most important leaders of the Kenya Land and Freedom Army, disappeared in 1955 and became a legend among the Gĩkũyũ, prompting speculation that he would return only when genuine *uhuru*, or freedom, was achieved in Kenya.[25] Ngũgĩ was aware of the political implications of Mathenge/Matigari's return, writing at the close of *Moving the Centre*, "I know, in a sense more deep than words can tell, that Matigari shall one day return to Kenya, to East Africa, for his world is shared by the essential East Africa once envisioned in the Arusha declaration and the glimpses of which we still get when looking at our history as East Africans" (*Moving*, 175).

Matigari moves even further from realistic narrative technique than *Devil on the Cross*, fusing genres in a carnival of Gĩkũyũ postmodernism. The novel is based on an oral story, as Ngũgĩ's note to the English edition indicates, and though it begins and ends with open-eyed and unsentimental references to cradling an AK-47, a military assault rifle, it has the quality of a prophetic vision. The fluid structure of the novel was influenced by film technique. As Ngũgĩ explained in a 1986 interview: "I write as if each scene is captured in a frame, so the whole novel is a series of camera shots" (Eyoh, 166). The novel, though focused on the events of one day, seems to take place in dream time, which is highly elastic, and at once both radically compressed and elongated. It contains simultaneously the past and the present and implies that past and present, and perhaps the future, are all categories of consciousness. Matigari is a figure from history who embodies the contemporary aspirations of the Kenyan masses and whose spirit lives on. The "reader/listener" is enjoined at the beginning of the novel: "May the action take place in the time of your choice!" and "May you allocate the duration of any of the actions according to your choice!" (*Matigari*, ix). The narrative invites the reader/listener's participation in the events of its past, present, and future.

Matigari also employs Ngūgī's Mau Mau aesthetics. The novel engages directly with a demythologized Christianity and links the legend of Mathenge and the possibility of his return with the promise in Luke's Gospel of Christ's Second Coming. One of the central biblical narratives from which *Matigari* borrows is Luke's account of the two despairing disciples, walking to Emmaus and meeting a man on the road who travels with them, but whom "their eyes were kept from recognizing" (Luke 24:16). It is nearing evening, and the disciples urge the man to stay with them, but when he breaks bread, they recognize him as Jesus Christ, and he vanishes. In *Matigari,* charting the course of a single representative day, during which the worsening weather reflects the rising tension in its protagonist, the recognition of Matigari by the 12 prisoners follows his breaking bread, at which the drunkard is moved to recite the words of the Eucharist. Whereas the novel de-emphasizes the metaphysical nature of Christ's promise of the Second Coming, it does employ the spirit of the Gospels and uses their language. Matigari warns, for example, that "Jesus will find you asleep . . . when he returns" (*Matigari,* 153). Ngūgī situates this religious truth in a political context:

> The God who is prophesied is in you, in me and in the other humans. He has always been there inside us since the beginning of time. Imperialism has tried to kill that God within us. But one day that God will return from the dead. Yes, one day that God within us will come alive and liberate us who believe in Him. I am not dreaming. He will return on the day when His followers will be able to stand up without worrying about tribe, race or colour, and say in one voice: Our labour produced all the wealth in this land. So from today onwards we refuse to sleep out in the cold, to walk about in rags, to go to bed on empty bellies. Let the earth return to those to whom it belongs. Let the soil return to the tiller, the factory to the worker . . . But that God lives more in you children of this land; and therefore if you let the country go to the imperialist enemy and its local watchdogs, it is the same thing as killing that God who is inside you. It is the same thing as stopping Him from resurrecting. That God will come back only when you want Him to. (*Matigari,* 156)

This passage emphasizes the role of imperialism in stunting the individual's spiritual nature but also challenges readers to perceive the relationship between personal and collective bondage and spiritual well-being. It challenges readers to accept their responsibility to choose. The arrival of a climate for a second coming and a national rebirth depends on the enabling will of the masses.

The figure in the novel who is changed most dramatically by Matigari's example is Gũthera. Like Warĩĩnga in *Devil on the Cross* and Wanja in *Petals of Blood*, Gũthera is a prostitute, but *Matigari* broadens the discussion of the oppression of women in the earlier novels. For example, Gũthera realizes that even the wife of the Minister for Truth and Justice, found naked with her driver in the Mercedes, den of illicit pleasure and "four-wheeled tomb," is oppressed, almost as if all women form a distinct social class, regardless of economic or other indicators. Gũthera asks, "What can we as women do to change our lives? Or will we continue to follow the paths carved out for us by men?" (*Matigari,* 140). She questions women's position more pointedly than Matigari does the location of truth, wondering about the "problems we women have to go through wherever we are! When that woman [the Minister's wife] goes home, her husband will beat her, demanding to know what she was doing in the wilderness with a man. When her lover goes home, he will beat his wife for demanding to know what he was doing in the wilderness with a woman" (151). Gũthera, however, "follows" Matigari to this realization (159). She is awakened to women's oppression by her man. She must learn to follow his lead in advancing to the ancestral homestead, accepting that in Matigari's words, "women were the cornerstones of the home" (27). The first practical expression of her newly forged revolutionary consciousness is highly problematic. Gũthera aids Matigari by breaking her own resolution, her 11th commandment, and obtaining Matigari's release by having sexual intercourse with a prison guard, again assuming the character of a prostitute. In this violation, and in the woman's sexual exchange of her body to gain freedom, her story parallels Warĩĩnga's. Warĩĩnga also sleeps with a despised man, a former abusive lover, to obtain the freedom of her comrades during the people's trek to Nairobi. A woman's major revolutionary contribution, it appears, is to manipulate her sexuality, as if her body's desirability is her best weapon. The limits of her role in the revolutionary struggle are demarcated by biology; even in the revolution against neocolonial oppression, anatomy is still destiny.

At the end of the novel, Matigari's and Gũthera's blood mingles in Kenyan soil, an image that may be read as a consecration of the land. The novel also has a second ending, which connects more directly with its opening, the scene of Matigari taking off the weapons of war at the sacred *mũgumo* tree. In the novel's second ending, protected in a timeless zone, far from the recent firestorm that claimed the lives of Matigari and Gũthera, Matigari, now reborn in Mũriũki, girds himself with the belt of war and raises an AK-47. He sees a "riderless horse," like the horse of the apocalypse in the Book of Revelation, save that this one awaits its rider. Like the transformed spirit of Matigari, the horse gazes at Mūriũki before galloping into the forest. Then Mūriũki, inspired by the memory of Matigari's hard struggle, assumes the challenge of his legacy. Matigari may also be resurrected in the people from all walks of life and all Kenyan nationalities, craving justice and peace, who sing communally the novel's last lines, "victory shall be ours!" (*Matigari,* 175). As at the end of *Devil on the Cross,* in which Joseph, who grew up nameless and abandoned in a junkyard, takes up the cause, so, too, at the end of *Matigari,* another man who was a child at the novel's beginning assumes the mantle of war. Mūriũki is first observed fighting with dogs and rats for waste food and other junk that he can take to his home in the car cemetery. Again, as in *Petals of Blood,* Ngũgĩ's concern for the next generation is evident. The members of this generation, the poorest and most abject, raised in such wretched conditions, have become the real dispossessed. They have lost their land and their families, and also their history and culture. If action is not taken, the novel suggests, they will have less patience for empty words, broken promises, and a squalid life amid the detritus of the wealthy's luxury.

The Adventures of Njamba Nene

Ngũgĩ's concern for the new generations of Kenyans, evident in his last three novels, is equally apparent in his series of three children's stories, *The Adventures of Njamba Nene,* first published in Gĩkũyũ between 1982 and 1986.[26] The titular hero, Njamba Nene, also the name of Wanja's heroic grandfather in *Petals of Blood,* seizes power in an adult world that, in Ngũgĩ's construction, is child centered. While not unconcerned with educating his reader in somewhat stridently didactic ways, a feature of the African folktale,[27] Ngũgĩ is not merely writing primers in Gĩkũyũ. These Gĩkũyũ stories are not just rewritten traditional folktales of origins and ancestral values but attempts to write the child reader into history.

The Adventures of Njamba Nene are imbued with the wisdom of oral stories, sayings, and proverbs told to Njamba Nene by his mother, who embodies the wisdom of the Wacũ in Gĩkũyũ orature.[28] She is a constant ethical presence governing his decisions. In the first story, he sings traditional songs, but his singing is abruptly stopped by his teacher when he begins a Mau Mau song about land ownership, indicating the proximity of revolutionary songs to traditional oral tales, and pointing to his mother's possible involvement with the Land and Freedom Army. At the end of the second story, Njamba Nene hears the Mau Mau general, about to initiate him into the battalion, repeat one of his mother's sayings and realizes that the goals of the revolutionary struggle are one with the ancestral wisdom passed down by his mother. Although these interconnected stories are permeated by his mother's oral wisdom, Mother Wacū appears only very briefly at the end of the first story and then is tortured to death at the beginning of the third.

The first story, *Njamba Nene and the Flying Bus*, set during the Emergency, introduces Njamba Nene's malicious African teacher and his fellow pupils, mostly drawn from the ranks of the rising middle classes who support the colonizers. The teacher ridicules him for being the malnourished and ill-clothed son of a laboring mother, and particularly for failing to be utterly servile before the supervising British missionary, Pious Brainwash, known because of his expanding girth as "Hangbelly." On the school trip to the museum in Nairobi, all the boys bring lunch money except for Njamba Nene, who carries food. They set off in a bus named *Go after Money*, which begins racing with another bus, *Money Matters*. The buses approach dangerously high speeds and begin to fly. The driver of *Go after Money* is thrown from the bus, which crashes in the forest, and just before it explodes, the resourceful Njamba Nene leads the other boys out through the emergency exit at the back where he has been exiled by their fear that his meal of the traditional staple, beans and maize, will cause him to fart. He comforts the others with his mother's wise words, prepares a fire, shares his provisions, and begins to lead them on a journey home. Facing a test of allegiance, they are saved by choosing to rely on Mau Mau fighters and forsake British soldiers. Back at school, instead of being rewarded, Njamba Nene is confronted by Hangbelly, who distorts the events of the journey, labels Njamba Nene a traitor, and expels him. The story ends with his reunion with his proud mother, but at the beginning of volume 2, he is a poor laborer.

His employer is a colonial sympathizer who has become rich by ruthlessly exploiting his employees. As in all the stories, the African colonial lackeys are the most actively malicious figures, but they serve invisible but malevolent white overlords, presented more prominently in illustrations than in the text, making arrogant gestures of command. Njamba Nene's teacher is murdered by Mau Mau forces, and his African employer, Mr. Mwendanda, whose name means "he who loves his belly" (Sicherman 1990, 165), is exposed as a collaborator and executed in the end by a people's court. As *Njamba Nene's Pistol* begins, Njamba Nene has not eaten for days, and he is tempted to steal a loaf of bread. He takes a loaf from a shop where payment is collected on an honor system, but the thought of his mother's disapproval makes him return the bread. He hears a news item on the store's radio about a young boy who is to be executed by the colonial authorities for carrying a gun, and another about a Mau Mau prohibition against anyone carrying loaves of bread, but when asked by a man in a wide-brimmed hat to transport bread to the Mau Mau fighters, Njamba Nene agrees. Soon he is overcome by hunger and removes a circular plug from the crust, intending to scoop out the heart of the loaf and replace the plug. He discovers that the loaf contains a pistol, which he later learns is the very weapon used to execute his teacher. In his amazed state, he is arrested by a British patrol and taken to an area where many Kenyans are detained and where a hooded informer is identifying those who have taken the Mau Mau oath. Outraged by seeing a British child tormenting prisoners, Njamba Nene uncovers his pistol, allowing the man in the wide-brimmed hat, who is among the detainees and is soon revealed as a famous Mau Mau leader, General Rũheni, to overcome the British and the Home Guards. Safely ensconced in a Mau Mau hideout in the forest at the story's end, Njamba Nene is embraced by the general, given the malicious white boy's clothes to wear and his pistol to keep, and promised he will be initiated into full Mau Mau membership that evening. The story ends with Njamba Nene realizing the truth of the liberator's ideology and watching with pride the gleaming of his pistol in the sun.

These are boys' adventure stories with a difference. They are also historical narratives designed to educate their readership in the heroism of the Mau Mau period, an episode underplayed in the postindependence curriculum. Criticism of the imposition of alien principles of education is one of the themes of the series.[29] In many ways, Ngũgĩ's work is a direct rejection of colonizing attitudes and the colonial education that he underwent in missionary schools.[30] Simon Gikandi, in a brief memoir of his Kenyan childhood in the 1950s, recalls the State of Emergency as "the period that no one spoke about."[31] He remembers that Ngũgĩ's novels for the first time gave voice to this national trauma. For Kenyan novelist Meja Mwangi, Ngũgĩ's *Weep Not, Child* was the first African response he encountered to the Mau Mau period, and "it encouraged me because it was closer to me than anything I had read before."[32] The significance of Ngũgĩ's contribution to children's historical understanding is apparent when one considers Nancy Schmidt's claim, in her useful classification of the themes of children's fiction about Africa up to 1981, that whereas many stories written by African writers concern nation building, most are apolitical (60–61).

These stories, like Ngũgĩ's other fiction, make extensive use of biblical plots and characters. In *Njamba Nene and the Flying Bus,* Teacher Kĩgorogoru warns his pupils about the long-threatened visit of the white missionary, and the teacher warns them to be ever "ready in body, mind and soul, so we may not be caught without oil in our lamps like the five foolish virgins in the parable" (6). The parable in Matthew 25 refers to the Second Coming, a narrative that occupies Waiyaki in *The River Between* and is a central theme in *Matigari.* Njamba Nene is a seemingly feeble hero, much loved by his mother, and he wears clothing marked by a rainbow of patches. This Joseph leads his classmates out of the land of potential starvation through his arcane knowledge of vegetation, fire, and hunting. Furthermore, his portion of maize and beans is distributed among a class of students as in the miracle of the loaves and the fishes. The journey they undertake from the burned bus leads them through the Bunyanesque Depression of Tears and the Valley of Laughter to a final encounter at the River of Life and the River of the Valley of Death. The boys' final trial leads not to Bunyan's celestial city but, after meeting with the Mau Mau fighters, to a longed-for home of justice and equality on earth. The central metaphor of *Njamba Nene's Pistol* is the bread of life and the hunger of its hero. Like Matigari in Ngũgĩ's last novel, who travels around Kenya seeking truth and justice, Njamba Nene repeats a single question: "How can I die of hunger in my own country?" (3). He learns to control this nagging hunger without resorting to useless prayers for manna. The story ends not with a feast but with an initiation into the Mau Mau army. At the story's closure, this spiritual bread is rendered into a stark maxim worthy of Mother Wacũ: "A gun in the hand of a freedom fighter is the bread of life" (31).

The stories display the success of the outcast and the rebel, whose revolutionary initiation leads him through a series of tests or trials (Osa, xxvi). Njamba Nene must not only display courage and independence of mind but also inspire others. He must undergo personal and psychological initiation, and initiation of a historical and political nature. Njamba Nene's personal initiation involves resisting mental colonization, apparent in his apathy toward the threatened visit of Pious Brainwash, a device designed to inculcate an internally monitored surveillance of thought and memory in the pupils, so as "to cultivate a small group of

Africans who had mouths, legs, arms, hearts, everything like those of white people, so that if freedom fighters ever won the war, this group would act as the eyes, the ears, and the feet of the white people" (*Njamba Nene and the Flying Bus,* 6). Njamba Nene refuses to conform to the dictates of the European curriculum by freely speaking Gĩkũyũ, and as a result he is punished for his adherence to "primitive languages" (4). His teacher mocks: "When will you learn to speak English? When hyenas grow horns?" (3). Njamba Nene is as unashamed of his mother tongue as he is of his poverty. Clearly his mother has taught him a national curriculum, and he draws on an extensive knowledge of Kenyan geography and history, and a rich store of folk wisdom. He has nevertheless been successful at this missionary school and has retained his personal integrity and his independence of action, based on his mother's tenets, whereas the other boys slavishly depend on the omnipresent guidance of their teacher. Significantly, too, he has not adopted an English name. When the boys' bus crashes in the bush, Njamba Nene is the only one who knows their precise location, and his poverty is rewarded by his possession of food instead of currency, useless in the forest. The other boys, who disdain the Kenyan diet, are reduced to begging for a single grain of maize.

Njamba Nene is also initiated into a historical understanding. At the beginning of *Njamba Nene's Pistol,* he has come to Limuru to find work in the Bata Shoe Company. Ironically, in the illustrations, Njamba Nene is portrayed as shoeless. It is 1953; the country is near collapse, and Njamba Nene's condition is grave. In one of the story's few sustained descriptions of social fragmentation, Ngũgĩ writes: "Njamba Nene would go to the Indian shops to see whether Manu, the owner of a large bakery in Limuru, had thrown any bread away. The bread was rotten and often covered in mould. It was often thrown in the same rubbish pits where the Indian children used to shit. But people did not mind the shit. Men, women and children scrambled for bread, just as dogs do for bones" (*Njamba Nene's Pistol,* 1). The bread of life here has a material reality, and Njamba Nene's subsequent carrying of the pistol-containing loaf is an initiation into this social reality. His act of bravery, albeit inadvertent, is an "initiation for the nation" (10). Furthermore, General Rũheni has been impressed by the knowledge of the allegorical geography of the forest Njamba Nene demonstrated after the bus crash. The general is struck by the extraordinary historical circumstances, when children transport guns and are hanged for doing so, and a young white boy, presumably Njamba Nene's age (as he later wears the boy's clothes), plays at "torturing and humiliating people in their own land" (22). This spectacle ignites Njamba Nene's outrage, and recalling Mother Wacū's words, he produces the pistol, though he is frightened and unaware of how to use the gun. He clearly perceives the scene from a child's perspective, and his anger presumably stems from his very similarity to the boy treating the adult prisoners like infants. After this episode, functioning as a material initiation into the movement, Njamba Nene is embraced by the general, who "stroked the pistol as though it were a favorite child" (31).

To get to this stage, Njamba Nene reenvisions his country's history. Rejecting the Anglocentric curriculum of his grammar school, designed to produce sycophantic colonial apologists, Njamba Nene draws on his alternative instruction from his mother. After the bus crashes, for example, he tackles the boys' predicament in straightforward temporal, spatial, and historical terms: "I'll explain how we can help ourselves. We must first of all find out where we have come from, and where we are now. Then and only then can we know which way to go" (*Njamba Nene and the Flying Bus,* 19). The force of warped official history that Njamba Nene must oppose is apparent upon his return to school, four weeks later. Pious Brainwash immediately distorts the events of the crash, claiming that the three students killed by the British were shot instead by "savages dressed in skins, with plaited hair" (33). He insists further that the other children were led from the exploding bus by the terrorist Njamba Nene, not for their safety but to join the rebels. John Bull, murdered by the British, is resurrected as a martyr who died because of his refusal to betray his country. This distortion is apparent to all, but none of the children protests. Njamba Nene's undaunted national spirit is acknowledged by his mother, who sings about the people's right to the land.

Njamba Nene's courage leads to his political initiation, the spark for which is witnessing a distortion of his own image, the small white boy, maltreating Kenyans. This leads Njamba Nene to embrace the narrator's notion of "our people" (*Njamba Nene's Pistol,* 23), becoming immersed in a collective enterprise, but his spirit is first apparent after the bus crash when he enjoins the others, "We must share tasks and ideas and burdens" (*Njamba Nene and the Flying Bus,* 21). He democratically organizes them into groups such as "the group which had been elected to think about the way to follow" (29) and instructs them to share their views and work together. Soon one of the social markers distinguishing the boys vanishes, and they all journey in similarly tattered clothes. This erasing of distinctions does not prevent the development of a political schism leading to John Bull's death. This testing of the bonds of mutual obligation partly brings Njamba Nene to the notice of the general, who articulates the communitarian ethic: "We must watch over one another. We must learn from each other to enable our minds and souls to grow together" (*Njamba Nene's Pistol,* 9). This is perhaps the weakest part of Ngũgĩ's polemic, as Njamba Nene, the leaderless leader, the individual with a communal consciousness, is clearly extraordinary, a fact proclaimed by his name. Although he ostensibly puts into practice a collective ethic during the boys' trek out of the forest and through the choice of life over death, Left over Right, and insists on shared wisdom and decision making, he is distinguished by his natural intelligence and fearlessness and his store of oral wisdom, the embodiment of the collective psyche. Distinguished in class terms from his student "comrades," by his inability to feel humiliation—even when unjustly taunted by his teacher—and by his ready acceptance by the adult Mau Mau community, Njamba Nene is seamlessly ideal and perhaps too wise and assured to be fully plausible as a child. His very weaknesses are made into an impenetrable armor.

The stories' political optimism and Njamba Nene's ideological initiation are most apparent in the utopian instances in the stories, pointing to future cultural and economic harmony in the nation. The first concerns Njamba Nene's experience in the forest after the bus crash. With possibly self-conscious reference to Rudyard Kipling's *Jungle Book* or Edgar Rice Burroughs's Tarzan books, Njamba Nene lives for a time in complete harmony with different types of animals. This intertextual fantasy seems out of character with the rest of the story, though animals, in Gĩkũyũ orature, always represent people,[33] and this animal empire may gesture toward a cooperative future. Njamba Nene's mother has taught him animals' habits, and he knows they may be tamed. He sings to the lion and hyena, lying beside him, and he instructs the other boys not to display fear. Wearing the animals' smell, the boys will be undisturbed by other animals. In the illustration, the animals, in profile, form a halo around Njamba Nene, and he stares indifferently into the lion's open maw. The second utopian account appears in *Njamba Nene's Pistol.* Reflecting on his growing hunger and the outrageous possibility of dying of starvation in his own country, Njamba Nene goes to the Limuru Hotel, where people come to read nationalist newspapers, which are "selling themselves" (5). This honor system amazes Njamba Nene, just denied his wages by his greedy employer. As the general later tells him, even without money, Njamba Nene could have helped himself to food, and he erred in pretending to pay for the bread before taking it and in violating the Mau Mau prohibition. Need alone determines access to food, and the store's workers focus on production, not profit. The general refers to bread selling itself as the "great change" (9), presumably part of a future economic overhaul.

Ngũgĩ's revolutionary children's stories may be distressing in their strident political rhetoric but also in their seeming celebration of children with guns, and it may be impossible to read *Njamba Nene's Pistol* without reflecting on the new child armies of East Africa, packed with kidnapped and orphaned children made to carry light, portable plastic weapons designed for operation by tiny hands. Although parallels with Kenya's neocolonial present are clear, the story does not advocate children taking up live action weapons or participating in violent struggle. Rather, the story places an obviously idealized child at the center of a historical moment to present Kenya's youth the realities of a critical period in the nation's history.

Chapter Four
Performing Revolution: Plays and Film

Ngũgĩ's plays have won awards and represented Kenya at international festivals, but they also indirectly caused Ngũgĩ's imprisonment. *The Trial of Dedan Kimathi* represented Kenya at the Second World African and Black Festival of Arts and Culture (FESTAC) in Lagos, Nigeria, in 1977, yet 26 copies of his Gĩkũyũ play *Ngaahika Ndeenda (I Will Marry When I Want)* were seized during a search of his home at the time of his detention (*Detained,* 16). Playwriting, then, is associated with some of the most dramatically uplifting and devastating moments of his career. Ngũgĩ's plays issue mainly from two periods, both enormously productive ones in which he was writing in different genres. The first period was at Makerere University College, a hothouse of creativity for Ngũgĩ personally and a landmark in the development of East African literature in English. The second period coincided with Ngũgĩ's involvement with the Kamĩrĩĩthũ Community Educational and Cultural Centre, for whose arts program he collaborated on two works. The Kamĩrĩĩthũ plays were written in Gĩkũyũ and performed by peasant, worker, and student actors before largely local peasant audiences, though the plays were enormously popular and attracted invitations to perform from as far away as Zimbabwe. Ngũgĩ's collaborative plays are related to Brechtian socialist drama, in combination with indigenous orature, such as the *gĩcaandĩ* performances his last novels draw upon so extensively.[1] This experience in community theater was a transforming one for Ngũgĩ. He has referred to this period as "the most exciting in my life and the true beginning of my education" (*Detained,* 76). His community-based Gĩkũyũ performance studies clearly influenced his last novels and his subsequent movement into film and video.

African theater has deep roots in traditional dance, masquerade, performative dialogue, and ritual, though precolonial African drama, as J. Ndukaku Amankulor points out, also treated political matters.[2] At least in West Africa, argues Soyinka, colonial theater history is "largely a history of cultural resistance and survival."[3] Ngũgĩ lamented the precariousness of East African theater in 1968 in the preface to *The Black Hermit:* "Drama in East Africa is mainly in the hands of the amateur. The European amateur has tended to produce plays of little appeal to Africans or, which is about the same thing, of little relevance to conditions and problems in East Africa. The African amateur was, and still is, to be found in schools and universities: here however he tends to produce plays with an eye on school certificate examinations. Thus in some schools an annual production of Shakespeare with African boys dressed in the costumes of Sixteenth century England, has become—like Speech Day—a ritual."[4] In his sweeping examination of linguistic cultural colonization, *Decolonising the Mind* (37–41), Ngũgĩ expands his concern about foreign domination of Kenya's theaters, especially in Nairobi, where in the late 1970s European plays and Broadway musicals were virtually the only fare. In fact, he argues that the development of English-language theater in Kenya at such venues as the Kenya National Theatre, built in 1952, was part of a systematic program of colonial cultural warfare to counteract the increasing militancy of insurgent nationalistic forces and also conversely to prepare an elite to assume the mantle of power after the departure of the colonizers (*Writers,* 2d ed., 60–63). Ngũgĩ's remarks about the health of indigenous Kenyan theater should be considered in the context of a much broader concern in the 1960s about the position of creative writing in East Africa.[5] The spare production of East African plays in this period was especially galling in relation to the almost prodigal productivity of West Africa, and especially Nigeria. This marked difference in volume of production may be attributed partly to the cultural consequences of Kenya's having been a settler colony, only dislodged after a bloody period of struggle. At least one of Soyinka's plays, with their explosive linguistic high jinks and roller-coaster shifts in level of discourse, was produced at Makerere toward the end of Ngũgĩ's residence there when he began writing for the stage, as he points out in his preface to *The Black Hermit* (vii).[6] Soyinka has written powerfully on the communicative potential of African theater, though the stylistic complexity of much of his dramatic work renders it a challenge for the mass audience Ngũgĩ strove to reach, which may account for the linguistic simplicity of Ngũgĩ's dramatic style. For Ngũgĩ, Soyinka "ignores the creative struggle of the masses" (*Homecoming,* 65).

In "Drama and the African World-View," Soyinka rejects a simplistic, polarized definition of the difference between Western and African drama as deriving from disparate individualistic or communal world-views. Rather, he defines the theatrical experience in terms of space, the milieu of the theater, which by its very arrangement of audience, actors, and performance area fosters the creation of "the communal self."[7] Ngũgĩ's theater often attempts to forge a communal spirit, the audience witnessing the merging of stylized dramatic performance and the details of local social conditions, present and past. As Soyinka points out, much African writing deals with the social contexts of day-to-day realities, and by doing so, "it gives clues to mental conditioning by previous history or colonial culture; or conversely shows the will to break free of such incubi in its projection of a future society" (Soyinka 1976, 67). In Ngũgĩ's later plays, such projections into the future are explicitly invited. The failure of the will to oppose oppression is a tragic result of the internalization of colonial inferiority, and the audience for Ngũgĩ's later plays was one most materially affected by this oppression. In the preface to *The Trial of Dedan Kimathi,* Ngũgĩ castigates Kenyan historians who do not force-fully attack imperialism, in terms of their responsibility to their audi-ence: "For whose benefit were these intellectuals writing?"[8] Ngũgĩ's didactic plays[9] are usually tragic or at least somber in tone, and starkly different from the carnivalesque mood shifting of Soyinka's. Ngũgĩ's earlier plays pose problems relating to cultural clashes for audience con-templation, whereas the later plays call for abandoning hairsplitting niceties and indecision in favor of urgent recourse to action. The later plays set explosive confrontations of opposing worldviews to ignite a change, a psychic and political gestalt, in the audience.

This Time Tomorrow

Ngũgĩ's early plays were collected in 1970 in the volume *This Time Tomorrow. The Rebels* from this collection is clearly a student play, per-formed at Makerere in 1961 and broadcast over the Uganda Broadcast-ing Service in 1962. It presents the common problem of a Western-educated son facing the rival claims of his family and village traditions, but it includes a twist on the basic pattern. The conventional plot is mocked in Peter Nazareth's Makerere play *Brave New Cosmos,* in which a prosperous but cynical graduate discovers his former college friend writ-ing for a drama competition "the usual play about the African village, and the chief being ill; about his son dramatically returning home from civilization in time to save his people, and all the rest of it."[10] In Ngũgĩ's play, Charles returns to the village from Makerere University College with his fiancée, Mary, a college-educated clergyman's daughter, only to discover that his father, Nguru, has prepared for him to marry Mumbi, the uneducated daughter of the chief. Mumbi, named after the mythical foremother of the Gĩkũyũ, has been circumcised; Mary, named after the mother of Jesus, has not. To marry the "unclean" Mary, Charles has been taught to believe, would introduce contagion into his village. Charles's dilemma is tragic, but he must choose between these competing responsibilities. He has pledged his heart to Mary and committed himself to a kind of pan-African communal ideal that will override the claims of tribal and village allegiance, but he owes obedience to his father, who has raised Charles and furnished his education, and also to the customs of his people. He moans to Mary that he is "torn between two worlds," words that echo a phrase from the Victorian poet Matthew Arnold's "Stanzas from the Grande Chartreuse": "Wandering between two worlds, one dead, / The other powerless to be born, / With nowhere yet to rest my head, / Like these, on earth I wait forlorn."[11] The echo of Arnold's famous lines about the crisis of faith and the awareness of being trapped in a historical interregnum signifies Charles's position amid shifting epochs and also his imprisonment in European modes of thought. He halfheartedly decides to return to the village, and Mary deplores his vacillating insincerity, especially when he cloaks his "weakness and irresolute heart" in beautiful words of "noble anguish."[12] She reminds him of his grandiose pan-African ideals, his teaching that the "strictures of religion and tribe" must loosen to unbind "the African prometheus" (*This Time Tomorrow*, 12).

Mary breaks off the engagement, and Mumbi runs away from the village, drowning in the river during her escape. Charles's decision to abandon Mary and his new principles as well as to embrace his father's wishes and the requirements of village traditions has led to disaster. At the very beginning, however, the play complicates this basic pattern by introducing a stranger who knows of a skeleton in the musty closet of Charles's father, Nguru. Nguru rebelled against his own father, even marrying an "unclean" woman, likely uncircumcised, and thus fell under a patriarch's curse. Nguru's hidden past is revealed only near the end of the drama. As a result, a play that appears to criticize the effects of "misshapen education" and the abandonment of principle (*This Time Tomorrow*, 15), to uphold modernity at any cost, and to give its most powerful words of righteous outrage to Mary in fact validates the power of tradition, the ability of a forgotten curse from the past to work its destructive magic, for however long delayed. Finally, the effect of the revealed curse complicates the basic polarity of tradition versus modernism.

The Wound in the Heart is another Makerere play, one that won the drama section of the 1962 Makerere Interhall English Competition. Its plot anticipates that of *A Grain of Wheat*. It tells of a man, released from detention after the Emergency, who returns home to discover that his wife was raped by his enemy and has given birth to his child. Ruhiu's wife has been raped by the white district officer, the man responsible directly or indirectly for Ruhiu's arrest and detention. In *A Grain of Wheat*, Gikonyo, who has given way under the oppression of detention, discovers that Mumbi has borne the child of his archenemy, the British collaborator Karanja. Gikonyo finally makes gestures of appeasement to Mumbi and her child, and their wounded, hybrid family even seems to be a model for the future. The outcome of *The Wound in the Heart,* on the other hand, with one exception, is the crescendo of death and destruction of classical Greek tragedy's catastrophe, and of Ngũgĩ's first two novels.

Ruhiu is a self-styled leader and prophet for his people, a Promethean character, to use Mary's allusion in *The Rebels*. Ruhiu is also a would-be savior, announcing before his years of detention, like Christ at the Last Supper, his imminent betrayal by one of the disciples: "He would one day be arrested and tortured for our sake" (*This Time Tomorrow*, 20). His homecoming is anticipated warily by the elders, as if they are chilled by his messianic assurance, an ominous warning that Ruhiu later associates with a curse. He has been brave under torture in detention, able to endure by thinking of his duty to his people, but now he is dismayed to learn that the present leader of the village believes that a brighter tomorrow may be realized by forgetting the past. Ruhiu is appalled:

> Your words are strange to my ears. How forget the past? How forget my yesterday of humiliation, my yesterday of whip-lashes on my back, my yesterday of sweat for another's stomach, my yesterday of shame, degradation, exploitation! For me there is no tomorrow without yesterday and I will so fan my wound alive that they will hurt hour by hour, a watchdog for a second betrayed by my rich brothers. No. I will keep my anger, my shame, my degradation sharp as the blade of a knife, smooth and elegant as the point of a spear aimed straight at the heart of my enemies. No. The fire of my anger, my shame is my legacy to my children. (*This Time Tomorrow*, 24–25)

Ruhiu's passionate words about cherishing the legacy of righteous anger anticipate the stance of Ngũgĩ's last novels, but here they smack of an unhealthy, obsessive egotism, and they preface the announcement of

Ruhiu's wife's rape, indicating his blindness to local realities. Ruhiu must accept that others have also suffered and been changed by the Emergency, and that the future will not be the utopia he envisioned. Too late, however, does Ruhiu modify his words of fire and fury, and his resolve to murder the child of rape. His wife, hearing his threat to murder her child, has run off and hanged herself, and he dies of grief. His mother, the voice of reason and moderation in the play, is left to raise the child, the living legacy of the wounds of the Emergency.

The play *This Time Tomorrow*, broadcast on the BBC Africa Service in 1967, like *The Wound in the Heart* and much of Ngũgĩ's post-1967 work, focuses on the legacy of the Emergency and independence. It is set in a slum, where the smell of urine and waste permeates the ironically named Uhuru, or freedom, Market, and the lunch stall of Njango and her daughter Wanjiro. Njango's husband was captured and shot during the Emergency, and most of her customers' lives were uprooted during that period. Her son lives elsewhere with an uncle who pays his school fees, and her daughter assists her in food preparation, though the girl dreams of escaping the poverty and stench of the slum and parading about the city in European clothes. Wanjiro also dreams of apocalyptic floods, dreams that unsettle her mother, who fears that her future in the market and the very existence of the slums are threatened by the draconian City Council, who, appropriating the rhetoric of the cooperative Harambee movement, is preparing to demolish the slum because its ugliness offends the sensibilities of foreign tourists. The wretched slum and its market represent the newly independent nation for the petty traders, workers, and peasants and provide a stark answer to the persistent question "what has this Uhuru brought us?" (*This Time Tomorrow*, 46).

Into this gloomy, disillusioned world come three intruders. The first is Asinjo, the young Wanjiro's boyfriend, who belongs to another tribe and has been unemployed. For these reasons, and because of her anxiety about the debased values of men severed from their village roots, Njango distrusts him. While Njango is away at a protest demonstration, he visits Wanjiro, saying that he now works as a taxi driver and that she must come and share his house, and cook and clean for him. The added enticement of "nice dresses and shoes" indicates that he caters to her fantasy of wanting to look like a foreigner (45), and that he may even lure her into prostitution. Certainly he is not offering an honorable marriage partnership, and when Njango hears of the compromising proposal, she despairs. The second intruder in the play is the Stranger, a man with good political credentials, in that he was a Mau

Mau freedom fighter who was detained. The Stranger appeals to the
people to recognize the nearly magical power of their united strength,
reminding them of the broken promise of *uhuru*. Finally he pleads in
vain to the demonstrators to unite against the police, who now are beating people, and he is arrested. His appeal, however, has resonated in
Njango, who voices the play's last words, a query about the future with
a regret that the people failed to unite against the authorities. The last
intruder is the journalist, who is present onstage, in a separate space,
when the play begins. He is writing a journalistic account of the events
witnessed onstage in portentous and flowery language. His disinterested
insincerity is indicated by his purple prose and his willingness to construct a distorted photographic image of the day's events that dramatizes but misrepresents the justice of the people's cause.

This Time Tomorrow is theatrically more ambitious than *The Rebels* or
The Wound in the Heart. A number of its scenes unfold on a bifurcated
stage, allowing the impression of the journalist languidly reflecting and
writing from a future vantage point about violent actions of the past
actually taking place simultaneously a few yards away. The play also
includes the songs of the dreamy Wanjiro, the sounds of shopkeepers
shouting their wares, the Inspector's loudspeaker, and the slogan-shouting
crowd coming from the demonstration. The ordinary, routine sounds of
babies crying and chickens crowing alternate with the shriek of police
sirens and finally the drone of the bulldozer come to raze the slum and
the Uhuru Market in the last scene. The play opens, however, with the
tapping of the journalist's typewriter and the cries of his editor for last-
minute news copy. His typewriting, instead of mirroring the social reality
its owner witnesses only a few feet away, like the bulldozer later,
smooths over the real misery of the people whose homes have been
destroyed. He uses a high-flown rhetoric with bombastic but empty Old
Testament allusions to justify the demolition. He exits the stage to interview the Police Inspector, breaking the contrapuntal time scheme of the
play and demonstrating clearly how truth is distorted. Njango alone
voices her regret and her belief in the power of solidarity at the end of
the play. In future plays, similar songs will be chanted but by a unified,
powerful chorus. Here, a bulldozer has the final word.

The Black Hermit

In 1962 *The Black Hermit* was produced by an international cast from
Makerere at the Uganda National Theatre as part of the Ugandan inde-

pendence celebrations. In many ways, the play is a rewriting and expansion of *The Rebels*. Its focus is the clash of tradition and modernity, though it gives much attention to issues of tribalism, racism, and religious strife. In his preface to Heinemann's 1968 edition, Ngũgĩ notes apologetically that he was certain that these three issues were the major problems besetting the newly independent African countries. By 1968, his position would appear closer to that of Remi's friend Omange in the play, who rails against neocolonialism, though Omange also targets all traditional customs. As Ngũgĩ said of *The Black Hermit* in this period, "The play is very confused, and I don't like to comment on it very much" (Sander and Munro, 55). Like *The Rebels* and Ngũgĩ's first two novels, *The Black Hermit* juxtaposes the bond between men and women with the relations between an individual, and his family and tribe. Like Charles in *The Rebels*, Remi decides to abandon his beloved, a white South African named Jane, to return to his village and his wife, but he rapidly manages to offend all those who have pleaded for his return. At the end of both plays, spurned partners commit suicide.

Remi, who does not appear until the second act, is the only educated member of his tribe. He cajoles his people to vote for the Africanist Party, or later the National Party (*Black Hermit,* 29, 63), which advocates intertribal harmony and cooperation, but his people want him to create a new Marua tribal political party to restore lost land and end taxation. Remi has a bitter personal history. His brother married Remi's first beloved, a girl he hoped to marry, when Remi was away at college. This is an important and somewhat mysterious event in the background of the present action, and its clearer development might have strengthened Remi's motivation in the play. We know only that Remi's brother died and that, grief stricken, his father rapidly declined, forcing a commitment from Remi to marry his deceased brother's wife. With the intercession of his mother, Remi yielded to his father's wishes but almost immediately went off to live as a "black hermit" in the city, spending his time not praying in church as his mother would wish but dancing and drinking in nightclubs, where he met Jane.

As Jane complains later, after the revelation that he is married, Remi has throughout their relationship mouthed high-flown, principled phrases while acting the part of a hypocrite. Earlier, in the second scene of act 2, he has met with and pompously dismissed two delegations from the village, one from the elders and the other comprising solely his mother's priest, Remi contemptuously complaining that he is not a savior while clearly thinking he can act like one. He holds the medicine bundle of the elders in one hand balanced by the pastor's Bible in the other, condemning them both as superstitious. This realization impels his return to the village, vowing to "serve our people, / Save them from traditions and bad customs, / Free them from tribal manacles" (*Black Hermit*, 45). Almost as soon as he sets foot on home soil, he insults the elders, the pastor, and even his mother by dismissing the elders' desire that he found a tribal party, attacking the destructiveness of religion, and soundly rejecting his wife Thoni. Hearing his cruel words, she runs off to commit suicide, stung by an absolute rejection from a man she has always loved, as she writes in a letter that he reads after her death.

It appears that Remi has returned to his village with a renewed commitment to the Africanist Party, though both he and Omange have deplored its falling away from early ideals. Remi, like the deluded heroes of Ngũgĩ's first two novels, never is convincing as an advocate of any political principles. Furthermore, Remi's insulting and humiliating responses to the requests for his return will almost certainly have severed whatever confidence the elders and the people have had in him. His return to the village with Omange is an unqualified disaster. While bombastically expounding a message of unity and reconciliation, he assumes the mantle of messianic demigod, arrogantly dismissing all traditional customs and even family ties, saying incredibly, "My stay in the city has taught me everything" (*Black Hermit*, 65). The most immediate consequence of his arrogance is the final rupture of his personal life. Just as he earlier rejected Jane, whom he deluded into loving him, so too he has driven away Thoni, who takes her love for him to a wretched death. The play ends with the fallout of his grief over Thoni muting his recent political diatribe. No indication is given of what Remi will do. He would appear to have burned all his bridges of escape and trapped himself at the center of all his dilemmas. This open, unsettled ending, like that of *The Rebels*, is perhaps a technique Ngũgĩ learned from the work of Bertolt Brecht, whose plays were performed at Makerere. *The Black Hermit*, however, provides few solutions to any of its problems, save that Remi's methods, whatever the intrinsic value of any of his principles, are utterly counterproductive. The public and the private domains are juxtaposed awkwardly in the play, and Remi and even his friend Omange, who wants to "spit on traditions," are highly flawed moral centers (70). Remi is a hedonistic, narcissistic, and hypocritical man, for whom political principles are mere topics of conversation and just the sort of "intellectual abstraction" he fatuously accuses Jane of entertaining (47).

The Trial of Dedan Kimathi

Written with Mĩcere Gĩthae Mũgo, *The Trial of Dedan Kimathi* is an imaginatively reconstructed historical drama. As its preface indicates, the play was to be the first in a series of plays on national heroes. As such, it is a secular variation on the medieval saint's play, a genre resurrected in the twentieth century by George Bernard Shaw, who added a socialist undercurrent to his story of Saint Joan. As Taban lo Liyong remarked, "Ngugi wants Mau Mau heroes to be saints" (Liyong 1980, 58). The play was written as a critical reply to Kenneth Watene's play *Dedan Kimathi,* which presents Kimathi in a much more equivocal light (Cook and Okenimkpe, 171). Ngũgĩ's play was Kenya's entry in the Second World African and Black Festival of Arts and Culture (FESTAC) in Lagos, Nigeria, in 1977 and was performed briefly the year before at Kenya National Theatre and at Kamĩrĩĩthũ. The play also had a successful series of performances by the Wazalendo Players in Britain in 1984, commemorating 100 years of resistance since the 1884 Berlin Conference.[13] The play is Ngũgĩ's most ambitious, fusing different time periods more successfully than *This Time Tomorrow* and blending the story of a martyr's death with a gesture in the direction of 400 years of Kenyan history. It attempts to show the seamless links between precolonial, colonial, and neocolonial oppression; the past and the present. In its mode of production, the play reflects its subject Dedan Kimathi's own experience in organizing a theater group, Gichamu, because *The Trial of Dedan Kimathi* is a collaborative work partly written in African languages and focused on raising its audience's political consciousness.

The play contains two types of trial, that of Dedan Kimathi by the colonial authorities, and the trial of collaborators and traitors by Dedan Kimathi and the Kenya People's Defense Council in the rebel-held areas. The effect of this intermingling of colonial and anticolonial trials is to expose the pretense of justice in the colonial trial while also revealing the vulnerability of Kimathi in the Mau Mau trials. The formal trial of Kimathi does not proceed far beyond the initial reading and rereading of the charge against him, and his repeated refusal to enter a plea and hence acknowledge the court and its power to charge, imprison, try, and sentence him. The court's illegitimacy is indicated further by its failure to provide the prisoner an adequate defense, its unintentional leaking of the preordained capital sentence before the trial has concluded, and its use of torture to extract a confession. Between the two trials, Kimathi meets with a settler, a politician, and a pastor, who represent colonial and neocolonial forces. The play clearly links these colonial sympathizers with the traitors tried in the forest, soundly castigating both groups of collaborators. The politician, using words repeated by Nderi wa Riera, the corrupt MP in *Petals of Blood* (153), claims, "We are all freedom fighters" (*Trial,* 47), wiping out distinctions between patriots and traitors with a single breath. The testing of notions of truth and justice on many fronts is one of the effects of the play's multiple trials, which include, as the authors point out in the preface, a trial of African literature itself ([vi]).

A second plot that finally merges with the trial of Kimathi concerns an attempted prison break. As the stage directions explicitly point out, it also symbolically enacts the involvement of the mothers of the nation with the moral education of the younger generation and displays the transformative power of Kimathi's legacy. The story is one Ngũgĩ will develop further in his second children's story, *Njamba Nene's Pistol*. It tells of a woman fruit seller who is rudely and provocatively searched by an English soldier. She adeptly distracts him from discovering a loaf of bread containing a gun that she is carrying. She escapes and immediately breaks up a fight between a young girl and boy in a dispute over money. These two destitute Kenyan orphans have been corrupted by living amid the vice and squalor of the city's slums and junkyards. The woman is generous to the boy and inspires him with the example of Kimathi, and later in the play, her disembodied words return to guide and encourage him. She persuades the boy to carry a loaf to Kimathi's prison as an initiation into manhood. He agrees, but outside the prison, he cannot find the contact to whom he must deliver the loaf. We learn later that this person was arrested. Undaunted, the boy, girl, and woman conspire to slip a gun to Kimathi inside the court.

Colonial law and the colonial subject are central concepts in the play. Just as the boy and girl are detached from family and tradition, so too are all colonial subjects alienated from a sense of identity as national citizens. They are, as it were, citizens of the imperial power by proxy. The white judge is the true citizen: "I am a Kenyan. By might and right" (*Trial,* 35). Dedan Kimathi's refusal to recognize the judge's law and the authority of his court implicitly questions the validity of colonial citizenship, democracy, and justice. Kimathi refuses to participate in a trial examining the violation of "a law . . . we had no part in . . . making" (25). For Kimathi, this is the law of the rich and of property; the law of the imperialist is a criminal "law of oppression" (25). He similarly dismisses the settler's law as the law of the gun. He also denies the politician's law of greed, and even the pastor's interpretation of God's law. For Kimathi, the settler's, politician's, and pastor's precepts manifest the cannibalistic law of the capitalist jungle, in which "creatures of prey [feed] on the blood and bodies of those who toil" (26). He especially repudiates the patronizing, paternalistic words of Shaw Henderson, who tries Kimathi's case and purports to dispense the stern kindness of the law of the father.

Kimathi, in effect, turns the tables in the courtroom and judges the judge and his court. He tries the colonial court as the embodiment of imperial exploitation. Kimathi says: "I recognize only one law, one court: / the court and the law of those who / fight against exploitation, / The toilers armed to say / We demand our freedom. / That's the eternal law of the oppressed, / of the humiliated, of the injured, the insulted!" (*Trial,* 27). Any other law for Kimathi is that of the slave. He further rejects any legal compromise with his colonial captors, such as any offer of conditional freedom, relating it to the unequal international legal agreements that led to dispossession: "Deals! Pacts! Treaties! How many nations have you wiped out, and later said: well, according to this treaty and that treaty, they had ceded their land and their lives" (33). Colonial law, finally, is reduced to the law of capital, which is antithetical to the law of the people. Ngũgĩ's next play, *I Will Marry When I Want,* concludes that the sword is the "poor people's lawcourt."[14]

The Trial of Dedan Kimathi suggests that the law of history dictates struggle and resistance. As the authors state in the preface: "The war which Kimathi led was being waged with even greater vigour all over Africa and in all those parts of the world where Imperialism still enslaved the people and stole their wealth. It was crucial that all this be put together as one vision, stretching from the pre-colonial wars of resistance against European intrusion and European slavery, through the anti-colonial struggles for independence and democracy, to post-independence struggle against neo-colonialism" (*Trial,* [vi]). Four hundred years of Kenyan history are recounted twice in the play in the form of a mimed progression, a moving *tableau vivant.* This mime indicates the omnipresence of the past within the present, the ever-buoyant spirit of heroes like Kimathi, and the regenerative will of the people. Kimathi is tortured during the second miming of history, indicating the source of his courage to withstand pain and to resist the demands for a confession, a negotiated cease-fire, or a betrayal of the whereabouts of General Mathenge. While the play obviously constructs Kimathi as heroic, its account of history is not altogether one-dimensional and idealized. For example, we see Kimathi judging a group of traitors that includes his own younger brother, Wambararia. Although there is a kind of participatory justice at work—this is a people's court—Kimathi is the leader, and because of his concern for his brother and his mentally ill mother, he does not sentence the convicts to death. The wisdom of Kimathi's clemency, taken against the advice of some of his comrades, including an eloquent female member of the court, is undermined by the obviously unrepentant prisoners' almost immediate escape. The play, furthermore, refers to factional divisions within the Mau Mau forces, and to the persistent debate about whether the armed struggle was a regional, even tribal, one rather than a national war of independence.

The Mau Mau war, as it is referred to in the play, saw full participation by women, and historically at least 5 percent of the fighters were female (Lonsdale, 456–57). The play's major subplot dramatizes women's role in carrying weapons and food to the forest. The central female character, like so many of Ngũgĩ's heroines, is a former prostitute who heard the call of "the humiliated, the injured, the insulted, the exploited, the submerged millions of labouring men and women of Kenya" (*Trial,* 19). Although later representing all "working mothers" (59), she is introduced initially as a "versatile" guerrilla supplier, showing "fearless determination and a spirit of daring": "She walks straight into the mouth of a gun" (8). During her interrogation, from which she escapes through an effective parody of stereotypically submissive feminine behavior, her interrogator refers to a female fighter he has heard of who is "lean, wiry and strong" and "fought like a tiger" (10). It appears that the successfully disguised, elusive woman is this legendary fighter. Immediately after her escape, the woman confronts the fighting children, initiating the boy into guerrilla activity by giving him a gun to transport. Later, the boy acknowledges that the girl too has encouraged him when his resolve wavered, and the three cooperate in an unsuccessful attempt to pass a gun to Kimathi in court; later, they may be said to celebrate Kimathi's symbolic escape (Killam 1980, 88). In a flashback to the second trial scene in the forest, Kimathi acknowledges female contributions to Mau Mau: "When this struggle is over / We shall erect at all the city corners / Monuments / To our women / Their courage and dedication / To our struggle" (73). Kimathi then solicits the opinion of the woman in the forest on his verdict, and she argues for an unsentimental judgment, to purify the ranks of the faithful. He disregards her opinion to the detriment of the cause.

The play is a socialist drama, with elements of folk opera, which has an epic social and historical sweep, and features representatives of different classes. The play achieves its breadth and accomplishes its various purposes concisely through the use of special dramatic effects. The boy, for example, mimics the actions of the Nairobi tourist, and Kenya's history unfolds in mime. The play's emotional appeal is made through mimed action, chanting, singing, and dancing. Dancing, for example, dramatizes Kimathi's prison dream of the unification of Kenya's tribal nationalities. The disembodied voice of the gun-carrying woman sounds like the call of conscience and motivates the boy. The divided stage, moreover, enhances the sense of the simultaneity of events in Kenya's past and present, and lighting and even silence economically partition microscenes.

These theatrical devices both intensify a nonintellectual, emotional response in the audience through the sensuality of movement and music and also encourage the audience to consider the play objectively as a somewhat self-conscious exchange of ideas. This Brechtian defamiliarization is accomplished partly by the inclusion of plays with the main play. For example, in the brief miming of Kenyan history, we see in miniature the grand sweep of which the Kimathi story is only a small but connected part. In addition, in the self-consciously theatrical colonial trial scenes, we observe on the stage an audience that is divided on racial, economic, and political lines watching a type of performance. Their outraged response to the trial is designed to objectively represent the reaction of the play's viewers. The play's audience is not to be composed and passive. When Kimathi wonders about his false neocolonial comforters, he asks, "What revolution will unchain these minds" (*Trial,* 47), also perhaps gesturing toward the audience. Clearly *The Trial of Dedan Kimathi* is designed as a revolutionary experience to unchain the minds of its audience. The objectified representation of this transformation within the play is the changed attitude of the boy, referred to as initiation into full manhood. The audience must not be merely distanced observers or "chequebook revolutionaries" (50) who pay no more than ticket-price lip service to the cause. The audience itself is on trial. Its members must be roused from complacency and respond emotionally and intellectually to the play, make choices, and fight against the ethnic and other divisions sown by colonialism and neocolonialism. The audience members must internalize Kimathi's spirit and become "creators of a new heaven on a new earth" (50).

I Will Marry When I Want

Originally written from 1976 to 1977 in Gĩkũyũ, *I Will Marry When I Want (Ngaahika Ndeenda)* was published in English translation in 1982. The play was cowritten by Ngũgĩ wa Mĩriĩ, composer, playwright, educator, and director of the Kamĩrĩĩthũ Educational and Cultural Centre. After initial composition, the script was developed at Kamĩrĩĩthũ in close collaboration during workshops with the peasant, worker, student theater group and performed to great acclaim. Ngũgĩ's involvement with this group was one of the most important experiences of his career, merging his cultural and political interests and providing an opportunity to learn directly from the peasantry. The theater's site is significant. Kamĩrĩĩthũ is the place where Ngũgĩ was born, and its inhabitants are a cross section of Kenyan society: factory and industrial workers, shopkeepers, city workers, intellectuals, and peasants; it has a complex colonial and neocolonial history (Sicherman 1990, 247–48). Like *The Trial of Dedan Kimathi,* the play created there is a type of socialist folk opera, freely mingling both action and dialogue with ritual dramatizations, mime, and song. The play is written in a lively style, rich with earthy humor and proverbial sayings. This linguistic flair is most marked in act 1, which presents the domestic sphere of Kĩgũũnda and Wangeci comically, before the direct statement later of somewhat formulaic political binaries. *I Will Marry When I Want* is also an African morality play, targeting the alliance of capitalism and Christianity as the enemy of cultural integrity and national cooperation. In passing, the play criticizes a number of other social problems from drunkenness and divorce to fawning on material luxuries, and it also celebrates virtues from respect for women to neighborliness.

The play explores two conflicts. The first is the disagreement between Wangeci and Kĩgũũnda about how to respond to their daughter Gathoni's involvement with John Mũhũũni, the son of Kĩgũũnda's wealthy boss, Ahab Kĩoi wa Kanoru (Kĩoi). Wangeci and Kĩgũũnda also disagree about whether they should sell their one-and-a-half-acre plot of land to Kĩoi and Ikuua wa Nditika, rich African directors of a company planning to establish an insecticide factory on the site. Kĩoi already owns most of Kĩgũũnda's land, which was "given to homeguards," and Kĩgũũnda labors for him (*I Will Marry,* 28). He cultivates and plants without enjoying the harvest, like the "pot that cooks without eating" (20). Their neighbors Gĩcaamba and Njooki, a worker and a peasant, who embody revolutionary ethics clothed in words of traditional wisdom, consistently advise them to avoid having anything to do with the devilish Kĩoi. The play's second major conflict is between Kĩgũũnda and Wangeci, and Kĩoi and his party. The two groups are starkly contrasted onstage in terms of dress, language, manners, wealth, and even physical distance. Kĩoi covets Kĩgũũnda's land, but he also wants to introduce him into the church, regarding Kĩgũũnda as an influential figure who will encourage other disgruntled factory activists to follow him into passive acceptance of all conditions, however unjust, as being divinely ordained. The point of entry into church membership for Kĩoi is Christian marriage, hence the play's title, and incredibly Kĩgũũnda and Wangeci readily accept this eventuality, though it requires expensive Western trappings. To finance the wedding dress and cake and other paraphernalia, Kĩgũũnda takes a loan from Kĩoi's bank using his cherished land title as collateral. Of course, the disastrous outcome is now inevitable, and the escalation of the first conflict—Gathoni's becoming pregnant and being abandoned by Kĩoi's son—precipitates Kĩgũũnda's confrontation with Kĩoi, who refuses to sanction a marriage between Gathoni and his son. Kĩgũũnda threatens Kĩoi but backs down, a possibly fatal mistake. Kĩgũũnda is fired from his job at the factory and becomes demoralized, and the play ends with his land being sold to pay the recalled bank loan. The four friends, Kĩgũũnda and Wangeci, and Gĩcaamba and Njooki, sing songs of resistance and unity.

As in *The Trial of Dedan Kimathi,* cultural and national solidarity is established through the reenactment of historical pageants within the play, dealing with significant moments in resistance history, such as, for example, the strike of 1948 and the Mau Mau war. The stark divisions between the patriots—Kĩgũũnda and Wangeci, and Gĩcaamba and Njooki—and their neocolonial exploiters are emphasized by their very different songs. The patriots sing resistance songs; the exploiters sing Christian hymns. The patriots' cultural cohesion also is demonstrated through proverbial sayings. Some of these are included for humorous effect or to foster the audience's recognition and identification. For example, Kĩgũũnda repeats the backhanded boast: "A man brags about his penis however small" (*I Will Marry,* 51), referring to his pride in his humble home. A number of proverbs relate homely folk wisdom. Some of these voice suspicions about Gathoni's courtship. Wangeci wonders if her daughter knows "that men have prickly needles," but Kĩgũũnda begs for a qualification recognizing men's traditional code of honor: "You should have said that it is the modern men / Who have got prickly needles" (21). Later, after Gathoni runs off with John for a romantic week in the beautiful coastal city of Mombasa, Wangeci reminds her annoyed husband that "a parent is never nauseated / By the mucus from his child's nose" (52). Parents, she reminds him, must accept their children's faults. When the now pregnant Gathoni runs off again to be a barmaid (often synonymous with being a prostitute), Gĩcaamba warns her friend Wangeci not to abandon Gathoni, for although "a hyena is very greedy . . . she does not eat her young" (104). Gathoni's actions, Gĩcaamba says, can be explained by another saying: "When a bird in flight gets very tired / It lands on the nearest tree" (104).

Many other proverbial sayings in the play relate to its political theme and convey bitter truths, warnings of ominous events, and injunctions to solidarity. Gĩcaamba complains of his exploitation at the factory. He bitterly compares his factory salary, and more generally the gains of the poor after independence, to the peanuts "thrown to a monkey / When the baby it is holding is about to be stolen!" (I Will Marry, 37). Referring to the fabulous wealth and arrogance of men like Kĩoi who exploit the poor's vulnerability, Wangeci comments that "a fool's walking stick supports the clever" (15), and later Gĩcaamba says: "Haven't you heard it said that / A rich man's fart does not stink?" (63). Stark observations on the inequalities of the present situation, however, do not forestall a warning of danger. Njooki, anxious about Kĩgũũnda and Wangeci's naive friendship with Kĩoi, warns that "a tooth smiles at a spear" (56); the tooth, believing the spear is its comrade, overlooks its own danger. Kĩoi will not change his ways, just as the colonial church is the same as the neocolonial church: "Did the leopard ever change its spots?" asks Gĩcaamba (59). To counter the bedbug- and scorpion-like Kĩois of the world, vigilance and unity are necessary. The people must never renege on their oath to the nation and begin, like Kĩoi, to forget that only "a vulture eats alone" (113). On the contrary, as the union leader intones, "if a bean falls to the ground / We split it amongst ourselves" (69).

In contrast to the use of traditional lore to convey socialist messages, hypocritical Christian pieties convey the egotism and greed of the wealthy capitalists. The play does acknowledge, however, that some indigenous Christian churches provided shelter for oathing ceremonies during the Mau Mau period, and it equates a revival of revolutionary spirit with the Second Coming. By and large, however, Christian groups are portrayed as exploiting the poverty and desperation of the masses while using the communal rhetoric of *harambee*, for example, to raise funds at the local level, and then in some cases sending a portion of the monies collected to America. The very prolixity of Christian denominations in the area signals their scavenging nature. Gĩcaamba resents the way that passive resignation to social stasis is misconstrued as a humble Christian acknowledgment of God's sanction of the status quo. Such hypocrisy covers up the miseries of hazardous, underpaid factory shift work and industrial pollution, the export of profits, and the inadequacy of infrastructural improvements in transportation, health, and education. Self-described Christians such as Samuel and Helen Ndugĩre mix Christian humility with union busting. For them, material prosperity indicates spiritual favor. For example, Helen says it is necessary to "show the wicked that everybody's share comes from Heaven, / Be it poverty or riches" (*I Will Marry,* 45). Similarly, such characters associate a blind mimicry of Western cultural traditions with spiritual purity, as in their insistence on the trappings of a Western wedding feast with Christian marriage. Patriotic peasants and workers must resist the drug of religion, remembering that earlier, "drunk with religion," their land was stolen (57). The deferred, otherworldly compensation of entry into the "Kingdom of God," instead of justice on earth, is mocked in song (61). This substitution is symbolically enacted when Kĩgũũnda's title deed disappears from its prominent place on the wall and is replaced by the ubiquitous phrase: "CHRIST IS THE HEAD OF THIS HOUSE, THE UNSEEN GUEST AT EVERY MEAL, THE SILENT LISTENER TO EVERY CONVERSATION" (74, 91). Kĩgũũnda's household, preparing for a Christian wedding, has become a poor parody of Kĩoi's. The play dismisses Christian/capitalist marriage in favor of a revolutionary union of "two patriots / Defending their home and nation" (64).

By the end of the play, Kĩgũũnda and Wangeci, through their experience of dispossession, have come to share the political opinions of Gĩcaamba and Njooki. They join the final dance and its songs, an affront to the historical colonial denial of such performances (*I Will Marry,* 67). These characters, unemployed and without shelter, will unite in a life-and-death revolutionary struggle, though their fortunes in the meantime are unclear. The play's ending is equally unclear about the fate of Gathoni, a pregnant barmaid. The play ends rather than concludes, though its message and even its outcome have been abundantly evident from the first scene, and any elaborate denouement or resolution would be superfluous. Audience members are enjoined to respond to the recital of exploitation and to perceive the only solution as lying in unified resistance to be undertaken whenever they want.

Mother, Sing for Me

The message of *I Will Marry When I Want* is elaborated further in Ngũgĩ's next, still unpublished play, *Maitũ Njugĩra*, translated as *Mother, Sing for Me*. Ngũgĩ prepared a translation of the play for a proposed London production, and its director added a foreword partly consisting of two poems by Bertolt Brecht. The title phrase is the name of a resistance song banned by colonial authorities, and it is mentioned briefly in adapted form in two other plays. Kĩgũũnda says, "Mother ululate for me," in *I Will Marry When I Want* (12), and in *The Black Hermit,* one of the elders, pleading with Remi to return to the village, tells him that "mothers cry for you" (39). *Mother, Sing for Me* is the subject of a detailed treatment in Ingrid Björkman's *"Mother, Sing for Me": People's Theatre in Kenya,* a performance and reception history of the play, especially valuable for conveying the enormous excitement generated by the entire Kamĩrĩĩthũ experience. The book also reveals the very real courage of the participants who worked against escalating state-sanctioned intimidation to provide a popular form of entertainment and consciousness-raising for a truly wretched populace. The play, a "polylingual musical drama" with Gĩkũyũ text and songs in more than eight Kenyan languages, points to Ngũgĩ's movement beyond Gĩkũyũ tradition to a consideration of the cultural legacy of other nationalities in Kenya.[15] In the play, he was addressing a much broader Kenyan public and attempting in a daring way "to put his theory of the writer's social role into practice" (Björkman, 4). The multiethnic audience that watched the play had to interact to grasp its shifting linguistic and cultural registers, and at moments, the audience broke through the conceptual fourth wall separating actors and audience, and joined the performers onstage (62, 87).

In Björkman's account, *Mother, Sing for Me* is a historical "political allegory" about land ownership and the neocolonial aftermath of independence (Björkman, 23), though as Celeste Fraser Delgado explains, the play reinterprets the birth of the nation, particularly regarding the question of land purchase at independence.[16] In *I Will Marry When I Want,* Wangeci recalls bitterly those who "roamed the whole land / Telling us that we should not buy land / For which we had all shed blood!" (*I Will Marry,* 73). In *Mother, Sing for Me,* the new African landlord, who takes over a settler's plantation and then manages it for an American multinational corporation, insists that the poor must purchase their land. This rich manager has the rebel leader Kariuki, who killed the white plantation owner, imprisoned and tortured. The manager fears that Kariuki, a mechanic, might unite the interests of workers and peasants. The play is set in the 1920s and 1930s at the time of the crisis over the hated *kipande,* or passbook and registration system. Like so many of Ngũgĩ's plays, however, *Mother, Sing for Me* encourages the audience to perceive a clear link between the events of the past and the politics of the present. The point of linkage in this play is the 1962 Lancaster House Conference at which the sale of Gĩkũyũ land was negotiated and which established one of the planks of the neocolonial system. This sensitive subject, or merely the play's use of Kenyan languages and its accessibility to a mass audience, certainly alarmed the Kenyan authorities, and the play's performances were halted, in effect making the play more famous and its history more mythic than might ever have been possible otherwise.

Sembene: The Making of African Cinema

Ngũgĩ's next dramatic productions were to be in film and video. Ngũgĩ's last novel, *Matigari,* was heavily influenced by film techniques, and Ngũgĩ at least has discussed a film adaptation of the novel "so that Matigari would return to East Africa as a visual image" (*Moving,* 175). Ngũgĩ has followed the path of Sembene Ousmane in moving away from novels toward film, seeing in the latter a more accessible medium for an illiterate mass audience in Africa. Between 1985 and 1986, he took a film course in Sweden and completed a short feature about antiapartheid sanctions entitled *Blood-Grapes and Black Diamonds,* presented at the 1986 Edinburgh Film Festival,[17] and "in company with two other African students, from Tanzania and Mozambique, [made] 'Africa in Sweden,' [a] documentary on images of Africa conveyed through Western media; for the film the three [interviewed] Swedes who have never been to Africa" (Sicherman 1990, 15). Ngũgĩ worked as an adviser on the 1982 film adaptation of Nadine Gordimer's short story "Oral History," directed by Peter Chappell, and using Gordimer's film script, in which some of the members of the Kamĩrĩĩthũ company appear.[18] At the end of *Moving the Centre,* Ngũgĩ tells of writing a script for *Kariũki,* a film project "involving film-makers from Zimbabwe, Tanzania, Mozambique, Zambia and Sweden" (*Moving,* 155).

 Sembene: The Making of African Cinema (1994) was directed by Ngũgĩ and Manthia Diawara, a filmmaker, scholar of African film, and professor at New York University. The film was produced by the Tisch School of the Arts, New York University, and Manthia/Ngũgĩ Productions in association with Channel 4 Television in the United Kingdom.[19] This documentary traces the career of Sembene Ousmane, the great Senegalese novelist who switched from writing novels to directing films as a better means of directly addressing a mass audience. As Diawara puts it elsewhere, Sembene's early novels were "utopian narratives of self-determination . . . which he later abandons in his films in favor of the criticism of postindependence regimes, satire, and socialist realism."[20] Ngũgĩ and Diawara's documentary is primarily a series of interviews with Sembene conducted in French (with English subtitles) at different locations in Senegal. The interviews are arranged thematically, but the film also proceeds chronologically, from Sembene's memory of his childhood to an injunction about revolutionary action in the present. Although he is more than willing to reflect upon his entire body of work, Sembene refuses to offer definitive interpretations of his films or to accept any special credit for their creation. Despite Sembene's evident vigor, there is an unavoidably elegiac tone to the film's presentation of a great artist near the end of his career. As he says, "Now, my future is behind me." The visual focus on Sembene, who has a commanding presence and speaks with enormous dignity and conviction, is intercut with shots of market scenes in Dakar and of people working, studying, and relaxing; in a sense, these people are the subject, the audience, and the inspiration of Sembene's own films, and Ngũgĩ and Diawara's film is interspersed with scenes from Sembene's work.

Sembene: The Making of African Cinema begins with a written statement of purpose that reads like the manifesto that prefaces *The Trial of Dedan Kimathi*, but that also has the interrogative, oral quality of the beginning of *Matigari*. The statement outlines the filmmakers' quest:

> What is Africa to me, said the poet. We asked ourselves what is African cinema? So we went home in search of African cinema. We landed in Ouagadougou, Burkina Faso, where every two years millions gather to celebrate African images. As we mingled with filmmakers, a host of media workers, and the Burkinabe People, it became clear to us that the one person who symbolized the struggle to make African cinema was Sembene Ousmane. His presence was felt everywhere. We followed him back to Senegal: the streets of Dakar; his Galle Ceddo home at Yoff, overlooking the sea; his . . . office in the city center; schools where he often goes to interact with the young; and finally the locations of his films. Among the latter was the Island of Goree, the last slave post on the Atlantic Ocean before Middle Passage. As we stood on a hill watching fishermen going out to sea, we remembered what everybody had

been telling us: with Sembene Ousmane we see the dawn of African cinema.

The poet's initial question, perhaps recalling David Diop's poem "Africa," is finally answered through images of West African people and their culture, land, and history. In part conjuring the presence of the griot, the oral poet, Ngũgĩ and Diawara set out in their filmed narrative of return to uncover the origins of African cinema, past and present, and to sing a praise song for Sembene Ousmane.[21]

One of the film's most arresting images shows Sembene before an ocean scape at home in Yoff addressing a small group facing away from the camera. Framed by this group and the roof of a balcony overlooking the sea, Sembene addresses his audience about his concept of film and his methods of creation while gesturing in silhouette against the beautiful expanse of ocean, like a breathing canvas or a blue blackboard. His films are shot, he explains, under an open sky, requiring that he always "play a bit with the sun," and he begins a new film's screenplay by first creating a frame. His ocean-backed gestures indicate that the Atlantic's fluid geography is one such imaginative performance space on which his celluloid dreams unfold, while also belonging to the locale of his characters' life and work. Cinema's attraction for him lies in its ability to unite diverse audiences and its democratic nature, which allows a free and open viewer response. He says that although he personally prefers literature, he felt compelled to use film as the medium for delivering his "ideology" because of its immediate, visceral appeal to a large audience. In strained social and political circumstances, he maintains, "literature is a luxury." He views himself as a type of modern griot, using different tools. Whereas the traditional griot is the sole director, writer, and actor, Sembene as a filmmaker can be the storyteller and also part of the audience. Cinema can communicate an ideology, maintain the oral tradition, and make history accessible.

The ocean backdrop of this scene also introduces a discussion of Sembene's early influences. To be creative in cinema, he says, one must study the history of the visual image, and he notes how Charlie Chaplin, whom he admired as a boy, was intimately familiar with the classics of film, theater, and animation. Chaplin's little tramp moreover is always vigilant and "returns blow for blow." Sembene also speaks of his father's quiet, sustained anticolonialism and antiracism, at a time when even the theaters in Senegal were racially segregated. Most importantly, Sembene's two grandmothers influenced him: "According to the local tradition, they were my 'wives.'" Later in the film, he will refer to African women's indomitable will as the reason for African survival.

Sembene reiterates the cardinal importance of understanding African history, especially cultural and political history, to grasp the present situation. Slavery, which Sembene sees continuing in France and America in the present, is an integral part of this history. Contemporary slavery is explored in one of Sembene's best-known films, *Black Girl,* which tells of a Senegalese girl, the envy of her friends, who goes to France as a maid, only to discover that fabled France is merely someone else's house to clean. Her future is a black hole in the starry sky. Her employers display on their apartment wall an elongated African mask, whose cultural content has been diminished to the status of a trinket or souvenir. Touring a slave house museum, a monument to African suffering and survival in the past, Sembene in Ngũgĩ and Diawara's film deplores the way that such sites have been reduced to the level of tourist attractions. Moreover, Sembene also repudiates Western aid for fostering in Africans a slavish dependency and helplessness, and he also deplores the exploitative nature of feudal class and gender relations, as well as aspects of Islam and Christianity. Such modern remnants of slavery denigrate Africa's spirituality, morality, and cultural integrity. In the past, Sembene concludes, African land was colonized, but now African minds are colonized: "We must keep this history in mind or we'll be slaves in the coming century."

Sembene's films counter the colonization of African historiography. He contends that African films about Africa's past must be accurate, and they must provide their audiences with heroes to emulate, though Sembene concedes that in his novels, the group, and not the individual, takes action. He maintains a profound interest in the historical revolutionary Samori who united parts of Senegal, Guinea, and Mali. Sembene wanted to counter the portrayal of Samori as a barbarian in French colonial school books. While stressing, in a meeting with a group of students, the need to acknowledge heroes of history, he also emphasizes the necessity of assuming personal responsibility to correct social injustice. To effect change, he cautions, hindrances from the past must be discarded, and violent action may be necessary: "If the branch is no good, don't let it kill the tree. No one can do this for us. Not the Germans, Russians, Americans, or French. To cauterize a wound, you need to heat the knife and plunge it, incandescent, into your flesh. There's no other way."

The narrative logic of *Sembene: The Making of African Cinema* clearly reflects the preoccupations of Ngũgĩ's own work. The film begins with

Sembene's influences, moves to his engagement with history, and ends with his injunction regarding personal responsibility and revolutionary action. Like Ngũgĩ, Sembene acknowledges the place of women in African history, and he sees the postcolonial artist as the inheritor of the oral tradition of the griot. Sembene also notes again and again the inter-sections of the past and the present, and he deplores material exploita-tion as well as the still more insidious legacy of mental colonization. For both Sembene and Ngũgĩ, heroes are important and problematic. Sem-bene acknowledges the need for heroes, and he clearly wishes to elevate the historical reputation of Samori, a figure like Ngũgĩ's Dedan Kimathi. Both Sembene and Ngũgĩ, however, warn of the insufficiency of heroes; individual sacrifice is critical. Sembene, perhaps more candidly than Ngũgĩ, admits the reluctance of postindependence generations to engage with a colonial past they regard as divorced from the reality of their lives, or to sacrifice present comfort and even the luxury of indifference for future justice. While clearly sharing Ngũgĩ's political views, Sem-bene in this film is less politically strident than Ngũgĩ in some of his polemical writing. *Sembene: The Making of African Cinema* ends with Sem-bene's warning against a naive attempt to rewrite the African past; he encourages a synthesis of old and new, and a recognition that "no artist is somebody without his or her community."

Chapter Five

Armed Words for
Mental Decolonization:
Nonfiction Prose

Ngũgĩ is arguably better known and more widely cited today as a theorist of African language, literature, culture, and politics than as a novelist or dramatist. Since the publication of *Matigari,* he has been enormously productive, and the last few years alone have witnessed a flamboyant burst of energy with the publication of a revised, expanded, and rewritten edition of one of his most famous and influential books, *Writers in Politics,* and the recent appearance of his Clarendon lecture series, *Penpoints, Gunpoints, and Dreams.* His polemical writing, with roots in the journalism he produced while a student at Makerere, is nevertheless closely associated with his creative fiction and his involvement in education. His first collection of essays, *Homecoming,* partly derived from his master's dissertation project on Caribbean literature undertaken at Leeds University, and the essays in his latest collection were delivered at Oxford University. Ngũgĩ prefaces *Homecoming* with the declaration that his essays are "an integral part of the fictional world" of his first novels (xv). Ngũgĩ's novels, conversely, may be read as extended illustrations of the cultural, economic, and political ideas in the essays. His position has remained strikingly consistent for more than 35 years, and from the beginning he has been concerned with history, politics, and economics, and with issues of language, education (canon formation and curricular reform), and culture. Even in the journalism written between 1961 and 1964, he expressed a concern for African languages, the growth of popular theater, and an Afrocentric curriculum; this early period, however, finds him still clinging to a politically liberal confidence in gradual, ameliorative change, and to an aesthetic valorizing individual expression and universal values (Lindfors 1981, 23–41).

With an increasing focus on the issue most often associated with his name, the linguistic integrity of African literature, Ngũgĩ's essays, like his fiction, are always rooted in a concern for history, especially the neo-

colonial legacy of colonialism, and a future-oriented cultural nationalism. The essays deal with the literatures of Africa and the African diaspora, and with African colonization. They also address the role of the
African writer and the intellectual's responsibility to a popular audience.
A number of essays explicate Ngūgī's own fictional or dramatic writing,
revealing the circumstances of its production and reception, or drawing
on these works in considering other, broader questions about Kenya's
cultural and political economy. These lucid, autobiographical essays,
showing the seamless intermingling of private and public domains,
are among his best writing. Partly because the essay collections are
often assemblages of delivered lectures, frequently repeated, modified,
and amplified, and because of the very consistency of Ngūgī's critical
stance, they do contain a good deal of overlapping and repetition.
Taken together, however, these volumes constitute an emergent "anti-
imperialist aesthetics of African literature."[1]

Ngūgī's essays must be read in the cultural contexts of Africa's independence movements to perceive how his intellectual points of reference
have remained remarkably fixed over nearly four decades. Although he
is critical of Léopold Sédar Senghor's obsequious relationship to Senegal's French colonial masters, Ngūgī's references to negritude are nearly
always positive, though he remains skeptical of an overemphasis on
racial difference. Negritude is a philosophy from the 1930s and 1940s of
positive "Africanness," evolved by Senghor and the Martinican theorist
Aimé Césaire, that distinguished "typical" African characteristics including emotion, sensuality, and naturalness.[2] Soyinka famously dismissed
the notion, saying that a tiger doesn't need to study its own tigritude;
Soyinka also condemned a naive, uncritical nativism as "neo-Tarzanism."[3]
Senghor was an example of Plato's philosopher king, a phrase that
Ngūgī applies in his most recent collection to the first president of
Ghana, Kwame Nkrumah, and the first president of Tanzania, Julius
Nyerere. Nkrumah is important for Ngūgī in calling neocolonialism the
last stage of imperialism, extending the analysis, which Ngūgī frequently cites, of V. I. Lenin in his pamphlet *Imperialism: The Highest Stage
of Capitalism,* about capitalism's violent monopoly stage.[4] Nyerere's Pan-
Africanism and African socialism are equally important for Ngūgī,[5]
though he is suspicious that Nyerere's formulation lacks a solid material
basis. Nyerere's and Ngūgī's African socialism also bears the character of
the Great Helmsman of the Chinese revolution, Mao Tse-tung. Mao's
emphasis on the progressive, revolutionary role of the peasantry was a
major innovation in classic Marxism and was welcomed as being tailor-

made for East Africa. The effective mystification of the tragic and cata-strophic consequences of some of Mao's most straitjacketed policies, openly embraced by some Western intellectuals in the late 1960s and early 1970s, must be considered when reading Maoist endorsements from this period.

The antiracist, Pan-African sentiments of W. E. B. Du Bois and Mar-cus Garvey, the latter of such importance in George Lamming's novel *In the Castle of My Skin,* have been of enduring significance for Ngũgĩ. Simi-larly, he has been inspired by African historian C. L. R. James, especially his *Black Jacobins,* and by Walter Rodney's influential *How Europe Under-developed Africa.* The link between African history and culture is provided for Ngũgĩ perhaps best by Guinea-Bissau's rebel leader and theorist Amílcar Cabral, who advocated a postcolonial "return to the source," because colonialism had interrupted the organic historical development of colonized peoples and nations; however, decolonized nations, he sug-gested, should progress beyond nationalism, or at least the European model of the nation-state, to avoid neocolonial hegemony.[6] Ngũgĩ often cites Jomo Kenyatta's *Facing Mount Kenya,* an anthropological study of the Gĩkũyũ, for reliable information about precolonial and colonial Gĩkũyũ cultural practices, but Ngũgĩ, who once nearly became Ken-yatta's biographer, also regards Kenya's first president as a betrayer of the promise of independence (*Detained,* 159–63). In terms of Kenyan national history, Ngũgĩ highly respects the historians Maina wa Kĩnyattĩ, former political detainee and editor of *Thunder from the Moun-tains* (among other books about the Mau Mau period), and also politi-cian and activist J. M. Kariuki, author of the autobiography *"Mau Mau" Detainee.* Perhaps the most significant figure for Ngũgĩ in terms of national political involvement, and the union of activism and radical cultural expression, is the general of the Kenya Land and Freedom Army, the independently declared first prime minister of the Kenya Par-liament, and the organizer of the Gichamu theater group, Dedan Kimathi. Like Cabral, Kimathi appears to have regarded cultural regen-eration as an integral part of armed struggle. Kimathi is a type of inspi-rational forefather for Ngũgĩ, a figure who put into practice a socialist ethos focusing on the injustices endured by the landless peasantry.

Ngũgĩ's aesthetic principles derive in large part from his national and political preoccupations. His writing, however, flowered first in the African renaissance of the early 1960s, and he frequently cites the fic-tional example and the extraliterary comments of the great Nigerian writers Chinua Achebe and Wole Soyinka. While referring to many

African writers from Ayi Kwei Armah to Ben Okri, as well as imperial and colonial writers from Joseph Conrad (whom he once regarded as a flawed critic of colonialism)[7] to Karen Blixen, Ngũgĩ was influenced perhaps most obviously by the example of three writers: Sembene Ousmane, George Lamming, and Okot p'Bitek. Sembene, socialist realist novelist and African filmmaker, is for Ngũgĩ a model of the engaged postcolonial cultural intellectual. Similarly, the Caribbean novelist George Lamming, especially his largely autobiographical novel *In the Castle of My Skin,* has inspired Ngũgĩ's novelistic practice. Finally, Ngũgĩ's former colleague, Ugandan poet Okot p'Bitek challenged Ngũgĩ to acknowledge the centrality of orature in African literature. These writers, however, could not prepare Ngũgĩ for the revolution in his outlook that began during his involvement with the Kamĩrĩĩthũ Community Educational and Cultural Centre. For inspiration and also to illustrate the crude workings of neocolonial power, Ngũgĩ's essays return again and again to this artistic blossoming and the state repression that crushed it. The experience exemplified for Ngũgĩ the fundamentally political nature of all art.

Perhaps the most significant influence on Ngũgĩ's thought remains Frantz Fanon, the Martinican psychiatrist and philosopher. Ngũgĩ has distanced himself from Fanon's widely acknowledged influence, remembering in early 1979 that even while writing *A Grain of Wheat,* he had wearied of Fanon's emphasis on trauma. In the 1960s, however, "Frantz Fanon became the prophet of the struggle to move the centre and his book, *The Wretched of the Earth,* became a kind of Bible among the African students from West and East Africa then at Leeds" *(Moving,* 2). Ngũgĩ cites Fanon's "Pitfalls of National Consciousness," from *The Wretched of the Earth,* along with Lenin's pamphlet on imperialism as canonical for students of African literature. The "Euro-African" literature of the 1960s, Ngũgĩ explains, "was really a series of imaginative footnotes to Frantz Fanon" *(Moving,* 66). The influence of Fanon's analysis of the creation of a national bourgeoisie during colonialism is everywhere in Ngũgĩ's writing. This class begins to identify with the departing white colonial authorities, their culture and values, and their disregard for indigenous culture; and rising to power, they mimic every aspect of their former colonial overlords. Colonialism thus is not merely a system of political, economic, and cultural exploitation but a profoundly destructive delayed-action psychological mechanism. It implants and sustains a mentality of inferiority and conformity, which is perhaps the most insidious, lingering, and devastating effect of colonial-

ism. In books such as *Decolonising the Mind,* Ngũgĩ applies and popular-
izes Fanon's notion of the colonized mentality and advocates that a
rejection of the colonizers' linguistic and cultural forms is a precondition
for achieving true freedom, though Ngũgĩ would always add that material circumstances must also change.

In his most recent collection of essays, Ngũgĩ's range of reference
expands exponentially. This widening engagement with intellectual
resources and traditions may have been designed partly to accommodate
the horizon of expectations of his Western audience, but it also draws his
analysis more obviously into the orbit of African philosophy, an increasingly vibrant field over the last decade.[8] As in his previous work, here
Ngũgĩ accentuates the positive in his discussion of African texts. While
grounded in an analysis of Plato, his inquiry considers, however briefly,
Michel Foucault, Edward Said, the postcolonial condition, magic realism, deconstruction, cyberspace, and even TV sitcoms such as *Family
Matters*. Ngũgĩ's critical contexts are still clearly postcolonial, but they
are also beginning to be informed, as these examples indicate, by cultural studies and postmodernism, though he remains adamantly opposed
to the perceived moral flux of the latter. Ngũgĩ occupies a somewhat
ambivalent position regarding the contemporary discourse on African
philosophy.

Moreover, there are significant differences between Ngũgĩ's work and
that of some African philosophers. For example, while deploring internalization of colonial stereotypes of Africans and endorsing links
between traditional Kenyan worldviews and those of Egypt and Greece,
and Said's concept of the Orient as the West's "Other," he does not
engage with V. Y. Mudimbe's influential, hermeneutically sophisticated
reading of "Africa" as a notional, ideological construct, or his critique of
ahistorical, utopian "myths of African socialism" (Mudimbe 1994, 43).[9]
Mudimbe could have Ngũgĩ in mind when he argues that those interested in African literature too often regard it merely "as a mirror of
something else, say, for instance, of Africa's political struggle" (Mudimbe 1994, 177). Mudimbe, born in Zaire, and a former Benedictine
monk and Duke University professor, refers to his theoretical investigation *The Idea of Africa* as "stories to my children" (Mudimbe 1994, 209);
and similarly, Kwame Anthony Appiah, a Ghanaian-born Harvard University professor, frames his account of African philosophy *In My Father's
House* with a memoir of home and a dedication to his family's children
(Appiah, viii).[10] Appiah, like Ngũgĩ, distrusts the racialist basis of Pan-
Africanism, and indeed, referring to Fanon's contempt for the so-called

native intellectuals' regard for traditional culture (Fanon 1968, 221), Appiah deplores such intellectuals' "fetishistic attitude toward the customs, folklore, and vernacular traditions of their people" (Appiah, 61). Simon Gikandi extends Appiah's critique to Ngũgĩ's theory of language (Gikandi 1992, 133–43). Gikandi argues, and some other critics agree,[11] that it fetishizes language as an ahistorical repository of an innate, romantic cultural harmony. Like Ngũgĩ, Gikandi would acknowledge with Appiah the "entanglement of African intellectuals with the intellectual life of Europe and the Americas" (Appiah, 68). Appiah, however, is much more unsympathetic toward the African postcolonial intellectuals' attempt to escape or deny a necessarily Western orientation, insisting that "ideologies, like cultures . . . *only* exist antagonistically; domination and resistance are a large part of what they are *for*. In the ferment of present-day African literary debate, it is as well to remember that the very meaning of postcolonial discourse subsists on these conflictual relations. Indeed, they are *the* topos of contemporary African literature" (72). Appiah warns of the danger of the African intellectual's fetishizing a marginal status and becoming an "otherness machine," in Sara Suleri's evocative phrase.[12] For Appiah, Ngũgĩ's view of the writer in politics is "avant-garde" and Western (Appiah, 149; Gikandi 1992, 133, 143). Ngũgĩ remains, nevertheless, committed to the integrity of his own specific personal and historical experience, particularly the armed struggle against colonial oppression. He also differs from these critics and shows his affinity for Fanon in his immediate concern for actively changing the wretched material conditions of the poor and dispossessed.

Homecoming

A somewhat heterogeneous selection of essays, lectures, and reviews written over a 10-year period, *Homecoming: Essays on African and Caribbean Literature, Culture, and Politics* celebrates the international Pan-African spirit of the late 1960s. It also focuses on the literature of the far-flung African diaspora and particularly the work of George Lamming. The collection begins with "Towards a National Culture," a manifesto calling for a type of African socialism like that advocated by Nyerere and Cabral. Ngũgĩ also reveres Okot p'Bitek in the essay, though in his introduction to p'Bitek's *Africa's Cultural Revolution,* he intimates that the poet was "in danger of emphasizing culture as if it could be divorced from its political and economic basis."[13] In a direct, plain style, Ngũgĩ calls for a renewal of African culture unstymied by the divisive tribalism fostered by colonialism, also a major concern of his 1962 essay "Kenya: The Two Rifts," which espouses ethnic and tribal harmony. In celebrating the African communal spirit, "Towards a National Culture" emphasizes the political drive behind negritude, a philosophy with which the essay has much in common. Ngũgĩ rejects the elevation of "the cult of the artist with its bohemian priests" (*Homecoming*, 6), a Eurocentric, Arnoldian[14] view responsible, Ngũgĩ intimates, for the infantilization and the virtual annihilation of African culture. The African elite nurtured on such an ideology merely perpetuated its own mental colonization. The alternative "national culture," however, is not an atavistic return to traditional cultural practices but a creative synthesis of old and new. To establish such a "cultural renaissance" (16), mental colonization must end through political change allowing first and foremost the masses access to land. A revolutionized political economy would lay the foundation for transforming all institutions blighted by colonialism.

"Towards a National Culture" crystallizes Ngũgĩ's position in the early 1970s on art and education. In it he makes one of his first calls for the study of African languages and for the recognition of language as the medium of culture. Furthermore, anticipating his interest of the late 1980s and 1990s, he points to the importance of film, which "has great possibilities in Africa, where many people are still illiterate" (*Homecoming*, 19). In addition, he refers to the cultural practice that informs his own adoption in his last novels of transformed and transforming genres, his Mau Mau aesthetics. He tells of how, during the anticolonial war, peasants "rediscovered the old songs—they had never completely lost touch with them—and reshaped them to meet the new needs of their struggle. They also created new songs and dances with new rhythms where the old ones were found inadequate" (11). Ngũgĩ suggests a similar artistic ferment will be created by shifting school and university curricula to focus on Africa. He also recommends a kind of Maoist sending down of students and intellectuals to the countryside to learn from the peasants, a recommendation recalling the enthusiasm for the Chinese cultural revolution, at least outside China, in the late 1960s and early 1970s. Ngũgĩ writes: "The universities and our schools should go to the countryside; there must be total involvement with the creative struggle of the peasants and workers. The present dangerous, unhealthy gap between intellectual and practical labour, between the rural and urban centres, would be bridged" (18). Ngũgĩ's advocacy of a radical retooling of educational institutions was linked to his successful reorganization of the English department and its curriculum at the University of Nairobi along national, postcolonial lines, the subject of the collection's appendix. This manifesto that launched a national debate had its humble beginning in a departmental memo.[15] Ngũgĩ's enthusiasm would lead a few years later to his involvement with the Kamĩrĩĩthũ Community Educational and Cultural Centre, whose theater program was part of its literacy work, which was based on the theories of Paulo Freire, who argued that literacy must be linked to the potential for a transformed material reality.[16]

"Church, Culture, and Politics," the last essay in the first part of *Homecoming*, is a sober indictment of the Christian Church in Kenya. Identifying himself as non-Christian, but saying that as a novelist he shares a Christian's interest in the inner life, and that as a Kenyan, he has a concern for the church's all-pervasive influence, Ngũgĩ bluntly informs his Presbyterian audience that "the missionary robbed people of their soul" (*Homecoming*, 32). The missionaries' advocacy of European customs and suppression of African cultural traditions were destructive, even unchristian. Handmaidens of colonial aggression and exploitation, missionaries insidiously advocated acceptance of poverty as spiritually ennobling while condemning political involvement as contemptuous of God's will. In so doing, "the Church became the greatest opponent of the African struggle for freedom" (33), and allied with the rich and powerful, the forces of Caesar, it oppressed the poor. Ngũgĩ's devastating conclusion, especially powerful given its first audience, is that "if Christ had lived in Kenya in 1952 . . . he would have been crucified" (34). The church must heal and reform itself, foster national harmony in line with traditional Kenyan cultural values, reject capitalism, and return to the communal ethic of the early church.

The African writer, Ngũgĩ states in "The Writer and His Past," locates characters in a living history. "The novelist," he claims, "is haunted by a sense of the past" (*Homecoming*, 39). This history, denied by historians as diverse as G. W. F. Hegel and more recently Oxford historian Hugh Trevor-Roper, is also overlooked in colonial fiction and film. More destructive than all these forces, however, Ngũgĩ maintains, is capitalism, which economically, politically, and socially has "disfigured the African past" (45). True African history, he suggests, is socialist history. In "The Writer in a Changing Society," Ngũgĩ situates his political concerns in the context of popular history, concluding that "African intellectuals must align themselves with the struggle of the African masses for a meaningful national ideal" (50). Other African writers, however, such as Achebe, Soyinka, and T. M. Aluko, fail to identify with the masses or promote radical political action, and here Ngūgī's account of African writers takes the form of modified evaluative criticism. After sometimes quite detailed textual analysis, he assesses the political stance of a work under review, weighing its sympathy for the masses and its advocacy of radical solutions to social problems. Although Achebe, for example, directly addresses an African audience in *A Man of the People*, Ngūgī regrets the novel's suggestion that mild social amelioration will solve the problems it outlines. Similarly, Ngūgī applauds Soyinka's exposure of intellectuals' "moral atrophy" (61) but deplores the glorification of the artist as an aloof moral center. Instead, the writer should investigate the "revolutionary struggle," contributing both "moral direction and vision" (66). Literary achievement is judged here by political measurements.

Shifting to the East African literary scene, Ngūgī laments its writers' conservatism. In the face of the volume of excellent writing coming from countries such as Nigeria and South Africa, Ngūgī wrote in 1969 that East Africans just before Kenya's independence in 1963 were awed and a bit discouraged. They forgot, he recalls, the rich history of East African literature in African languages. East African literature of the 1960s often deals with the scars of colonization and with a love for the land, but "so far the East African novel has not radically departed from the Western mainstream. There has been little experimentation in language or in structure, or in the narrative method" (*Homecoming,* 73). Although it would be nearly a decade before Ngūgī heeded the radical implications of his own words, he hails Okot p'Bitek's innovations in poetry. In *Song of Lawino,* p'Bitek draws on traditional oral sources while also exposing the psychological effects of Westernization (*Homecoming,* 74–77).

Ngūgī locates in the literature of the African diaspora a similar concern for colonial alienation. He dates his revolutionary first encounter with Lamming's *In the Castle of My Skin* to 1961. Its effect was more profound and lasting than that produced by any European literature because the novel "evoked through a child's growing awareness a tremendous picture of the awakening collective social consciousness of a small village" (*Homecoming,* 81). Ngūgī values Lamming's novel as a careful account of awakening to oppression, but he is also interested in its views of Africa. In detailed readings of a number of Caribbean novels, including those of Lamming, John Hearne, and V. S. Naipaul,[17] Ngūgī examines Africa's representation, uncovering images of Africa as an icon of barbarity or as the mythical homeland of all creation. These images answer a variety of symbolic, spiritual, and psychological needs in the works' protagonists, but the central yearning is for a sense of identity, a respite from a nagging awareness of emptiness and exile. Identification with Africa, Ngũgĩ feels, is better fostered through an understanding of shared historical experience and economic exploitation than through the creation of a unifying "religion of skin colour" (108). Race is an important marker in Caribbean literature, hinting at the violence of slavery and sexual degradation lingering below its surface, but Ngũgĩ concludes that the vital link between Caribbean and African literature is economic.

The final two essays in *Homecoming* solely concern *In the Castle of My Skin*. The first provides a detailed close reading of the novel as "a study of colonial revolt" (*Homecoming,* 110), tracing its movement from colonial inertia to an anticipation of neocolonial dispossession. Ngũgĩ locates the novel's strength in its melding of the narrator G's awakening consciousness with the painful, slowly developing miscomprehension of the people of the village in Barbados, "Little England."[18] Ngũgĩ follows G's examination of the roots of gender conflict in slavery and the roots of personal alienation in colonial education and a feudal relationship to the landlord, Mr. Creighton. The villagers' hatred of the landlord is redirected to their immediate black overlords, and they ignore the landlord and the "black Jesus" Mr. Slime, the secret agent of their ultimate betrayal (Lamming, 159). The novel's final irony is that the people's total dispossession from their land coincides with the glimmer of a dawning political awareness, articulated in the novel most clearly by Trumper, who has returned from America with a radicalized consciousness of racial injustice. The novel ends, like Naipaul's *Miguel Street,*[19] with a disillusioned departure. In his final essay about Lamming, Ngũgĩ again explores Lamming's handling of political irony and his central theme of exile, from history, race, class, and self. The only effective escape from this alienated self-exile, Ngũgĩ concludes, is through action, which springs from political awareness.

Writers in Politics

Ngũgĩ is a relentless reviser of his work, and this is nowhere more apparent than in the 1997 "revised and enlarged" edition of his influential 1981 collection of essays *Writers in Politics*. Essays have been deleted, new essays added, and in some cases essays from the first edition have

been almost totally rewritten. Ngũgĩ's rewriting has focused and clari-
fied the thrust of his writing, eliminating numerous examples, illustrations, and digressions. Even the three parts of the book are renamed for
greater impact. Part 1 in the 1981 edition, for example, bears the somewhat prosaic title "Literature, Education: The Struggle for a Patriotic
National Culture"; the second edition's part 1 announces a "War of
Images." The revised edition removes many extended quotations, and
epigraphs from Marcus Garvey and Karl Marx. It also eliminates direct
references to the original lectures' genre and audience, and places its discussion in a contemporary, late-1990s, context. For example, the first
lecture is subtitled "The Politics of the Canon," referring to the debate
in the last two decades over curricular revision in the Western academy
and especially in departments of English, and also to the debate in
Nairobi in the late 1970s that Ngũgĩ addresses in *Homecoming*.

The focus of the revised *Writers in Politics* remains the politics of writing and writers. The book provides Ngũgĩ's most sustained materialist
reading of the intersection of history, culture, and politics, but its leftist
literary analysis is not always especially subtle or nuanced, unlike that
of, for example, Aijaz Ahmad, Fredric Jameson, or Abdul JanMohamed.
Ngũgĩ's analysis does not engage with the thought of some of Marxism's
most challenging twentieth-century interpreters, such as Louis Alt-
husser and Antonio Gramsci. It does not always succeed, moreover,
in what Ngũgĩ calls the necessity of going "beyond the cliché and the
slogan" (*Writers,* 2d ed., 118).[20] Ngũgĩ advances a reflexive model of
socialist realism, and evaluative and legislative critical strategies. He
endorses demonic versus angelic interpretive binaries and inevitably
rehearses a prescriptive view of the stages of world history, leading from
slavery and imperialism, through colonialism and neocolonialism, to
socialism. He enjoins cooperation between Africa and the African diaspora, on the one hand, and the socialist countries in Asia and Latin
America, on the other, in opposition to international imperialism and its
domestic "comprador allies" (156). As he writes in "Writers in Politics,"
all writers must fight imperialism, and they either advance or retard
social progress by their grasp of class struggle and their own class preju-
dices (70–71). The African writer "must reject, repudiate, and negate
his roots in the native bourgeoisie and its spokesmen, and find his true
creative links with the pan-African masses over the earth in alliance with
all the socialistic forces of the world" (75). Saying this, Ngũgĩ fully
acknowledges his own liberal position in the early 1960s, anticipating a
period when the scars of history could be healed and his writing could

explore individual angst, divorced from material social conditions
(73–74). By 1975, Ngũgĩ's attitudes have hardened, and he demands
that the African writer "must actively support and in his writing reflect
the struggle of the African working class and its class allies for the total
liberation of their labour power" (75).

The collection's inaugural essay, "Literature and Society," connects
colonial history and cultural imperialism and views writing as a social
process, materially related to the processes of its production, reproduction, and reception. Ngũgĩ discusses the place of Africa and the African
writer in the web of international imperialism, as in *Homecoming,* examining contentions that Africa lacked a history or culture before the
arrival of the white man. He refers to the denigration of African qualities such as blackness in the English language, and the universalizing of
European cultural norms when African cultural norms were dismissed as
having at best only "local" relevance. Colonial literature, such as the
novels of H. Rider Haggard, Joseph Conrad, Joyce Cary, and Karen
Blixen, presented African characters as either diabolical demons or objects
of pity. Such novels manifest racism, due to ignorance, contempt, or
patronizing and paternalistic pity, and finally offer "an aesthetic of
acquiescence" (*Writers,* 2d ed., 16).

Ngũgĩ writes, as in *Homecoming*'s "Towards a National Culture,"
about the retooling of the cultural and linguistic weapons of colonialism, such as Christian hymns, to resist oppression:

> The Mau Mau took up similar hymns but now turned them into songs of
> actual political engagement in an actual political universe. They called
> for visible material freedom. The battle was no longer for some invisible
> new heaven but for a real heaven on their own earth. They called on the
> youth, asked them to hearken to their leaders and take up real arms
> against a visible colonial state. The songs called on the people to give up
> drunkenness; prostitution; fear; self-abnegating social practices that only
> harmed themselves. They urged the youth to step up political agitation
> among the masses. With justice on their side they would emerge victori-
> ous. (*Writers,* 2d ed., 21)

Such a cultural program led a reinvigorated people "to seize the initia-
tive in history" (21). In addition, the forces of resistance published in
African languages and later in European languages: "Here once again
Africans turned that which was meant to imprison them into a weapon
of struggle. They took the languages of Europe to denounce colonialism
or simply to assert their negritude" (22). Ngũgĩ cites African writers like

Sembene Ousmane, who wrote anticolonial works in colonial languages. He concludes that African writing should be regarded as central to the study of twentieth-century literature because it best demonstrates the political and economic forces of the century: "African literature is an essential part of those cultural forces that destroyed the hegemony of imperialism in the world. They may not have created a new world but by their struggles they have cleared the ground for new foundations" (25).

"Literature and Society" frequently cites Marx and Fanon, but also Mao Tse-tung. Mao's influence is especially apparent in Ngũgĩ's remarks about literary criticism. Although he states that all criticism has an ideological basis of some type, he suggests a type of legislative criticism, necessarily limited, but that limitation justified by present conditions: "At the very least people should strive to detect in African or any other literature, what is positive, humanistic, revolutionary in the work as art—supporting it, strengthening it—and rejecting what is negative and anti-humanist in the same or other works" (*Writers,* 2d ed., 24). His formula for good criticism, and by extension for the writing of good literature, resembles that advanced in Mao's *Talks at the Yenan Forum on Literature and Art,* which Ngũgĩ cites earlier in the essay. Mao, writing in the remote caves of Yenan, where his forces had fled to escape the onslaught of Chiang Kai-shek and to fight the Japanese invasion, declared that "revolutionary literature and art [must] . . . help the masses to propel history forward."[21] Ngũgĩ's rewritten conclusion to the second edition of his essay refers to the new forces that threaten the very survival of Africa at the end of the twentieth century. To offset crisis, he maintains, the persuasive potential of literature must be exploited to the maximum to move people to radical action.

Ngũgĩ's approach to a national literature curriculum ("Literature and Society" is subtitled "The Politics of the Canon") pits an Afrocentric against a Eurocentric curriculum. The latter, he argues, is akin to "self-mutilation of the mind" (*Writers,* 2d ed., 29). Drawing on the prototypical figures of early postcolonial discourse, Prospero and Caliban from Shakespeare's *The Tempest* and Crusoe and Friday from Daniel Defoe's *Robinson Crusoe,* Ngũgĩ writes that a Eurocentric curriculum teaches Kenyan readers to "see how Prospero sees Caliban, or how Crusoe sees Friday, but hardly ever how Caliban or Friday sees Prospero and Crusoe" (30). *The Tempest* and *Robinson Crusoe* belong to the third order of importance in Ngũgĩ's proposed curriculum, after first Pan-African and African diasporan literature, and second the literature of Asia and Latin

America. What joins the first two orders is the defining quality of literature worthy of the name: an account of struggle against oppression. Like Mao, Ngũgĩ demands that literature affirm the positive and critique the negative, and always "reflect the grandeur of our history" (35). Similarly, in "Literature and Double Consciousness," Ngũgĩ views the whole of Afro-American literature as the story of resistance to global economic and political repression. W. E. B. Du Bois, from whose work Ngũgĩ draws the impetus for his essay, advocated education and democracy to forestall a "second slavery."[22] Du Bois and Ngũgĩ wish to reverse the effects of "double consciousness," the perspective of looking at the self from the negative point of view of someone else. Ngũgĩ concludes, however, that class-based economic exploitation is a more serious barrier than racism to human progress.

"Return to the Roots" is a powerful early statement of Ngũgĩ's position on the politics of language articulated at greater length later in *Decolonising the Mind.* He begins with a consideration of the debate among African writers in the early 1960s about the relative value of writing in African languages or the languages of the colonizers. In particular, he cites the virulent reaction against Obiajunwa Wali's now famous pronouncement in 1963, a year after the Conference of African Writers of English Expression at Makerere, that writing in European languages was a dead end for African culture and that true African literature could be written only in African languages. Proponents of African writing in English suggested that English, for example, united members of diverse linguistic groups against colonialism. Even Ngũgĩ, at one time, advocated this position, but at least by 1979 he regarded Kenyan novels written in English as belonging not to African but to "Afro-saxon literature" (*Writers,* 2d ed., 57). Language, he asserts, is the basis of a people's material and cultural life, and the repository of historical memory. Ngũgĩ traces the repression of Kenya's languages to the 1940s, the period of increasing opposition to colonial rule, when English was promoted in schools and the newly erected theaters and cinemas to assimilate an elite class of Kenyans who would assume the mantle of neocolonial power. Independent Kenya has maintained and even encouraged such a policy. The colonial authorities banned the Gĩkũyũ edition of Kenyatta's *Facing Mount Kenya;* neocolonial authorities have suppressed Ngũgĩ's Gĩkũyũ texts, while their English translations are readily available. Such practices result from internalized linguistic inferiority and foreign cultural imperialism, and as Ngũgĩ laments in "Freedom of Expression," they build "linguistic prisons" (81) and deny citizens the "right to write" (78).

Some of Ngũgĩ's best and most poignant essays are his personal, autobiographical reflections, such as "A Novel in Politics," an account of the writing and publication of his early novels and *Petals of Blood*. Just as "Freedom of Expression" begins with an extended reflection on his baby Mũmbi's fight for self-assertion, and "Kamau Brathwaite: The Voice of Pan-African Presence" tells about the renaming of Edward[23] and his evocation of Ngũgĩ's mother in a poem written for Mũmbi, so the heart of Ngũgĩ's memoir of the launch of *Petals of Blood* is a meditation on his mother. He remembers that while she labored on her farm to pay his school fees, his mother encouraged and closely monitored his progress in school. The minuteness of her inquiries led him for years to believe that she was literate. She attended his book launch in July 1977, a celebration ominously followed by the withdrawal of the license for public performances of *I Will Marry When I Want* at Kamĩrĩĩthũ in November and Ngũgĩ's detention in December. When his mother died, more than a decade later, Ngũgĩ was in exile. Also present at the launch was a cabinet minister and Ngũgĩ's former economics teacher, Mwai Kĩbaki, who taught him about capitalism's inequalities almost 15 years earlier. To some extent, Ngũgĩ provides here a series of early intimations of the growth of the novelist's mind and his emergence as an engaged political writer. The signal event, galvanizing his perception of the writer's social responsibility, was wrestling with the "dreadful indulgence called fiction" during the tortured six-year gestation of *Petals of Blood*: "My pursuit of literature which I then thought was fiction had brought me full circle to the facts of economics" (*Writers*, 2d ed., 87, 89).

In other essays in *Writers in Politics*, Ngũgĩ commends the spirit of resistance in the writing of Kenyan patriots such as J. M. Kariuki. Ngũgĩ's account of his missed meetings with the author of *"Mau Mau" Detainee* (1963) is chilling, given that the essay's composition marked Kariuki's assassination by forces loyal to Kenyatta and Moi in 1975. For Ngũgĩ, Kenyatta betrayed independence, and his successor was a colonial collaborator. Ngũgĩ celebrates Kariuki's advocacy of universal education, national and Pan-African unity, anti-imperialism, and self-reliance. Ngũgĩ wants to resurrect a man whose name means "a generation resurrected." Ngũgĩ, furthermore, demands recognition for Mau Mau as the force that "broke the back of the British Empire it being the first armed struggle against colonialism anywhere in the Empire" (*Writers*, 2d ed., 99).

The revised edition of *Writers in Politics* ends with a warning about the new world order's threat to Africa's survival. In a series of short speeches delivered mostly in Asia in the 1990s, Ngũgĩ deplores the combined might of a unified Europe, Japan, and America, and their far-reaching instruments: the international lending agencies such as the International Monetary Fund and the World Bank, Free Trade Blocs, the G7 Group of Industrialized Countries, and the United Nations Security Council. These organizations, Ngũgĩ feels, have colluded with African civilian and military dictatorships, and only international and especially "Third World" solidarity can effectively oppose them. To prevent Africa's absolute collapse and recolonization, a Pan-African alliance must be formed in dialogue with the socialist forces of Asia and South America to resist the new imperial order. Ngũgĩ calls on "writers and all cultural workers" to assume a committed position "at the forefront of this struggle" (*Writers,* 2d ed., 131).

Detained: A Writer's Prison Diary

In December 1977, a few days after preparing his students at Nairobi University to begin a historical study of the novels of Chinua Achebe, Ngũgĩ was arrested and began a yearlong detention as prisoner K677 in Cell 16 of Kamĩtĩ Maximum Security Prison, where Dedan Kimathi was hanged. In his account of this period, *Detained: A Writer's Prison Diary,* Ngũgĩ describes his apprehension on the last day of December 1977 in biblical terms and, in passing, offers a materialist reading of *Genesis:* "Two Land-Rovers with policemen armed with machine-guns, rifles and pistols drove into the yard. A police saloon car remained at the main gate flashing red and blue on its roof, very much like the Biblical sword of fire policing the ejection of Adam and Eve from the legendary Garden of Eden by a God who did not want human beings to eat from trees of knowledge, for the stability of Eden and his dictatorship over it depended on people remaining ignorant about their condition" (*Detained,* 15). Ngũgĩ's reference to knowledge here probably gestures to his recent liberating work with the Kamĩrĩĩthũ Community Educational and Cultural Centre. This is significant because Ngũgĩ was never formally charged, and he attributed his detention to his involvement with community-based consciousness-raising. Kamĩrĩĩthũ combined theater production with literacy classes, along the lines advocated in *Pedagogy of the Oppressed,* by Paulo Freire. Freire advanced a plan for literacy work that placed potent key words and the act of reading itself directly into the context of the new literates' liberating grasp of their own material social reality. Learning to read words becomes an approach to "decoding" the condition of oppression itself (Freire, 83), and to direct involvement in transforming material reality. Hence the new literates in the Kamĩrĩĩthũ project learned to read and to express significant moments in their lives in writing and public performance. Ngũgĩ's Kamĩrĩĩthũ plays were written collectively, and he realized in prison that it was his linguistic liberation work that was frowned upon by the state. The state regarded his work with the peasants, in their own language, as more dangerous than the political message of his recently published English-language novel *Petals of Blood,* which the peasantry would be unable to read. The Kamĩrĩĩthũ experience and Ngũgĩ's resulting detention galvanized his understanding of state oppression and of the real power of language. Henceforth, he resolved to write only in Gĩkũyũ, and his prison cell became the workshop for his first Gĩkũyũ novel, translated as *Devil on the Cross.*

Detained collects texts and documents relating to Ngũgĩ's detention, including the detention order signed by then minister for home affairs Daniel arap Moi, who became president a year later. The book is partly a diary, written concurrently as events unfold, and also a memoir reflecting from a later perspective on these earlier events. The text is multifaceted, almost a library of Ngũgĩ's current concerns. It contains a type of writer's manifesto in its account of the slow genesis of *Devil on the Cross;* a reflection on Kenya's history, literature, and politics; and even a history of detention in colonial Kenya. In addition, *Detained* collects letters from prison and documents concerning Ngũgĩ's dismissal from, and his attempt to regain his position at, the University of Nairobi. As a result, the book is a hybrid in terms of genre, more diverse and diffuse than the prison diary so much admired by Ngũgĩ, J. M. Kariuki's *"Mau Mau" Detainee.* The prison diary in its different forms is sadly one of the central genres of African literature, and while in prison Ngũgĩ read Kwame Nkrumah's autobiographical account of his colonial imprisonment in James Fort Prison in 1948, from which Ngũgĩ learned the technique of writing on the prison's hard toilet paper. During his more recent nearly seven-year detention, however, the Kenyan historian Maina wa Kĩnyattĩ was denied permission to read Ngũgĩ's work (*Penpoints,* 58). Ngũgĩ also read the South African prison poems of Dennis Brutus, *Letters to Martha,* during his detention. Imprisonment by colonial authorities has been a reality for many of Africa's most respected elder political leaders, such as Nelson Mandela, and detention by neocolonial governments has not been an uncommon experience for Africa's writers. The prison is even referred to as Africa's university. Other celebrated African prison diaries

include Soyinka's *The Man Died* and the South African Breyten Breyten-
bach's *True Confessions of an Albino Terrorist.*[24]

Ngũgĩ writes that detention begins with dreams of release. His
began more prosaically with internal segregation and a war of biblical
quotations traded with the prison chaplain. Much of the time he also
spent in historical reflection. He recalls a contract signed in 1967 for "A
Colonial Affair," an account of settler life, and its legacy in contemporary Kenya. He traces the history of colonial and neocolonial detention
and the development of national theater. He reflects on Kenya's famous
colonial political prisoners, Harry Thuku and Jomo Kenyatta. The routine of prison life interrupts these thoughts, causing despair that he is
becoming "part of the life of the caged" (*Detained,* 119). He is buoyed,
however, by the spirit of resistance in other prisoners, and when the
prison superintendent cautions him not to write, Ngũgĩ resolves to
begin a diary immediately, despite his impatience with autobiography.
After a regular warder rebukes him as a detached intellectual partly
"responsible for the cultural plight of Kenya" (130), Ngũgĩ is outraged
and that evening commences his novel in Gĩkũyũ. From a scrap of
newspaper, he learns of two corrupt members of Parliament who have
been punished when bigger political fish have escaped the judicial net,
and he seizes on this information for the central theme of his novel,
adding to it the news of South African transplant surgeon Professor
Barnard's visit to Kenya. In this period, Ngũgĩ also listens to the folktales and political songs of other prisoners, which may also have made
their way into his novel. He reads of his detention by accident in
Newsweek and on the advice of other detainees resists the expectation of
release, offered by the "gigantic judicial hoax" of the Detainees's Review
Tribunal (150). He learns later to give more credence to the seemingly
absurd "dove theory of freedom," discovering on his release that doves
have hovered near his home since his arrest.[25] With Kenyatta's death,
Ngũgĩ is released, but not before an agonizing final six months during
which the toilet paper manuscript of his novel is seized and then finally
returned. He emerges from prison with two manuscripts and begins the
long and finally hopeless attempt to be reinstated at the University of
Nairobi.

Ngũgĩ's detention has been for him a distinction, albeit a dubious
and tragic one, and one he has declined to repeat. It has made him one
of Kenya's "political untouchables" (*Detained,* 21), but detention has
also symbolically authorized him as a spokesperson for neocolonial
oppression and for the oppressed masses. Detention connected him

directly to, and confirmed his interpretation of, Kenya's history of resistance. Looking at the other detainees and hearing their stories, Ngũgĩ recognized that they belonged to "groups that span the whole history of post-independence upheavals in Kenya" (123). He comes to see his own incarceration as representative of a shift in political consciousness in the country: "I am part of a living history of struggle" (124). Ngũgĩ was detained by the government of Jomo Kenyatta, who was himself detained by colonial authorities. Detention brought into diamond clarity what Ngũgĩ had always said, and more loudly said in the 1970s, about the neocolonial, parrotlike status of postindependence Kenya. Ngũgĩ was released upon the declaration of a general amnesty following Kenyatta's death, but repression continued. Henry Chakava, Ngũgĩ's former student and Nairobi publisher, writes of the death and kidnapping threats and also the very real abductions and beatings Chakava suffered, especially in the period after Ngũgĩ's release from detention, because of Chakava's involvement with the country's most famous artist.[26] Such tactics are designed to implant a dread of such terror in the population at large so that they will internalize the disciplinary regimen of the state.

In *Detained,* the committed artist's incarceration without sentence or trial becomes an allegory for the confinement of the nation. Ngũgĩ refers to the neocolonial Kenyan nation itself as a prison, and his own nearly two-decade long exile as a type of exported imprisonment. In Kamĩtĩ, he soon grasped that "my detention is not a personal affair. It's part of the wider history of attempts to bring up the Kenyan people in a reactionary culture of silence and fear" that may become their "destiny" (*Detained,* 28, 63). Even Ngũgĩ's release, heralded by the news of Kenyatta's death, occasions for Ngũgĩ a somber reflection on this leader, the nation's history, and its destiny. The book contains a number of biblical allusions, from the reference to Adam and Eve's expulsion from the Garden of Eden at Ngũgĩ's arrest, to his hearing the trembling of the walls of Jericho in messages of support, and more generally his condemnation of the "colonial Lazarus" of neocolonialism, which is forever being raised from the dead (63). These allusions give the text a troubled, fateful quality. Ngũgĩ, of course, had no knowledge of when his detention would end and whether it would end in freedom or death. His psychological terror in prison, mingled with soul-destroying boredom, was matched by the anxiety of some of those outside the prison's walls confined by a dread of such treatment.

Barrel of a Pen

Two years after the publication of *Detained* and *Writers in Politics,* another volume of essays appeared. Like the chapters of *Writers in Politics,* the essays in *Barrel of a Pen: Resistance to Repression in Neo-colonial Kenya* were first conference papers and speeches, but this volume also reproduces songs from *The Trial of Dedan Kimathi,* dialogue from *I Will Marry When I Want,* and excerpts from *Detained* and Maina wa Kĩnyattĩ's collection of Mau Mau poems and songs, *Thunder from the Mountains.* Ngũgĩ's title appears to derive from Bulwer-Lytton's phrase about the pen being mightier than the sword, and also from Mao's epigram about truth issuing from the barrel of a gun, and it clearly links cultural work and armed struggle, writing and fighting.[27] Ngũgĩ employs another variation on this phrase in the title of his latest collection, *Penpoints, Gunpoints, and Dreams.* The impetus behind *Barrel of a Pen*'s publication was a widely perceived increase in political and cultural repression in Kenya in early 1982, though as Ngũgĩ points out, the repression had been in place from the dawn of independence: "The distance between the barrel of a gun and the point of a pen is very small: what's fought out at penpoint is often resolved at gunpoint" (*Barrel,* 9). Focusing on the relationship between widespread political suppression and the neocolonial rewritings of history, Ngũgĩ's pen-gun analogy ultimately figures the engaged writer's participation in violent struggle.

What Ngũgĩ calls the "scholarly attempt at the ideological burial of Mau Mau" derives from a sector of the scholarly community in Kenya who contend that Mau Mau was a localized Gĩkũyũ rebellion and not a national liberation movement. For celebrating this phase in Kenya's history as heroic and for writing in Gĩkũyũ, Ngũgĩ has been branded by such scholars—later referred to as "state intellectuals" (*Decolonising,* 102)—as a Gĩkũyũ nationalist, instead of a Kenyan nationalist, whereas his sympathies obviously lie with Pan-Kenyan and Pan-African unity. Ngũgĩ's analysis of Kenyan history's rewriting and erasure is informed by his reading of Fanon's account of the colonial bourgeoisie and neocolonialism. Echoing Fanon, Ngũgĩ names political and military leaders in Kenya with direct links to the colonial government as "white settlers in black skins" (*Barrel,* 18).[28] Writing about the time when Elspeth Huxley's *The Flame Trees of Thika* was being shown on Kenyan Television and a ballet based on *Alice in Wonderland* was being performed at the Kenya National Theatre, Ngũgĩ deplores the historic suppression of indigenous cultural expression. He regards the annihilation of Kamĩrĩĩthũ as one of the worst examples of Moi's repressive policies. Reproducing passages from *Detained* and *I Will Marry When I Want*, Ngũgĩ explains how women's participation in drama was used as part of the authorities' pretext for withdrawing the license for the theater, and finally for its total destruction. Ngũgĩ regards women's involvement in Kamĩrĩĩthũ as part of a long historical line of female cultural resistance to colonial and neocolonial repression.

In *Barrel of a Pen*, Ngũgĩ again tackles one of his central concerns, the role of the postcolonial intellectual.[29] As he wrote in *Writers in Politics*, the knowledge and ability of the intellectual traditionally was public property (*Writers*, 2d ed., 150), but in the neocolonial period, when not silenced or exiled, the intellectual is often alienated from his or her community by language or by fear of the repercussions of expression, a type of self-censorship. The Brechtian artist, writes Ngũgĩ in "Freedom of the Artist: People's Artists versus People's Rulers," is not "the poet laureate or the court singer to the status quo" (*Barrel*, 61) who regards history as static and is encouraged and rewarded by the established powers.[30] The artist exemplified and celebrated by Brecht, rather, is "the trumpeter of a new world" (61), resembling the educator whose "education should give people the confidence that they can in fact create a new heaven on this earth" (90). Although Ngũgĩ believes that no artist working within a capitalist system is free, he implies that correct thinking, clear observation, and courageous social criticism will liberate the postcolonial artist's creative expression in any circumstances. He echoes Mao's call for far-reaching criticism of catastrophic state policies, the Hundred Flowers campaign, which was followed in China by the draconian Anti-Rightist campaign that suppressed those who had offered criticism and many who had not, based on a quota system for different work units. The Anti-Rightist campaign was partly an outgrowth of Mao's obsession with the moral imperative of continuous class struggle; the campaign was a repressive social movement intended to root out those taking the so-called capitalist road. Ngũgĩ issues a modified Maoist appeal: "Let a hundred schools of drama contend in the villages" (66). While acknowledging that political and economic freedom is essential for robust cultural expression, Ngũgĩ calls for postcolonial intellectuals even in neocolonial conditions not merely to reproduce "petrified museum culture" (81) but to give voice to the vibrancy of true national culture, even exploiting modern technology such as film and video.

Decolonising the Mind

Decolonising the Mind: The Politics of Language in African Literature is one of Ngũgĩ's deservedly best-known and most frequently cited works, with one of his most brilliant and memorable titles. The book offers a lucid and sustained Fanonean reading of the internalization of colonial racial and cultural stereotypes. It focuses on the question of the African writer's linguistic medium, intended audience, and purpose in writing. *Decolonising the Mind,* nevertheless, is largely a recapitulation of Ngũgĩ's earlier thoughts on these subjects, especially in *Homecoming* and *Writers in Politics.* Ngũgĩ, in fact, introduces the book as a "summary" of his earlier ideas (*Decolonising,* 1). Although these essays, like those in his previous three volumes, began as lectures, causing some of the repetition within those books, *Decolonising the Mind* is more fully synthesized into a sustained argument on the politics of language. Near the beginning of the volume, published in 1986, Ngũgĩ strikes a proudly elegiac note, saying that the book is his "farewell to English as a vehicle for any of my writings" (xiv). Only 2 of the 21 essays in Ngũgĩ's subsequent 1993 collection *Moving the Centre* were originally published in Gĩkũyũ, and in the preface to that volume, Ngũgĩ laments the shortage of African-language translation and the total absence of journals or newspapers in Gĩkũyũ. This situation was rectified somewhat with the launch of the Gĩkũyũ journal *Mũtiiri* at New York University in 1994.

The autobiographical impulse is strong in *Decolonising the Mind,* which is one of the reasons for its success, and Ngũgĩ everywhere creates a synthesis of personal and national politics. He also softens the sometimes wooden and pontificating tone of *Barrel of a Pen,* acknowledging in the preface: "Inevitably, essays of this nature may carry a holier-than-thou attitude or tone. I would like to make it clear that I am writing as much about myself as about anybody else" (*Decolonising,* xii). In the collection's first essay, "The Language of African Literature," Ngũgĩ writes of a trajectory beginning with the 1884 Berlin Conference and extending to the 1962 Makerere University College Conference on African Writers of English Expression (attended by Soyinka and Achebe, among other illustrious figures). Years later, Ngũgĩ is struck by how the Makerere conference organizers and he personally blithely overlooked the program's omission of many famous African-language writers, whose form of expression he had come to accept as genuinely African.

In the powerful third section of the essay, Ngũgĩ tells his own story of growing up in Gĩkũyũ. He describes the fertility of his early linguistic environment, rich with a diversity of storytelling and language games, and of his early schooling until 1952 in his mother tongue. At the time of the Emergency, he began learning English, and his proficiency set him on a rapid helicopter ride to higher education at the elite Alliance High School and then at Makerere and Leeds. Ability in the language of the colonizer was richly rewarded; inability or reluctance to learn it and to forget the mother tongue was punished. He remembers: "One of the most humiliating experiences was to be caught speaking Gĩkũyũ in the vicinity of the school. The culprit was given corporal punishment— three to five strokes of the cane on bare buttocks—or was made to carry a metal plate around the neck with inscriptions such as I AM STUPID or I AM A DONKEY" (11). Ngũgĩ adds to this catalog of horrors in *Moving the Centre:* "In some cases, our mouths were stuffed with pieces of paper picked from the wastepaper basket, which were then passed from one mouth to that of the latest offender" (*Moving,* 33). Exposure of native speakers was policed by a system of informers.

Language for Ngũgĩ is communicative, but it belongs to the production process, and it also embodies the culture, history, and self-identity of a people. The colonial introduction of English, with its devaluing of indigenous languages and cultures, contributed to an alienation that Ngũgĩ refers to in *Writers in Politics* as "double consciousness." The optimistic postindependence generation of African writers in English, an indigenous elite, became cynical with the rise of overt neocolonial oppression and began using traditional peasant forms and a more direct address, but they were ambivalent about a shift to African languages. Indigenous languages remained vibrant among the peasantry and had their champions in "organic vernacular intellectual[s]" such as Gakaara wa Wanjau (Pugliese, 177), and even at the Makerere conference in the voice of Obiajunwa Wali. Ngũgĩ concludes that "African literature can only be written in African languages" (*Decolonising,* 27), and that only such writing with the correct political perspective can foster cultural and mental decolonization.

The two middle essays in *Decolonising the Mind* divide their discussion according to genre. "The Language of African Theatre" testifies about Ngũgĩ's by now well-known invitation to join the coordinated literacy and theatrical work at Kamĩrĩĩthũ, and how his life was changed. Theater had always been an organic part of traditional lifeways, though with colonialism, the theater's continuity was shattered, only reemerging with a more nationalistic thrust in the 1950s and after independence, when theater was imposed on the people from above. At Kamīrīīthū, the theatrical language was Gīkūyū, a language immediately connecting the village audience with its own history, the subject of the plays performed. Kamīrīīthū's Gīkūyū-language drama interspersed action and dialogue with song, dance, and mime. Authenticity of linguistic and historical detail was scrupulously monitored through full and open dialogue between everyone in the theater and the village, the living archive of Gīkūyū linguistic expertise. Even the prop guns were fashioned by a man who had made guns for the Mau Mau fighters. The success and then destruction of the theater ensured its enduring fame but also inspired Ngũgĩ's first fiction in Gīkūyū. He was arrested five days after instructing his University of Nairobi students to prepare for an Achebe course informed by a study of Lenin and Fanon. Defying his detention and connecting with a tradition of resistance, Ngũgĩ acquired improvised writing materials—a pen for writing an appeal to the authorities and rough toilet paper—and tackled the difficulty of Gīkūyū orthography and the question of finding a fictional form to reach a peasant audience. Ngũgĩ chose a pared-down story with a highly dramatic and suspenseful plot, incorporating elements of Gīkūyū fable, parable, praise song, and myth. Writing about a country in which outrageous occurrences had become commonplace, Ngũgĩ introduced fantastic satire to escalate the narrative interest of actual events to incendiary levels. The published novel was widely distributed in Kenya and, in less than a year, sold 15,000 copies, the beginning of its popular "appropriation" (*Decolonising,* 68).

Decolonising the Mind concludes with an examination of another signal experience in Ngũgĩ's career, like Alliance's linguistic colonialism, the Makerere conference, participation in people's theater, and detention. What he refers to as "the great Nairobi literature debate" was the widespread discussion in the English Department at the University of Nairobi in 1968 and 1969 about the future direction of literature teaching. One of the opening salvos, "On the Abolition of the English Department," is included in the appendix of *Homecoming*. Ngũgĩ maintains that Kenyan, East African, and African literatures must be the focus of the department, and that orature must be the core of the curriculum. Ngũgĩ dismisses as absurd the elevation of European literature as having universal application and the deflation of African literature as having only local application. The university debate continued at a September 1974 conference on the teaching of African literatures in

Kenyan schools, a conference that recommended the centrality of Swahili
literature in a national school curriculum. For Ngũgĩ, both debates were
"really about the direction, the teaching of literature, as well as of history, politics, and all the other arts and social sciences, ought to take in
Africa today" (*Decolonising,* 101). Restating a demand for the reform
of political and economic conditions as a necessary ground for nurtur-
ing cultural expression, *Decolonising the Mind* ends with "a call for the
rediscovery of the real language of humankind: the language of struggle" (108).

Moving the Centre

Like Ngũgĩ's collections published before *Decolonising the Mind, Moving
the Centre: The Struggle for Cultural Freedoms* is an assemblage of disparate
and often very brief public lectures and presentations that rehearse the
central concerns of his work, often with the same illustrations and examples. It was designed to bring together his final words in English.[31] Like
Decolonising the Mind, it often skillfully and effectively mingles an evocative personal narrative with its restatement of postcolonial positions. For
example, the first essay in the collection, "Moving the Centre: Towards a
Pluralism of Cultures," focuses on a groundbreaking period in Ngũgĩ's
career: his years as a graduate student at Leeds University in the 1960s.
Ngũgĩ tells of how, deeply influenced by Fanon, his ambivalence about
writing novels in English began his linguistic journey home to Gĩkũyũ.
He also explains how his interest in the novels of Joseph Conrad, located
at the empire's center, shifted to an interest in the novels of George
Lamming, located at the empire's periphery. Ngũgĩ's abiding interest in
the language of African literature and in curricular reform is everywhere
apparent in *Moving the Centre,* and he welcomes plurality, diversity, and
difference, the hallmarks of postcolonial literary analysis, which was
gaining widespread acceptance, influence, and prestige—and shifting
toward the center of academic studies—in the early 1990s.

Writing in the shadow of "globalization" and the new economic
world order, Ngũgĩ emphasizes the so-called Third World's history of
oppression, and the ties between cultural and moral values, on the one
hand, and economic and political values, on the other. Ngũgĩ again
reads the history of oppression in *The Tempest, Robinson Crusoe,* and *Heart
of Darkness,* but also surprisingly in J. M. Coetzee's *Foe,* which would
appear to give voice to the very voicelessness that Ngũgĩ deplores.
Ngũgĩ rehearses his query about the universality of European experi-

ence, but he extends his analysis in *Writers in Politics* and *Decolonising the Mind,* claiming a dialectical relationship for the universal and the local. Showing the influence of contemporary interest in cultural studies, Ngũgĩ argues against the adoption of English as a global language, because of its imperial legacy, though all languages pack ideological baggage: "The oppressor nation uses language as a means of entrenching itself in the oppressed nation. The weapon of language is added to that of the Bible and the sword in pursuit of what David Livingstone, in the case of nineteenth-century imperialism, called 'Christianity plus 5 percent.' Today he would have probably described the same process as Christianity, debt, plus 40 percent in debt servicing" (*Moving,* 31). Instead of the adoption of the language of power, English, Ngũgĩ suggests as a better candidate Kiswahili, which does not carry a similar load of oppression and disgrace. While the omnivorous appetite of English gobbles up the world for Anglo-American interests, the means by which it engulfs other linguistic cultures are insidiously disguised in the media and entertainment industries. The omnipresence of such cultural imagery and ideas refigures the globe in "the image of the West" (53).[32] In the words of Ngũgĩ's onetime colleague Taban lo Liyong, a poet and now professor at the University of Venda, South Africa: "The poor of the world who buy silence with sweets and ice-cream / Will keep McDonald and the General in business / Regardless of ideology, change of regime, whims of the boss."[33]

The intellectual's role concerns Ngũgĩ in the second section of *Moving the Centre,* and he puts forward his by-now-familiar position in the context of his personal experience of exile. He writes of the slowly rising despair of the late 1960s and 1970s after the intoxicating optimism of independence.[34] Ngũgĩ hints at a failure in that period to anticipate that achieving African socialism required more than merely notional support; it was a failure that led to the virtual supremacy of neocolonial forces. Ngũgĩ never fails, however, to enjoin resistance to imperial oppression, among intellectuals in particular, through the use of African languages and an alliance with the peasantry, resistance to official, state-sanctioned retelling of history, and vocal outrage at suppression of scholarship. Writers' imprisonment has made texts like *Detained* a major branch of African literature, but Ngũgĩ contends that African writers are also psychologically imprisoned and mentally exiled through the legacy of colonial education and neocolonial politics. One of colonialism's most debilitating effects is the internalization of racism, the subject of the third section of *Moving the Centre.* Racism insidiously obscures its ideological

links to Western European capitalism that in turn associates Africa with
profit and pleasure, and reinforces the myth of racial superiority "at the
heart of the Western bourgeois civilisation" (*Moving,* 135). In colonial
literature, racism hides behind fine phrases or action-packed adventures,
leaving youthful readers ambiguously positioned. At Alliance High
School, for instance, Ngũgĩ enjoyed air adventure stories and identified
with English fighter pilots while his brother, who encouraged Ngũgĩ to
stay in school, was being bombed in the forests of Mount Kenya by the
Royal Air Force. Resistance to such narrative double-crossing, internalized inferiority, and racism comes through awareness of the 500-year
history of struggle against it, even in England, and the inspiration of
resistance fighters like Nelson Mandela.

Moving the Centre concludes with a bittersweet evocation of Ngũgĩ's
homeland. He tells of the creation of the African novel *Matigari* while
exiled in England, and of writing an African film script at Yale. Exile is a
condition both galling and poignant. He realizes, for instance, that with
his students at Ivy League Yale, in the heart of America's comfort and
privilege, he is free to discuss issues that in his homeland "would land all
of us in prison for anything between one and ten years" (*Moving,* 157).
He recalls a visit to the colorful and lively Swahili coast of Tanzania in
1987, when a grand feast marking the end of the Muslim Ramadan fast
was followed by a beautiful ocean journey at night. At such a time,
home is a tantalizingly near but absent presence, and the experience
makes him recall Makerere, his first time away from home: "It was
Makerere and Uganda which made me discover my sense of being a
Kenyan" (165). Most of Ngũgĩ's novels were written outside Kenya, and
they all evoke a powerful sense of the soil of East Africa: "Writing has
always been my way of reconnecting myself to the landscape of my birth
and upbringing" (156). This nostalgic piece of personal travel writing
evokes Ngũgĩ's dreams about the post-neocolonial union of Kenya, Tanzania, and Uganda; about writing, homecoming, and identity; and
about an abiding love for the land and the people of his home.

Penpoints, Gunpoints, and Dreams

Ngũgĩ's most recent collection of essays, subtitled *Towards a Critical Theory of the Arts and the State in Africa,* extends the spatial metaphor of *Moving the Centre.* The latter speaks of moving away from a Eurocentric
worldview in favor of the discovery of new centers. *Penpoints, Gunpoints,
and Dreams,* however, extends *Decolonising the Mind*'s notion of empty

space to include performative space, a contested political space for reflection and action. This volume collects the Clarendon Lectures in English Literature that Ngũgĩ delivered at Oxford University in 1996. It consolidates and amplifies the position worked out in his previous essay collections on the African intellectual, art and the neocolonial state, language, and orature. Ngũgĩ acknowledges harping on his familiar concern about language in the lectures, and provides a justification. "The responsibility of Africa's artists and intellectuals to return to the languages of the people," he states, "has been my theme in books, and in my talks, over the last ten years. This is because I do not want the issue to be forgotten" (*Penpoints,* 128). The volume generally lacks the autobiographical focus of *Decolonising the Mind* and the last section of *Moving the Centre,* their linkage of the personal and the political, and as a result their narrative drive, though it does broaden the context of Ngũgĩ's remarks. *Penpoints, Gunpoints, and Dreams* locates its discussion of Ngũgĩ's familiar concerns against the background of Greek philosophy, stressing the connections between the land of Socrates and Plato, and the civilizations of Egypt and the Nile Valley stretching all the way to Uganda and Kenya. Ngũgĩ also places his analysis in the context of the writing of other theorists, previously unmentioned in his essays, such as Bakhtin, Said, and Foucault. More optimistically than ever before, Ngũgĩ celebrates the power of art and the artist and their role in creating a space for dreams of freedom.

Ngũgĩ begins by showing how the state attempts to constrain and exploit this very power, being suspicious of the nearly divine dynamism of the creator, the wildly unrestrained questioning in the act of creation, and art's refusal to mask the truth or remain silent. Recalling that Plato admitted into his Republic only artists who would portray rulers positively, Ngũgĩ counters that good art, even written to praise the emperor, may expose oppression, and like Rudyard Kipling's *Kim,* "undermin[e] . . . [its] very avowal of allegiance" (*Penpoints,* 31). Ominously, of course, the state may attempt to make the artist disappear through imprisonment, torture, death, or exile. Even when not removed "from the territorial stage" (35), the artist, like a prophet crying in the wilderness of the nation, may simply be ignored.

Ngũgĩ's examination of the politics of postcolonial performance space is informed by a reading of renowned English director Peter Brooks and influential French philosopher Michel Foucault. In the neocolonial nation, Ngũgĩ writes, all space, geographically and conceptually, is fought over by the powerful state, which fears the free zone of a people's theater slipping outside the bounds of the dramatic performance. Space in a postcolonial nation is never "empty," in Brooks's formulation, and may be divided internally according to geography, race, class, and gender. The national space, both the idea of the nation and its boundaries, is contested. Ngũgĩ's example is the colonial suppression of ritual performances of the Ituĩka ceremony, and the neocolonial repression of performances at Kamĩrĩĩthũ and in Nairobi (*Penpoints*, 64). The Kenya National Theatre, site for the first performances of *The Trial of Dedan Kimathi*, is located near the colonial-era Norfolk Hotel, which overlooks the spot of the 1922 massacre of the peasants who marched and danced for Harry Thuku's release. Performances of *The Trial of Dedan Kimathi*, a play marked to represent the nation at a Pan-African festival in Nigeria, were slotted into a tight scheduling space between a French ballet and an English farce. Every night of the play's brief run, the audience broke the conceptual fourth wall separating audience and actors, and they sang and danced inside and outside the theater, breaking out of the enclosed free space of the theater and, in the state's view, challenging its control of national space. Ngũgĩ invokes Foucault's analysis of the ideological context in which public spectacles of horrific punishment in Europe were replaced in the eighteenth century, during the rise of nascent capitalism and of more intrusive church and state power. Spectacle was replaced by the silent discipline of the penitentiary that was ultimately to internalize its surveillance inexorably within the body of the condemned.[35] Ngũgĩ conjures Foucault's powerful Benthamite image and his ideological analysis to demonstrate how the space of the writer is policed in the neocolonial state. Exile, like Ngũgĩ's own nearly two-decade-long exile from Kenya, is exported imprisonment. In a country such as Kenya, where any gathering of five or more people requires a permit, all "performances" of normal human interaction, such as weddings and funerals, become potentially subversive. The neocolonial police state delimits and disciplines the space of the nation.

Internalized surveillance operates through control of thought and language, and intellectuals in Kenya, Ngũgĩ contends, either sanction or confront such impositions. To assess the performance of the African intellectual, Ngũgĩ examines the postcolonial uses made of Plato's allegory of the cave, as in Ayi Kwei Armah's novel *The Beautyful Ones Are Not Yet Born*, a raucous cry of despair about postindependence Ghana. For Ngũgĩ, this intellectual may be either a neocolonial interpreter for those outside the cave, a liberal interpreter uselessly lamenting personal bondage, like Caliban, or a rebel interpreter working as the people's guide. To guide the people, the African intellectual must speak in African languages like the traditional Gĩkũyũ "oral intellectual" (*Penpoints,* 96), but although African artists in every field have drawn on the oral heritage, some of their work has enabled the theft of Africa's legacy. Orature models Ngũgĩ's dream of Africa's future because of its circular nature, which "assumes a dynamic interplay of margins and centres" (115), an intriguing construct, though a somewhat ambiguous political paradigm for post-neocolonial Africa. Interestingly, Ngũgĩ perceives cyberspace's relationship to orature: "Cyberspace, where we can already see the narrowing of the gap between signs, icons, and voices, is nearer to the world of the oral. In cyberspace resides the possible merger of the four aesthetic systems of the written, the oral, the theatrical, and the cinematic. Cyberspace orature may turn out to be the great oral aesthetic system of the future" (118). *Penpoints, Gunpoints, and Dreams* concludes by enjoining African artists and intellectuals to acknowledge their roots in orature, and to dream this legacy into the free space of Africa's future.

Notes and References

Chapter One

1. Chinua Achebe, "The Novelist as Teacher," in *Morning Yet on Creation Day: Essays* (London: Heinemann, 1975), 42–45.

2. Ngũgĩ wa Thiong'o, *Writers in Politics,* 1st ed. (London: Heinemann, 1981), 31; hereafter cited in text as *Writers,* 1st ed.

3. Karen Rothmyer, "About a Seized Kenyan Writer, and Fiction by Him," *New York Times,* 10 May 1978, A27; hereafter cited in text.

4. Ngũgĩ wa Thiong'o, *Moving the Centre: The Struggle for Cultural Freedoms* (London: James Currey, 1993), 162; hereafter cited in text as *Moving.*

5. Ngũgĩ wa Thiong'o, *Detained: A Writer's Prison Diary* (London: Heinemann, 1981), 29–43; hereafter cited in text as *Detained.*

6. Patrick Brantlinger, "Victorians and Africans: The Genealogy of the Myth of the Dark Continent," *Critical Inquiry* 12, no. 1 (Autumn 1985): 166–203.

7. Taban lo Liyong, "Interview with Taban lo Liyong," interview by Bernth Lindfors, *Mazungumzo: Interviews with East African Writers, Publishers, Editors, and Scholars,* ed. Bernth Lindfors, Papers in International Studies, Africa Series, no. 41 ([Athens, Ohio]: Ohio University Center for International Studies, 1980), 57; hereafter cited in text as Liyong 1980. Ngũgĩ refers to meeting Achebe in *Decolonising the Mind: The Politics of Language in African Literature* (London: James Currey, 1986), 5; hereafter cited in text as *Decolonising.*

8. Joseph Conrad, *Heart of Darkness,* ed. D.C.R.A. Goonetilleke (Peterborough, Ont.: Broadview, 1995), 66–67.

9. John Lonsdale, "The Conquest State of Kenya, 1895–1905," in *Unhappy Valley: Conflict in Kenya and Africa* (London: James Currey, 1992), 13; hereafter cited in text. Lonsdale's phrase, slightly modified, is repeated in B. A. Ogot and W. R. Ochieng', eds., *Decolonization and Independence in Kenya, 1940–93* (London: James Currey, 1995), xiv.

10. Adam Hochschild, *King Leopold's Ghost: A Story of Greed, Terrorism, and Heroism in Colonial Africa* (Boston: Houghton Mifflin, 1998), 27, 51. See Henry M. Stanley, *Through the Dark Continent,* 2 vols. (1878; reprint, New York: Dover, 1988); John Bierman, *Dark Safari: The Life Behind the Legend of Henry Morton Stanley* (New York: Knopf, 1990).

11. Joseph Thomson, *Through Masailand with Joseph Thomson,* edited and abridged by Roland Young (Chicago: Northwestern University Press, 1962), 82.

12. John Boyes, *John Boyes, King of the Wa-Kikuyu, a True Story of Travel and Adventure in Africa, Written by Himself,* ed. C. W. L. Bulpett (London: Methuen, 1911), 96; hereafter cited in text.

13. D. A. Masolo, in an account of African epistemology in his *African Philosophy in Search of Identity* (Bloomington: Indiana University Press, 1994), writes of how before the European arrival, "Kenyans living in the vicinity of the mountain had frequently gone barefoot to the mountaintop to pray" (223).

14. K. Michael Barbour, introduction to *The First Ascent of Mount Kenya,* by H. J. Mackinder (London: Hurst, 1991), 22–25. Mackinder's *First Ascent* is cited hereafter in text.

15. Ngũgĩ wa Thiong'o, *Petals of Blood* (London: Heinemann, 1977), 111; hereafter cited in text as *Petals.*

16. Zöe Marsh and G. W. Kingsnorth, *A History of East Africa: An Introductory Survey* (Cambridge: Cambridge University Press, 1972), 146.

17. Ngũgĩ wa Thiong'o, *A Grain of Wheat,* rev. ed. (London: Heinemann, 1986), 98; hereafter cited in text as *Grain.*

18. Charles Chenevix Trench, *Men Who Ruled Kenya: The Kenya Administration, 1892–1963* (London: Radcliffe, 1993), 4–5; hereafter cited in text.

19. Carl G. Rosberg Jr. and John Nottingham, in *The Myth of "Mau Mau": Nationalism in Kenya* (New York: Frederick A. Praeger, 1966), suggest that Mau Mau may originate in a 1948 investigation by the district commissioner of Nakuru into a "politico-religious sect," and they note the resemblance of the phrase to the Gĩkũyũ word for oath, *muma* (331–32; hereafter cited in text). Similar conclusions are drawn by John Lonsdale in *Unhappy Valley* (426).

20. *Mau Mau,* written by David Koff, produced and directed by Anthony Howarth and David Koff, 52 min., Anthony David Productions, 1979, videocassette.

21. See Oginga Odinga, *Not Yet Uhuru: The Autobiography of Oginga Odinga* (London: Heinemann, 1967), 120 (hereafter cited in text); Maina wa Kinyatti, ed., *Kenya's Freedom Struggle: The Dedan Kimathi Papers,* with a foreword by Ngũgĩ wa Thiong'o (London: Zed, 1987), 16–17 (hereafter cited in text); Ngũgĩ wa Thiong'o, *Barrel of a Pen: Resistance to Repression in Neo-colonial Kenya* (London: New Beacon, 1983), 12 (hereafter cited in text as *Barrel*).

22. Josiah Mwangi Kariuki, *"Mau Mau" Detainee: The Account by a Kenya African of His Experiences in Detention Camps, 1953–60* (Harmondsworth, Middlesex: Penguin, 1964), 50–51; hereafter cited in text.

23. Donald L. Barnett and Karari Njama, *Mau Mau from Within: Autobiography and Analysis of Kenya's Peasant Revolt* (New York: Monthly Review, 1966), 53–55; hereafter cited in text.

24. Ali A. Mazrui, "Mau Mau: The Men, the Myth, and the Moment, a Foreword," in *Mau Mau: Twenty Years After, the Myth and the Survivors,* by Robert Buijtenhuijs (The Hague: Mouton, 1973), 11.

25. In an early piece of journalism, Ngũgĩ attacked the movement. Bernth Lindfors writes: "Considering his later post-Leeds shift to a more

extreme leftist position on social and political matters, it is rather surprising to find in some of his early writing a condemnation of the Land Freedom Army, an endorsement of western Christianity as 'the best challenge to Communism or any form of totalitarianism,' and a stern warning against sending Kenyan students 'to any obscure half-civilised country that calls itself Communistic and Socialistic.'" Bernth Lindfors, "Ngugi wa Thiong'o's Early Journalism," *World Literature Written in English* 20 (Spring 1981): 29; hereafter cited in text as Lindfors 1981.

See, too, Richard Peck's account of an early story "The Wind," which he describes as "an anti–Mau Mau piece," and *The River Between* in "Hermits and Saviors, Osagyefos and Healers: Artists and Intellectuals in the Works of Ngũgĩ and Armah," *Research in African Literatures* 20, no. 1 (Spring 1989): 28–29.

26. Robert Buijtenhuijs, *Mau Mau: Twenty Years After, the Myth and the Survivors* (The Hague: Mouton, 1973), 74–77.

27. Wunyabari O. Maloba, *Mau Mau and Kenya: An Analysis of a Peasant Revolt* (Bloomington: Indiana University Press, 1993), 3; hereafter cited in text.

28. Similarly, Maina wa Kinyatti, in his introduction to *Kenya's Freedom Struggle,* agrees that the movement lacked "theoretical and ideological analysis of world imperialism and capitalism"; its program was "patriotic nationalism" and not "dialectical materialism" (Kinyatti, 11–12).

29. See Lonsdale's excellent account, which briefly refers to Ngũgĩ, of Mau Mau's "moral economy" and the ideological struggle over its legacy between historians of the Left and Right, in *Unhappy Valley,* 266–302. See Peter Simatei's account of Ngũgĩ's position in the debate about fictional interpretations of Mau Mau, in "Versions and Inversions: Mau Mau in Kahiga's *Dedan Kimathi: The Real Story,*" *Research in African Literatures* 30, no. 1 (Spring 1999): 154–61.

30. Ngũgĩ wa Thiong'o, in *Homecoming: Essays on African and Caribbean Literature, Culture, and Politics* (London: Heinemann, 1972), writes that "the oath was not a simple avowal to attend a Sunday afternoon picnic; it was a commitment to sabotage the colonial machine and to kill if necessary" (28; hereafter cited in text as *Homecoming*). See Maina wa Kinyatti, *Kenya's Freedom Struggle,* on the purpose of oathing (Kinyatti, 2–3), and his transcription of the verbal component of the oaths (Kinyatti, 133–38). On oathing, see also Waruhiu Itote (General China), *"Mau Mau" General* (Nairobi: East African Publishing House, 1967), 273–84; hereafter cited in text.

31. E. S. Atieno-Odhiambo, in "The Invention of Kenya," in Ogot and Ochieng', *Decolonization and Independence in Kenya,* regards these developments as a consequence of the loyalist and Home Guard forces "winning" the armed struggle and thus defeating both the Mau Mau fighters and the "white tribe" of settlers. He traces the conservatives' appropriation of the nationalistic rhetoric of Mau Mau to the period when the participants in the Mau Mau struggle were being ushered off the political stage (41–43).

32.   Michael T. Kaufman, "Kenya's Political Detainees Freed," *New York Times,* 13 December 1978, A8.

33.   I am indebted here to the work of Carol Sicherman, *Ngugi wa Thiong'o: The Making of a Rebel, a Source Book in Kenyan Literature and Resistance* (London: Hans Zell, 1990) (hereafter cited in text as Sicherman 1990), and to an interview conducted with Ngũgĩ shortly after his release from detention, which is included in appendix 2, "A Discussion between Ngugi and Myself," of Amooti wa Irumba's "Ngugi wa Thiong'o's Literary Production: A Materialist Critique," Ph.D. diss. (University of Sussex, 1980), ii-lxxxvi.

34.   Peter Nazareth, "Interview with Peter Nazareth," interview by Bernth Lindfors, *Mazungumzo: Interviews with East African Writers, Publishers, Editors, and Scholars,* ed. Bernth Lindfors, Papers in International Studies, Africa Series, no. 41 ([Athens, Ohio]: Ohio University Center for International Studies, 1980), 84; hereafter cited in text as Nazareth 1980.

35.   In "Ngugi wa Thiong'o's Early Journalism," Bernth Lindfors writes: "Between May 1961 and August 1964 Ngugi wrote nearly eighty pieces for the Nairobi press, contributing first to the *Sunday Post,* then preparing a fairly regular weekly or fortnightly column for the *Sunday Nation,* and finally working full time as a junior reporter and editorial commentator for the *Daily Nation* in the months between his graduation from Makerere and his departure for postgraduate studies at Leeds University in England" (Lindfors 1981, 24).

36.   "Kenya: Unity of Kenyan Organizations Abroad," *African Communist* 112 (1988): 69.

37.   Charles Cantalupo, introduction to *Ngũgĩ wa Thiong'o: Texts and Contexts,* ed. Charles Cantalupo (Trenton, N.J.: Africa World Press, 1995), x.

38.   Ngũgĩ wa Thiong'o, *Writers in Politics: A Re-engagement with Issues of Literature and Society,* 2d ed., rev. and enl. (Oxford: James Currey, 1997), xii; hereafter cited in text as *Writers,* 2d ed. See Ella Shohat, "Notes on the 'Post-Colonial,'" *Social Text* 31–32 (1992): 99–113; and Anne McClintock, "The Angel of Progress: Pitfalls of the Term 'Post-Colonialism,'" *Social Text* 31–32 (1992): 84–98.

The term "postcolonial" has been applied so freely that "there is a danger of its losing its effective meaning altogether," as Bill Ashcroft, Gareth Griffiths, and Helen Tiffin point out in their general introduction to *The Post-colonial Studies Reader* (London: Routledge, 1995), 2, which includes two essays by Ngũgĩ. Patrick Williams deftly situates the problems with the term in the context of a discussion of Ngũgĩ's treatment of intellectuals, in "'Like Wounded Birds'? Ngugi and the Intellectuals," *Yearbook of English Studies* 27 (1997): 201–3.

39.   Bruce Robbins, *Secular Vocations: Intellectuals, Professionalism, Culture* (London: Verso, 1993), 152.

40.   Stephen Slemon, "Post-colonial Allegory and the Transformation of History," *Journal of Commonwealth Literature* 23, no. 1 (1988): 157–68. Chris

Tiffin, "The Voyage of the Good Ship 'Commonwealth,' " *Kunapipi* 14, no. 2 (1992): 12–21. See Helen Tiffin's handling of the "postcolonial" as a "set of discursive practices" in her introduction to *Past the Last Post: Theorizing Post-colonialism and Post-Modernism,* ed. Ian Adam and Helen Tiffin (Calgary: University of Calgary Press, 1990), vii. See Robert J. C. Young, *Colonial Desire: Hybridity in Theory, Culture, and Race* (London: Routledge, 1995), 159–66, for a deft and lucid historical analysis of colonial and postcolonial discourse.

41. Simon Winchester, *The Professor and the Madman: A Tale of Murder, Insanity, and the Making of the "Oxford English Dictionary"* (New York: Harper-Collins, 1998), 78. John Willinsky, *Empire of Words: The Reign of the OED* (Princeton, N.J.: Princeton University Press, 1994), 3, 202–3.

42. Ngũgĩ wa Thiong'o, *Penpoints, Gunpoints, and Dreams: Towards a Critical Theory of the Arts and the State in Africa* (Oxford: Clarendon, 1998), 2; hereafter cited in text as *Penpoints.*

43. Chinua Achebe, in *Morning Yet on Creation Day,* counters this view, saying that in the Nigerian colonial experience, the English language united individuals from a large number of ethnic nationalities speaking hundreds of different languages (57). Henry Indangasi mourns the death of a universal implied reader in Ngũgĩ's Gĩkũyũ texts and suggests that Ngũgĩ's construction there of his ideal reader as a Gĩkũyũ peasant or worker contains "an element of wishful thinking" (197); Indangasi also objects to Ngũgĩ's designation of Kenya's languages as Soviet-style "national languages" (199), in "Ngugi's Ideal Reader and the Postcolonial Reality," *Yearbook of English Studies* 27 (1997): 193–200.

44. B. A. Ogot, "The Construction of a National Culture," in Ogot and Ochieng', *Decolonization and Independence in Kenya,* 214–36.

45. Albert S. Gérard, *African Language Literatures: An Introduction to the Literary History of Sub-Saharan Africa* (Harlow, Essex: Longman, 1981), 312.

46. "Editorial," *Zuka,* no. 1 (September 1967): [4].

47. Sam Mbure, poet and president of the Kenya Writers Association, acknowledges Ngũgĩ's material support, advice, and encouragement in "Ngugi wa Thiong'o and the 'Young Poet,' " in Cantalupo, *Ngũgĩ wa Thiong'o: Texts and Contexts,* 29–32. Cristiana Pugliese writes of the dire political consequences that faced Gakaara wa Wanjau resulting from his association with Ngũgĩ. See Cristiana Pugliese, "The Organic Vernacular Intellectual in Kenya: Gakaara wa Wanjau," *Research in African Literatures* 25, no. 4 (Winter 1994): 181–84; hereafter cited in text.

48. Frantz Fanon, *The Wretched of the Earth,* trans. Constance Farrington (New York: Grove, 1968), 221; hereafter cited in text as Fanon 1968. Kwame Anthony Appiah, *In My Father's House: Africa in the Philosophy of Culture* (New York: Oxford University Press, 1992), 61; hereafter cited in text.

49. Tsenay Serequeberhan, *The Hermeneutics of African Philosophy* (New York: Routledge, 1994), 11.

50. Chinua Achebe, *Morning Yet On Creation Day,* 19.

51. Gayatri Chakravorty Spivak, *The Post-colonial Critic: Interviews, Strategies, Dialogues,* ed. Sarah Harasym (New York: Routledge, 1990), 56.

52. Ngũgĩ wa Thiong'o, *Devil on the Cross,* trans. Ngũgĩ wa Thiong'o (London: Heinemann, 1982), 59; hereafter cited in text as *Devil.*

53. Antonio Gramsci, "The Formation of Intellectuals," in *The Modern Prince and Other Writings,* trans. Louis Marks (New York: International Publishers, 1957), 118–25.

54. Nuruddin Farah, "Bastards of Empire," *Transition* 5, no. 1 (Spring 1995): 26–35. Ngũgĩ refers to Farah's work in narrative as "a metaphor for postcolonial Africa," in "Nuruddin Farah: A Statement of Nomination to the 1998 Neustadt Jury," *World Literature Today* 72, no. 4 (Autumn 1998): n.p.

55. Homi K. Bhabha, *The Location of Culture* (London: Routledge, 1994), 13.

56. Homi K. Bhabha, introduction to *Nation and Narration,* ed. Homi K. Bhabha (London: Routledge, 1990), 1–7.

57. Carol M. Sicherman, "Ngugi wa Thiong'o and the Writing of Kenyan History," *Research in African Literatures* 20, no. 3 (1989): 347–70.

58. Fredric Jameson, "Third-World Literature in the Era of Multinational Capitalism," *Social Text* 15 (1986): 65–88.

59. Aijaz Ahmad, "Jameson's Rhetoric of Otherness and the 'National Allegory,' " *Social Text* 17 (1987): 3–25.

Chapter Two

1. Ngũgĩ has said that the prize money was a major motivation behind writing the first version of *The River Between.* Reinhard Sander and Ian Munro, " 'Tolstoy in Africa': An interview with Ngugi wa Thiong'o," in *Critical Perspectives on Ngugi wa Thiong'o,* ed. G. D. Killam (Washington, D.C.: Three Continents Press, 1984), 49–50; hereafter cited in text.

2. Ngũgĩ wa Thiong'o, *Secret Lives and Other Stories* (London: Heinemann, 1975), [X]; hereafter cited in text as *Secret Lives.*

3. David Cook and Michael Okenimkpe, *Ngũgĩ wa Thiong'o: An Exploration of His Writings,* 2d ed. (Oxford: James Currey, 1997), 156; hereafter cited in text.

4. Kimani Njogu, "Living Secretly and Spinning Tales: Ngugi's *Secret Lives and Other Stories,*" in *Ngũgĩ wa Thiong'o: Texts and Contexts,* ed. Charles Cantalupo (Trenton, N.J.: Africa World Press, 1995), 336.

5. David Cook, ed., *Origin East Africa: A Makerere Anthology* (London: Heinemann, 1965), 70–76; hereafter cited in text.

6. D. H. Lawrence, "Figs," in *The Complete Poems of D. H. Lawrence,* vol. 1, ed. Vivian de Sola Pinto and Warren Roberts (New York: Viking, 1964), 282–84; "Bare Fig-Trees," 298–300.

7. Some critics suggest a biographical explanation for this uncertainty. See Abdul R. JanMohamed, *Manichean Aesthetics: The Politics of Literature in*

Colonial Africa (Amherst: University of Massachusetts Press, 1983), 207–8 (hereafter cited in text); Richard Peck, "Hermits and Saviors, Osagyefos and Healers: Artists and Intellectuals in the Works of Ngũgĩ and Armah," *Research in African Literatures* 20, no. 1 (Spring 1989): 29–30.

8. Charles E. Nnolim, "Background Setting: Key to the Structure of Ngugi's *The River Between*," in *Critical Perspectives on Ngugi wa Thiong'o*, ed. G. D. Killam (Washington, D.C.: Three Continents Press, 1984), 141.

9. Ngũgĩ wa Thiong'o, *The River Between* (London: Heinemann, 1965), 10; hereafter cited in text as *River*.

10. G. D. Killam, *An Introduction to the Writings of Ngugi* (London: Heinemann, 1980), 35; hereafter cited in text as Killam 1980.

11. Micere Githae-Mugo, *Visions of Africa: The Fiction of Chinua Achebe, Margaret Laurence, Elspeth Huxley, and Ngugi wa Thiong'o* (Nairobi: Kenya Literature Bureau, 1978), 128–30; Cook and Okenimkpe, *Ngũgĩ wa Thiong'o*, 30. For a discussion of a variety of other explanations of Waiyaki's failure, see Peck, "Hermits and Saviors," 29, 43.

12. Some critics read the novel's closure as a celebration of love as reconciliation. See Killam, *An Introduction to the Writings of Ngugi*, 29–33; and Michael Rice, "*The River Between*—a Discussion," in Killam, *Critical Perspectives on Ngugi wa Thiong'o*, 132–35.

13. Micere Githae-Mugo, *Visions of Africa*, 56–58; Judith Cockrane, "Women as Guardians of the Tribe in Ngugi's Novels," in Killam, *Critical Perspectives on Ngugi wa Thiong'o*, 90–94; Florence Stratton, *Contemporary African Literature and the Politics of Gender* (London: Routledge, 1994), 60.

14. See, for example, Asma El Dareer, *Woman, Why Do You Weep? Circumcision and Its Consequences* (London: Zed Books, 1982); Efua Dorkenoo, *Cutting the Rose: Female Genital Mutilation: The Practice and Its Prevention* (London: Minority Rights, 1994); Hanny Lightfoot-Klein, *Prisoners of Ritual: An Odyssey into Female Genital Circumcision in Africa* (New York: Haworth, 1989); Alice Walker and Pratibha Parmar, *Warrior Marks: Female Genital Mutilation and the Sexual Blinding of Women* (New York: Harcourt Brace, 1993).

15. See Dennis Hickey, "One People's Freedom, One Woman's Pain: Ngugi wa Thiong'o, Alice Walker, and the Problem of Female Circumcision," in Cantalupo, *Ngũgĩ wa Thiong'o: Texts and Contexts*, 231–45. Hickey indicates that Kenyatta's *Facing Mount Kenya* was written as a dissertation under the supervision of Bronislaw Malinowski, a structural-functionalist anthropologist who regarded culture as a complex, indivisible whole (242–43).

16. Ornella Moscucci, "Clitoridectomy, Circumcision, and the Politics of Sexual Pleasure in Mid-Victorian Britain," in *Sexualities in Victorian Britain*, ed. Andrew H. Miller and James Eli Adams (Bloomington: Indiana University Press, 1996), 60–78; Roy Porter, *The Greatest Benefit to Mankind: A Medical History of Humanity* (New York: Norton, 1997), 364.

17. Theodore Natsoulas, "The Politicization of the Ban on Female Circumcision and the Rise of the Independent School Movement in Kenya: The

KCA, the Missions, and Government, 1929–1932," *Journal of Asian and African Studies* 33, no. 2 (May 1998): 138.

18. Vivienne Walt, "Senegalese Women Break with Tradition," *Guardian Weekly* 159, no. 2 (12 July 1998): 19; Joelle Stolz, "Putting a Stop to Excision in Burkina Faso," *Le Monde Diplomatique*, 25 October 1998, 6–7.

19. Cosmo Pieterse and Dennis Duerden, eds., "Ngugi wa Thiong'o," in *African Writers Talking: A Collection of Radio Interviews* (New York: Africana Publishing Corporation, 1972), 122; hereafter cited in text.

20. Ngũgĩ wa Thiong'o, *Weep Not, Child* (London: Heinemann, 1964), 104; hereafter cited in text as *Weep Not*.

21. Eustace Palmer, *An Introduction to the African Novel* (New York: Africana Publishing Corporation, 1972), 2; Killam, *An Introduction to the Writings of Ngugi*, 37–41; Micere Githae-Mugo, *Visions of Africa*, 52–54, 80–82.

22. Sola Soile, "Myth and History in Ngugi's *Weep Not, Child*," in Killam, *Critical Perspectives on Ngugi wa Thiong'o*, 171–72; Cook and Okenimkpe, *Ngũgĩ wa Thiong'o*, 60–61.

23. JanMohamed, in *Manichean Aesthetics*, interprets the novel's closure as inconclusive and therefore "anticlimactic" (194); Micere Githae-Mugo, in *Visions of Africa*, sees the novel's true closure projecting beyond the novel's ending into the future (133).

24. "Koina" was "Koinandu" in the novel's first edition.

25. Peter Nazareth, *An African View of Literature* (Evanston, Ill.: Northwestern University Press, 1974), 132–38, 147–48 (hereafter cited in text as Nazareth 1974); C. Ponnuthurai Savan, "Conrad's Influence on Ngugi," *Kucha* 1, no. 1 (1977): 39–44; Bu-Buakei Jabbi, "Conrad's Influence on Betrayal in *A Grain of Wheat*," *Research in African Literatures* 11, no. 1 (Spring 1980): 50–83; Jacqueline Bardolph, "Ngugi wa Thiong'o's *A Grain of Wheat* and *Petals of Blood* as Readings of Conrad's *Under Western Eyes* and *Victory*," *Conradian* 12, no. 1 (1987): 32–49; Byron Caminero-Santangelo, "Neocolonialism and the Betrayal Plot in *A Grain of Wheat*: Ngũgĩ wa Thiong'o's Re-Vision of *Under Western Eyes*," *Research in African Literatures* 29, no. 1 (Spring 1998): 139–52.

26. JanMohamed, *Manichean Aesthetics*, 218–20, 222; James Decker, "Mugo and the Silence of Oppression," in *The World of Ngũgĩ wa Thiong'o*, ed. Charles Cantalupo (Trenton, N.J.: Africa World Press, 1995), 45–57.

27. The postscript on Kurtz's report on the "Suppression of Savage Customs" reads: "Exterminate all the brutes!" Joseph Conrad, *Heart of Darkness*, ed. D. C. R. A. Goonetilleke (Peterborough, Ont.: Broadview, 1995), 142, 117.

28. Govind Narain Sharma, "Ngugi's Christian Vision: Theme and Pattern in *A Grain of Wheat*," in Killam, *Critical Perspectives on Ngugi wa Thiong'o*, 201–10.

29. Neil Lazarus, *Resistance in Postcolonial African Fiction* (New Haven, Conn.: Yale University Press, 1990), 213 (hereafter cited in text); Nazareth, *An African View of Literature*, 148–51.

Chapter Three

1. Hansel Nolumbe Eyoh, "Ngugi wa Thiong'o: Interviewed by Hansel Nolumbe Eyoh," *Journal of Commonwealth Literature* 21 (1986): 166; hereafter cited in text.

2. James Ngugi, "Editorial," *Zuka*, no. 2 (May 1968): [4].

3. Roger A. Berger, "Ngũgĩ's Comic Vision," *Research in African Literatures* 20, no. 1 (Spring 1989): 2–3.

4. In Conrad's *Heart of Darkness,* Africa is similarly "a place of darkness" for Marlow (*Heart of Darkness,* ed. D. C. R. A. Goonetilleke [Peterborough, Ont.: Broadview, 1995]), 67.

5. Killam, *An Introduction to the Writings of Ngugi,* 114; Cyril Treister, "Review: An Addition to the Genre of the Proletariat Novel," in *Critical Perspectives on Ngugi wa Thiong'o,* ed. G. D. Killam (Washington, D.C.: Three Continents Press, 1984), 267; Jacqueline Bardolph, "East Africa," in *The Commonwealth Novel since 1960,* ed. Bruce King (London: Macmillan, 1991), 56.

6. Clara Tsabedze, *African Independence from Francophone and Anglophone Voices: A Comparative Study of the Post-independence Novels by Ngugi and Sembène* (New York: Peter Lang, 1994).

7. Killam, *An Introduction to the Writings of Ngugi,* 96–118; Eustace Palmer, "Ngugi's *Petals of Blood,*" in Killam, *Critical Perspectives on Ngugi wa Thiong'o,* 271–84; hereafter cited in text.

8. Clifford B. Robson, *Ngugi wa Thiong'o* (London: Macmillan, 1979), 101; Lewis Nkosi, "A Voice from Detention," *West Africa,* no. 3162 (20 February 1978): 334–35; Stewart Crehan, "The Politics of the Signifier: Ngugi wa Thiong'o's *Petals of Blood,*" in *Postcolonial Literatures: Achebe, Ngugi, Desai, Walcott,* ed. Michael Parker and Roger Starkey (London: Macmillan, 1995), 101–26.

9. Eustace Palmer, "Ngugi's *Petals of Blood,*" 165; Jacqueline Bardolph, "East Africa," 54–56. Lewis Nkosi argues that "*Petals of Blood* is not so much a novel as an attempt to think aloud about the problems of modern Kenya," in "A Voice from Detention," 334–35. Homi Bhabha perceptively suggests in a review that *Petals of Blood* founders on the horns of a formal dilemma: the socialist realist novel's close resemblance to the classic realist novel. The result of "Ngugi's failure to find an appropriate and original form," Bhabha argues, is the creation of a perfect hero, the failure to integrate the murder plot with the novel's socialist theme, and the idealization of historical change, in "African Praxis," *Times Literary Supplement,* 12 August 1977, 989.

10. Simon Gikandi, *Reading the African Novel* (London: James Currey, 1987), 146; Simon Gikandi, "Ngũgĩ's Conversion: Writing and the Politics of Language," *Research in African Literatures* 23, no. 1 (Spring 1992): 139; hereafter cited in text as Gikandi 1992.

11. Bernth Lindfors, *Popular Literatures in Africa* (Trenton, N.J.: Africa World Press, 1991), 81; hereafter cited in text as Lindfors 1991.

12. Joseph McLaren, "Ideology and Form: The Critical Reception of *Petals of Blood,*" in *The World of Ngũgĩ wa Thiong'o,* ed. Charles Cantalupo (Trenton, N.J.: Africa World Press, 1995), 87–88.

13. Jomo Kenyatta, *Suffering without Bitterness: The Founding of the Kenya Nation* (Nairobi: East African Publishing House, 1968), 343.

14. Katherine Frank, "Feminist Criticism and the African Novel," *African Literature Today* 14 (1984): 34–48; Florence Stratton, "The Shallow Grave: Archetypes of Female Experience in African Fiction," *Research in African Literatures* 19 (1988): 143–69; Charles A. Nama, "Daughters of Moombi: Ngugi's Heroines and Traditional Gikuyu Aesthetics," in *Ngambika: Studies of Women in African Literature,* ed. Carole Boyce Davies and Anne Adams Graves (Trenton, N.J.: Africa World Press, 1986), 139–49. Emmanuel Ngara, "The Portrayal of Women in African Literature," *Kunapipi* 11, no. 3 (1989): 34–40.

15. This potential revolution fails to convince, Neil Lazarus and James A. Ogude argue, because peasants and workers are present only in romanticized type characters like Karega, contrived authorial mouthpieces spouting slogans. "Ngugi's workers experience monopoly capitalism and imperialism, not concrete lived experience," claims Ogude, who sees Ngũgĩ's "predicament" as the absence of a proletariat in Kenyan history, which forced him to create a historical fantasy (4). Ogude perhaps underestimates the effect of the novel's hybridized genres and the centrality of the vacillating Munira, who is poised helplessly between Karega's idealized, usable past and a vague hope for a transformed future. See Neil Lazarus, *Resistance in Postcolonial African Fiction,* 213 (hereafter cited in text); and James A. Ogude, "Imagining the Oppressed in Conditions of Marginality and Displacement: Ngugi's Portrayal of Heroes, Workers, and Peasants," *Wasafiri,* no. 28 (Autumn 1998): 3–9.

16. Ngũgĩ wa Thiong'o, "On Writing in Gikuyu," *Research in African Literatures* 16 (1985): 152.

17. Christopher Wise, "Resurrecting the Devil: Notes on Ngũgĩ's Theory of the Oral-Aural African Novel," *Research in African Literatures* 28, no. 1 (Spring 1997): 134–40; Gĩtahi Gĩtĩtĩ, "Recuperating a 'Disappearing' Art Form: Resonances of 'Gĩcaandĩ' in Ngũgĩ wa Thiong'o's *Devil on the Cross,*" in Cantalupo, *The World of Ngũgĩ wa Thiong'o,* 114.

18. Albert S. Gérard, *African Language Literatures: An Introduction to the Literary History of Sub-Saharan Africa* (Harlow, Essex: Longman, 1981), 308, notes the existence of Gĩkũyũ adaptations of *The Pilgrim's Progress* in upper-grade primary-school readers.

19. See John Lonsdale, "The Moral Economy of Mau Mau: Wealth, Poverty, and Civic Virtue in Kikuyu Political Thought," in *Unhappy Valley: Conflict in Kenya and Africa* (London: James Currey, 1992), 442–43, on the Christian belief and rituals of Mau Mau fighters.

20. Alec J. C. Pongweni, "The Chimurenga songs of the Zimbabwean War of Liberation," in *Readings in African Popular Culture,* ed. Karin Barber (Bloomington: Indiana University Press, 1997), 63–72.

21.   David Sweetman, "Adding to the Howl of Anguish," *Times Literary Supplement,* 18 June 1982, 676; Andrew Gurr, *"Journal of Commonwealth Literature* and the Implied Reader," *Journal of Commonwealth Literature* 21 (1986), 4–8; Reed Way Dasenbrock, review of *Devil on the Cross, World Literature Today* 58, no. 1 (Winter 1984): 153.

22.   Nama, "Daughters of Moombi," 146; Ngara, "The Portrayal of Women in African Literature," 39; Jennifer Evans, "Women and Resistance in Ngugi's *Devil on the Cross,"* in *Women in African Literature Today,* ed. Eldred Durosimi Jones (London: James Currey, 1987), 131–39; hereafter cited in text.

23.   Mary Louise Pratt, *Imperial Eyes: Travel Writing and Transculturation* (London: Routledge, 1992), 166.

24.   Ngũgĩ wa Thiong'o, *Matigari,* trans. Wangũi wa Goro (Oxford: Heinemann, 1987), 65; hereafter cited in text.

25.   Simon Gikandi, "The Epistemology of Translation: Ngũgĩ, *Matigari* and the Politics of Language," *Research in African Literatures* 22, no. 4 (Winter 1991): 161–67.

26.   Ngũgĩ wa Thiong'o, *Njamba Nene na Mbaathi ĩ Mathagu* (Nairobi: Heinemann Educational Books, 1982); *Njamba Nene and the Flying Bus,* trans. Wangũi wa Goro, 1986. Ngũgĩ wa Thiong'o, *Bathitoora ya Njamba Nene* (Nairobi: Heinemann Educational Books, 1984); *Njamba Nene's Pistol,* trans. Wangũi wa Goro, 1986. Ngũgĩ wa Thiong'o, *Njamba Nene na Cibũ Kĩng'ang'i* (Nairobi: Heinemann Educational Books, 1986). My focus here is primarily on the first two stories translated into English by Wangũi wa Goro; *Njamba Nene and the Flying Bus* and *Njamba Nene's Pistol* are hereafter cited in text. An earlier version of some of this discussion of *The Adventures of Njamba Nene* appears in a forthcoming essay collection entitled *Voices of the Other: Colonial and Postcolonial Children's Literature* (Garland), ed. Roderick McGillis.

27.   Osayimwense Osa, *African Children's and Youth Literature* (New York: Twayne, 1995), xi (hereafter cited in text); Nancy J. Schmidt, *Children's Fiction about Africa in English* (Owerri: Conch Magazine, 1981), 132 (hereafter cited in text).

28.   Kĩmani wa Njogu, "Decolonizing the Child," in Cantalupo, *The World of Ngũgĩ wa Thiong'o,* 135.

29.   In "Ngũgĩ wa Thiong'o's Mau Mau for Children," *Children's Literature Association Quarterly* 20, no. 3 (Fall 1995): 129–34, Frederick Hale concludes that the series is "poorly developed and transparently propagandistic" because it simplifies the complexities of Mau Mau's contribution to Kenyan independence "into a crassly dualistic presentation of history" (133).

30.   Carol Sicherman, "Ngugi's British Education," in *Ngũgĩ wa Thiong'o: Texts and Contexts,* ed. Charles Cantalupo (Trenton, N.J.: Africa World Press, 1995), 35–46.

31.   Simon Gikandi, "Moments of Melancholy: Ngũgĩ and the Discourse of Emotions," in Cantalupo, *The World of Ngũgĩ wa Thiong'o,* 71.

32. Meja Mwangi, "Interview with Meja Mwangi," interview by Bernth Lindfors, *Mazungumzo: Interviews with East African Writers, Publishers, Editors, and Scholars,* ed. Bernth Lindfors, Papers in International Studies, Africa Series, no. 41 ([Athens, Ohio]: Ohio University Center for International Studies, 1980), 74.

33. Rose Njoki Gecau, *Kikuyu Folktales* (Nairobi: East African Literature Bureau, 1970), 3–4; Schmidt, *Children's Fiction about Africa in English,* 172, 178.

Chapter Four

1. Gĩtahi Gĩtĩtĩ, "Recuperating a 'Disappearing' Art Form: Reso-nances of 'Gĩcaandĩ' in Ngũgĩ wa Thiong'o's *Devil on the Cross,*" in *The World of Ngũgĩ wa Thiong'o,* ed. Charles Cantalupo (Trenton, N.J.: Africa World Press, 1995), 109–27.

2. J. Ndukaku Amankulor, "English-Language Drama and Theater," in *A History of Twentieth-Century African Literatures,* ed. Oyekan Owomoyela (Lincoln: University of Nebraska Press, 1993), 140.

3. Wole Soyinka, *Art, Dialogue, and Outrage: Essays on Literature and Culture* (London: Methuen, 1988), 134.

4. Ngugi wa Thiong'o, *The Black Hermit* (Oxford: Heinemann, 1968), vii; hereafter cited in text.

5. Taban lo Liyong, "Can We Correct Literary Barrenness in East Africa?" in *The Last Word: Cultural Synthesism,* by Taban lo Liyong (Nairobi: East African Publishing House, 1969), 23–42. L. A. Mbughuni more optimistically reviews East African dramatic production in the period, concluding with an attack on the formal weaknesses of Ngũgĩ's early plays, in "Old and New Drama from East Africa: A Review of the Works of Four Contemporary Dramatists: Rebecca Njau, Ebrahim Hussein, Peninah Muhando, and Ngugi," *African Literature Today* 8 (1976): 85–98.

6. Soyinka's *The Lion and the Jewel* was performed by the Makerere College Dramatic Society in November 1963, a production reviewed by Ngũgĩ in *Transition* 3, no. 12 (January–February 1964): 55, although this performance is not included in James Gibbs's production history of the play in "The Masks Hatched Out," *Theatre Research International* 7, no. 3 (1982): 181. Five months before the production of *The Black Hermit* in November 1962, moreover, Soyinka read from his plays at Makerere's Conference of African Writers of English Expression, 11–17 June 1962, as noted by Bloke Modisane in "African Writers' Summit," *Transition* 2, no. 5 (July–August 1962): 5–6. The confer-ence was attended and enthusiastically reviewed by Ngũgĩ. In addition, through Gerald Moore, director of extramural studies at Makerere, Ngũgĩ may have been familiar with two other plays by Soyinka: *The Trials of Brother Jero* and *A Dance of the Forests.* In a theater review published in the month of the con-ference, Moore refers to these plays. See "Macbeth and African Drama," *Transi-tion* 2, no. 4 (June 1962): 27–28.

7. Wole Soyinka, *Myth, Literature, and the African World* (Cambridge: Cambridge University Press, 1976), 42; hereafter cited in text as Soyinka 1976.

8. Ngugi wa Thiong'o and Micere Githae Mugo, *The Trial of Dedan Kimathi* (Oxford: Heinemann, 1976), [iv]; hereafter cited in text as *Trial*.

9. F. Odun Balogun, *Ngugi and African Postcolonial Narrative: The Novel as Oral Narrative in Multigenre Performance* (St. Hyacinthe, Quebec: World Heritage Press, 1997), 37.

10. Peter Nazareth, "Brave New Cosmos," in *Origin East Africa: A Makerere Anthology,* ed. David Cook (London: Heinemann, 1965), 174.

11. Matthew Arnold, "Stanzas from the Grande Chartreuse," in *Victorian Prose and Poetry,* ed. Lionel Trilling and Harold Bloom (New York: Oxford University Press, 1973), 600.

12. Ngugi wa Thiong'o, *This Time Tomorrow* (Nairobi: East African Literature Bureau, [1970]), 13; hereafter cited in text.

13. Carol Sicherman, "Ngugi wa Thiong'o as Mythologizer and Mythologized," in *From Commonwealth to Post-Colonial,* ed. Anna Rutherford (Sydney, New South Wales: Dangaroo, 1992), 262–69.

14. Ngũgĩ wa Thiong'o and Ngũgĩ wa Mĩriĩ, *I Will Marry When I Want* (Oxford: Heinemann, 1982), 101; hereafter cited in text as *I Will Marry*.

15. Ingrid Björkman, *"Mother, Sing for Me": People's Theatre in Kenya* (London: Zed Books, 1989), viii; hereafter cited in text. Björkman indicates that the play was "written by Ngugi wa Thiong'o" [vii], whereas the blurb on the back cover of *I Will Marry When I Want* refers to "the Gikuyu musical by the two Ngũgĩs, *Mother, Cry for Me."*

16. Celeste Fraser Delgado, "MotherTongues and Childless Women: The Construction of 'Kenyan' 'Womanhood,' " in *The Politics of (M)Othering: Womanhood, Identity, and Resistance in African Literature,* ed. Obioma Nnaemeka (London: Routledge, 1997), 130–46.

17. Manthia Diawara, *African Cinema: Politics and Culture* (Bloomington: Indiana University Press, 1992), 117.

18. Robert Cancel, "Nadine Gordimer Meets Ngũgĩ wa Thiong'o: Text into Film in 'Oral History,' " *Research in African Literatures* 26, no. 3 (Fall 1995): 41–46.

19. A video of *Sembene: The Making of African Cinema* may be viewed at the Avery Fisher Center for Music and Media, Bobst Library, New York University (VCA 8221). The executive producer of the film, Mary Schmidt Campbell of the Tisch School of the Arts, is negotiating the film's general release, which has been delayed because of problems relating to the film's music; Manthia Diawara informed me of this by telephone in the summer of 1998.

20. See Manthia Diawara, "Toward a Regional Imaginary in Africa," in *The Cultures of Globalization,* ed. Fredric Jameson and Masao Miyoshi (Durham, N.C.: Duke University Press, 1998), 113; a slightly different version of this text appears in Diawara's *In Search of Africa* (Cambridge, Mass.: Harvard University Press, 1998), 141.

21. See Diawara's discussion of the narrative of return in *In Search of Africa*, 86–119.

Chapter Five

1. Chidi Amuta, *The Theory of African Literature: Implications for Practical Criticism* (London: Zed Books, 1989), 96.
2. Albert Gérard, in "Is Anything Wrong with African Literary Studies," in *Research Priorities in African Literatures*, ed. Bernth Lindfors (New York: Hans Zell, 1984), refers to the "negritude fallacy" of homogenized Africanness (22); Tsenay Serequeberhan offers a cogent critique of Senghor's "ethnophilosophy" in *The Hermeneutics of African Philosophy*, 6, 42–53.
3. Wole Soyinka, "NEO-TARZANISM: The Poetics of Pseudo-Tradition," *Transition* 48 (1975): 38–44.
4. V. I. Lenin, *Imperialism: The Highest Stage of Capitalism* (New York: International Publishers, 1939), 88–89. For an alternative reading of the inevitability of colonialism and imperialism, see V. Y. Mudimbe, *The Invention of Africa: Gnosis, Philosophy, and the Order of Knowledge* (Bloomington: Indiana University Press, 1988), 2–5.
5. Serequeberhan regards Nkrumah's "universal scientific socialism" as yet another European imposition on Africa rather than a distinctively "African socialism" (*Hermeneutics of African Philosophy*, 34–41). For a critical reading of the achievements and challenges of postindependence Africa and "African socialism" of the 1960s, see onetime Nyerere adviser René Dumont, *False Start in Africa*, 2d ed. (New York: Praeger, 1970).
6. Serequeberhan, *Hermeneutics of African Philosophy*, 102–15; Anthony Arnove, "Pierre Bourdieu, the Sociology of Intellectuals, and the Language of African Literature," *Novel: A Forum on Fiction* 26, no. 3 (Spring 1993): 282–83. Basil Davidson, *The Search for Africa: History, Culture, Politics* (New York: Times Books, 1994), 239–43.
     For the indigenous postcolonial elite to lose their cultural alienation from the masses, Cabral insists on the intellectual's committing "class suicide" and breaking the association with the elite (Davidson, *The Search for Africa*, 219–26). Cabral holds that such a "reconversion of minds—of mentalities" is indispensable for "assimilated intellectuals," in "National Liberation and Culture," *Transition* 45 (1974): 12–17. This "reconversion of minds" recalls the title of Ngũgĩ's collection *Decolonising the Mind*.
7. C. P. Sarvan, "Racism and the 'Heart of Darkness,'" *International Fiction Review* 7, no. 1 (1980): 9.
8. V. Y. Mudimbe, *The Idea of Africa* (Bloomington: Indiana University Press, 1994), 201–2 (hereafter cited in text as Mudimbe 1994); Emmanuel Chukwudi Eze, "Introduction: Philosophy and the (Post)colonial," in *Postcolonial African Philosophy: A Critical Reader*, ed. Emmanuel Chukwudi Eze (Cambridge: Blackwell, 1997), 1–21.

9. See Ioan Davies, "Negotiating African Culture: Toward a Decolonization of the Fetish," in *The Culture of Globalization,* ed. Fredric Jameson and Masao Miyoshi (Durham, N.C.: Duke University Press, 1998), 125–32, for an account of the politics of African cultural identity in Mudimbe, Appiah, and Ngũgĩ.

10. Like Appiah, Manthia Diawara frames his more recent account of African modernism, *In Search of Africa,* with a memoir of his return to Guinea, from which his family was exiled years before, to locate a childhood friend.

11. Anthony Arnove, "Pierre Bourdieu, the Sociology of Intellectuals, and the Language of African Literature," 284; William Slaymaker, "Mirrors and Centers: A Rortyan Reading of Ngũgĩ's Liberation Aesthetics," *Research in African Literatures* 26, no. 4 (Winter 1995): 95–96.

12. Sara Suleri, *Meatless Days* (Chicago: Chicago University Press, 1989), 105.

13. Ngũgĩ wa Thiong'o, introduction to *Africa's Cultural Revolution,* by Okot p'Bitek (Nairobi: Macmillan, 1973), ix–xiii.

14. Matthew Arnold, *Culture and Anarchy* (1869), ed. Samuel Lipman (New Haven, Conn.: Yale University Press, 1994).

15. Carol Sicherman, "Revolutionizing the Literature Curriculum at the University of East Africa: Literature and the Soul of the Nation," *Research in African Literatures* 29, no. 3 (Fall 1998): 129.

16. Paulo Freire, *Pedagogy of the Oppressed* (Harmondsworth, Middlesex: Penguin, 1972); hereafter cited in text.

17. V. S. Naipaul visited Makerere a few years after Ngũgĩ's period of study. See Paul Theroux, *Sir Vidia's Shadow: A Friendship across Five Continents* (Toronto: McClelland and Stewart, 1998).

18. George Lamming, *In the Castle of My Skin* (Burnt Mill, Harlow, Essex: Longman, 1953), 29; hereafter cited in text.

19. V. S. Naipaul, *Miguel Street* (London: Penguin, 1971).

20. John Povey, in his review of the first edition of *Writers in Politics* in *World Literature Today* 55, no. 4 (Autumn 1981), writes: "Those tired clichés exemplify what is so dismaying about this book. No matter what one's general sympathy for much of Ngugi's view, his diction is banal, and that is a devastating accusation to launch at a writer. But use of secondhand phrases from socialist tracts, as George Orwell properly reminded us, is not accidental but is clear evidence of avoiding original thought. There are excellent reasons to teach Kenyan children in Swahili rather than in English, as Ngugi advocates. His recommendation carries less credence when couched in slogans such as 'Neocolonial profit hunting adventures' or 'imperialist cultural domination in the cultural struggle.' The only familiar animal I missed was the legendary 'fascist hyena' " (717).

21. Mao Tse-tung, *Talks at the Yenan Forum on Literature and Art* (Beijing: Commercial Publishing House, 1972), 45.

22. W. E. B. Du Bois, *The Souls of Black Folk* (New York: Penguin, 1989), 11.

23.   Kamau Brathwaite, "Limuru and Kinta Kunte," in *Ngũgĩ wa Thiong'o: Texts and Contexts,* ed. Charles Cantalupo (Trenton, N.J.: Africa World Press, 1995), 1–11.

24.   Oliver Lovesey, "Chained Letters: African Prison Diaries and 'National Allegory,' " *Research in African Literatures* 26, no. 4 (1995): 30–45.

25.   Jack Mapanje, *The Chattering Wagtails of Mikuyu Prison* (Oxford: Heinemann, 1993), 82–83, writes of a similar prophetic appearance of flying geese when he was a political prisoner in Malawi.

26.   Henry Chakava, "Publishing Ngugi: The Challenge, the Risk, and the Reward," *Matatu: Journal for African Culture and Society* 15–16 (1996): 183–200.

27.   Georg M. Gugelberger refers to it as a "Sartreian and Mayakovskyan title" in " 'When Evil-Doing Comes like Falling Rain': Brecht, Alioum Fantouré, Ngugi wa Thiong'o," *Comparative Literature Studies* 24, no. 4 (1987): 380.

28.   Frantz Fanon, *Black Skins, White Masks,* trans. Charles Lam Markmann (New York: Grove Press, 1967).

29.   The postcolonial intellectual has largely been ignored in studies of Ngũgĩ. A notable exception is Patrick Williams's " 'Like Wounded Birds'? Ngugi and the Intellectuals," *Yearbook of English Studies* 27 (1997): 201–18. Williams responds to Edward Said's demand for analysis of the intellectual's construction in terms of image, signature, and intervention. Ngũgĩ's intellectual, for Williams, is an important though deeply conflicted figure, and one who has evolved throughout Ngũgĩ's writing. In Ngũgĩ's later works, Williams finds positive representations of intellectuals, including even Gatuĩria in *Devil on the Cross,* who, like Ngũgĩ himself, successfully combines a grasp of theory and political activism.

30.   Gugelberger finds more of Brecht's influence in Ngũgĩ's essays and novels than in his plays ("When Evil-Doing Comes like Falling Rain," 377–83).

31.   Ngũgĩ wa Thiong'o, "Ngũgĩ wa Thiong'o: Moving the Centre: An Interview by Charles Cantalupo," in Cantalupo, *The World of Ngũgĩ wa Thiong'o,* 208.

32.   See Manthia Diawara, "Toward a Regional Imaginary in Africa," in Jameson and Miyoshi, *The Cultures of Globalization,* 103–24, on cultural and economic globalization in Africa, and the space of the West African market as a site of resistance. Some of this material also appears in chapter 5 of Diawara's *In Search of Africa,* 134–62.

33.   Taban lo Liyong, "Ministers to the Toothless," *Ariel: A Review of International English Literature* 29, no. 2 (April 1998): 111.

34.   In "(Re)turn to the People: Ngũgĩ wa Thiong'o and the Crisis of Postcolonial African Intellectualism," in Cantalupo, *The World of Ngũgĩ wa Thiong'o,* Neil Lazarus commends Ngũgĩ's "contribut[ion] to the reanimation of radical African intellectualism" (12).

35.   Michel Foucault, *Discipline and Punish: The Birth of the Prison,* trans. Alan Sheridan (New York: Vintage, 1995), 195–228.

Selected Bibliography

PRIMARY SOURCES

Novels

Weep Not, Child. London: Heinemann, 1964.
The River Between. London: Heinemann, 1965.
A Grain of Wheat. London: Heinemann, 1967.
Petals of Blood. London: Heinemann, 1977.
Devil on the Cross. Trans. Ngũgĩ wa Thiong'o. London: Heinemann, 1982.
A Grain of Wheat. Rev. ed. London: Heinemann, 1986.
Matigari. Trans. Wangũi wa Goro. Oxford: Heinemann, 1987.

Short Stories

Secret Lives and Other Stories. London: Heinemann, 1975.

Children's Stories

Njamba Nene and the Flying Bus. Trans. Wangũi wa Goro. Nairobi: Heinemann, 1986.
Njamba Nene's Pistol. Trans. Wangũi wa Goro. Nairobi: Heinemann, 1986.
Njamba Nene na Cibũ Kĩng'ang'i. Nairobi: Heinemann, 1986.

Plays

The Black Hermit. Oxford: Heinemann, 1968.
This Time Tomorrow. Nairobi: East African Literature Bureau, [1970].
Ngugi wa Thiong'o and Micere Githae Mugo. *The Trial of Dedan Kimathi.* Oxford: Heinemann, 1976.
Ngũgĩ wa Thiong'o and Ngũgĩ wa Mĩriĩ. *I Will Marry When I Want.* Oxford: Heinemann, 1982.

Films

Sembene: The Making of African Cinema. 1994. Directed by Ngũgĩ wa Thiong'o and Manthia Diawara. Produced by the Tisch School of the Arts, New York University, and Manthia/Ngũgĩ Productions in association with Channel 4 Television U.K. Assistant production coordination by Njeeri wa Ngũgĩ. Translation by Francois Manchuelle. 60 minutes. Videocassette.

Essays and Nonfiction Prose

Homecoming: Essays on African and Caribbean Literature, Culture, and Politics. London: Heinemann, 1972.

Detained: A Writer's Prison Diary. London: Heinemann, 1981.

Writers in Politics. 1st ed. London: Heinemann, 1981.

Barrel of a Pen: Resistance to Repression in Neo-colonial Kenya. London: New Beacon, 1983.

Decolonising the Mind: The Politics of Language in African Literature. London: James Currey, 1986.

Moving the Centre: The Struggle for Cultural Freedoms. London: James Currey, 1993.

Writers in Politics: A Re-engagement with Issues of Literature and Society. 2d ed., rev. and enl. Oxford: James Currey, 1997.

Penpoints, Gunpoints, and Dreams: Towards a Critical Theory of the Arts and the State in Africa. Oxford: Clarendon, 1998.

SECONDARY SOURCES

Bibliographies

Sicherman, Carol. *Ngugi wa Thiong'o: A Bibliography of Primary and Secondary Sources, 1957–1987.* London: Hans Zell, 1989.

———. *Ngugi wa Thiong'o: The Making of a Rebel, a Source Book in Kenyan Literature and Resistance.* London: Hans Zell, 1990.

Books and Parts of Books

Amooti wa Irumba, Katebalirwe. "Ngugi wa Thiong'o's Literary Production: A Materialist Critique." D. Phil. diss., University of Sussex, 1980.

Balogun, F. Odun. "Ngugi's *Devil on the Cross:* The Novel as Hagiography of a Marxist." In *Postcolonial Literatures: Achebe, Ngugi, Desai, Walcott,* ed. Michael Parker and Roger Starkey, 127–42. London: Macmillan, 1995.

———. *Ngugi and African Postcolonial Narrative: The Novel as Oral Narrative in Multigenre Performance.* St. Hyacinthe, Quebec: World Heritage Press, 1997.

Bardolph, Jacqueline. *Ngugi wa Thiong'o.* Paris: Présence Africaine, 1991.

Björkman, Ingrid. *"Mother, Sing for Me": People's Theatre in Kenya.* London: Zed Books, 1989.

Boehmer, Elleke. "The Master's Dance to the Master's Voice: Revolutionary Nationalism and the Representation of Women in the Writing of Ngugi wa Thiong'o." In *Postcolonial Literatures: Achebe, Ngugi, Desai, Walcott,* ed. Michael Parker and Roger Starkey, 143–54. London: Macmillan, 1995.

Cantalupo, Charles, ed. *Ngũgĩ wa Thiong'o: Texts and Contexts.* Trenton, N.J.: Africa World Press, 1995.

———, ed. *The World of Ngũgĩ wa Thiong'o.* Trenton, N.J.: Africa World Press, 1995.

Cook, David, and Michael Okenimkpe. *Ngũgĩ wa Thiong'o: An Exploration of His Writings.* 2d ed. Oxford: James Currey, 1997.

Crehan, Stewart. "The Politics of the Signifier: Ngugi wa Thiong'o's *Petals of Blood.*" In *Postcolonial Literatures: Achebe, Ngugi, Desai, Walcott,* ed. Michael Parker and Roger Starkey, 101–26. London: Macmillan, 1995.

Davies, Ioan. "Negotiating African Culture: Toward a Decolonization of the Fetish." In *The Cultures of Globalization,* ed. Fredric Jameson and Masao Miyoshi, 125–45. Durham, N.C.: Duke University Press, 1998.

Delgado, Celeste Fraser. "MotherTongues and Childless Women: The Construction of 'Kenyan' 'Womanhood.' " In *The Politics of (M)Othering: Womanhood, Identity, and Resistance in African Literature,* ed. Obioma Nnaemeka, 130–46. London: Routledge, 1997.

Dramé, Kandioura. *The Novel as Transformation Myth: A Study of the Novels of Mongo Beti and Ngugi wa Thiong'o.* Syracuse, N.Y.: Maxwell School of Citizenship and Public Affairs, Syracuse University, 1990.

Evans, Jennifer. "Women and Resistance in Ngugi's *Devil on the Cross.*" In *Women in African Literature Today,* ed. Eldred Durosimi Jones et al., 131–39. London: James Currey, 1987.

Gikandi, Simon. "Character and Consciousness in *Petals of Blood.*" In *Reading the African Novel,* 134–48. London: James Currey, 1987.

Gurnah, Abdulrazak. "Transformative Strategies in the Fiction of Ngũgĩ wa Thiong'o." In *Essays on African Writing,* ed. Abdulrazak Gurnah, 142–58. Oxford: Heinemann, 1993.

Gurr, Andrew. *Writers in Exile: The Identity of Home in Modern Literature.* Brighton: Harvester, 1981.

JanMohamed, Abdul R. "Ngugi wa Thiong'o: The Problems of Communal Regeneration." In *Manichean Aesthetics: The Politics of Literature in Colonial Africa,* 185–223. Amherst: University of Massachusetts Press, 1983.

Kamenju, Grant. "*Petals of Blood* as a Mirror of the African Revolution." In *Marxism and African Literature,* ed. Georg M. Gugelberger, 130–35. Trenton, N.J.: Africa World Press, 1986.

Killam, G. D. *An Introduction to the Writings of Ngugi.* London: Heinemann, 1980.

———, ed. *Critical Perspectives on Ngugi wa Thiong'o.* Washington, D.C.: Three Continents Press, 1984.

Larson, Charles R. "The 'Situational' Novel: The Novels of James Ngugi (Kenya)" and "Characters and Modes of Characterization: Chinua Achebe (Nigeria), James Ngugi (Kenya), and Peter Abrahams (South Africa)." In *The Emergence of African Fiction,* 113–66. Bloomington: Indiana University Press, 1972.

Lindfors, Bernth. *"Petals of Blood* as a Popular Novel." In *Popular Literatures in Africa,* 79–86. Trenton, N.J.: Africa World Press, 1991.

Lovesey, Oliver. " 'The Sound of the Horn of Justice' in Ngũgĩ wa Thiong'o's Narrative." In *Postcolonial Literature and the Biblical Call for Justice,* ed. Susan VanZanten Gallagher, 152–68. Jackson: University Press of Mississippi, 1994.

Maughan-Brown, David. "Not Yet the Freedom." In *Land, Freedom, and Fiction: History and Ideology in Kenya,* 230–65. London: Zed Books, 1985.

——. "Ngugi wa Thiong'o (James Ngugi)." In *Twentieth-Century Caribbean and Black African Writers,* 2d series, ed. Bernth Lindfors and Reinhard Sander, 145–69. Detroit, Mich.: Gale Research, 1993.

Mugo, Micere Githae-. *Visions of Africa: The Fiction of Chinua Achebe, Margaret Laurence, Elspeth Huxley, and Ngugi wa Thiong'o.* Nairobi: Kenya Literature Bureau, 1978.

Nama, Charles A. "Daughters of Moombi: Ngugi's Heroines and Traditional Gikuyu Aesthetics." In *Ngambika: Studies of Women in African Literature,* ed. Carole Boyce Davies and Anne Adams Graves, 139–49. Trenton, N.J.: Africa World Press, 1986.

Nazareth, Peter. "Is *A Grain of Wheat* a Socialist Novel?" In *An African View of Literature,* 128–54. Evanston, Ill.: Northwestern University Press, 1974.

——. "The Second Homecoming: Multiple Ngugis in *Petals of Blood.*" In *Marxism and African Literature,* ed. Georg M. Gugelberger, 118–29. Trenton, N.J.: Africa World Press, 1986.

Palmer, Eustace. "James Ngugi." In *An Introduction to the African Novel,* 1–47. New York: Africana Publishing, 1972.

Robson, Clifford B. *Ngugi wa Thiong'o.* London: Macmillan, 1979.

Sicherman, Carol. "Ngugi wa Thiong'o as Mythologizer and Mythologized." In *From Commonwealth to Post-Colonial,* ed. Anna Rutherford, 259–75. Sydney, New South Wales: Dangaroo, 1992.

Stratton, Florence. "Gender on the Agenda: Novels of the 1980s by Ngũgĩ and Achebe." In *Contemporary African Literature and the Politics of Gender,* 158–70. London: Routledge, 1994.

Tsabedze, Clara. *African Independence from Francophone and Anglophone Voices: A Comparative Study of the Post-independence Novels by Ngugi and Sembéne.* New York: Peter Lang, 1994.

Articles

Arnove, Anthony. "Pierre Bourdieu, the Sociology of Intellectuals, and the Language of African Literature." *Novel: A Forum on Fiction* 26, no. 3 (Spring 1993): 278–96.

Bamiro, Edmund O. "Recasting the Centre: Ngũgĩ wa Thiong'o and the Africanization of English." *Kunapipi* 16, no. 2 (1994): 65–76.

Bardolph, Jacqueline. "Ngugi wa Thiong'o's *A Grain of Wheat* and *Petals of Blood* as Readings of Conrad's *Under Western Eyes* and *Victory.*" *Conradian* 12, no. 1 (May 1987): 32–49.

Berger, Roger A. "Ngũgĩ's Comic Vision." *Research in African Literatures* 20, no. 1 (Spring 1989): 1–25.

Bhabha, Homi. "African Praxis." Review of *Petals of Blood. Times Literary Supplement,* 12 August 1977, 989.

Caminero-Santangelo, Byron. "Neocolonialism and the Betrayal Plot in *A Grain of Wheat:* Ngũgĩ wa Thiong'o's Re-vision of *Under Western Eyes.*" *Research in African Literatures* 29, no. 1 (Spring 1998): 139–52.

Cancel, Robert. "Nadine Gordimer Meets Ngũgĩ wa Thiong'o: Text into Film in 'Oral History.' " *Research in African Literatures* 26, no. 3 (Fall 1995): 36–48.

Chakava, Henry. "Publishing Ngugi: The Challenge, the Risk, and the Reward." *Matatu: Journal for African Culture and Society* 15–16 (1996): 183–200.

Dasenbrock, Reed Way. Review of *Devil on the Cross, World Literature Today* 58, no. 1 (Winter 1984): 153.

Eyoh, Hansel Nolumbe. "Ngugi wa Thiong'o: Interviewed by Hansel Nolumbe Eyoh." *Journal of Commonwealth Literature* 21 (1986): 162–66.

Frank, Katherine. "Feminist Criticism and the African Novel." *African Literature Today* 14 (1984): 34–48.

Gikandi, Simon. "The Epistemology of Translation: Ngũgĩ, *Matigari,* and the Politics of Language." *Research in African Literatures* 22, no. 4 (Winter 1991): 161–67.

———. "Ngũgĩ's Conversion: Writing and the Politics of Language." *Research in African Literatures* 23, no. 1 (Spring 1992): 131–44.

Gugelberger, Georg M. " 'When Evil-Doing Comes like Falling Rain': Brecht, Alioum Fantouré, Ngugi wa Thiong'o." *Comparative Literature Studies* 24, no. 4 (1987): 370–86.

Gurnah, Abdulrazak. "*Matigari*: A Tract of Resistance." *Research in African Literatures* 22, no. 4 (Winter 1991): 169–72.

Gurr, Andrew. "*Journal of Commonwealth Literature* and the Implied Reader." *Journal of Commonwealth Literature* 21 (1986): 4–8.

Hale, Frederick. "Ngũgĩ wa Thiong'o's Mau Mau for Children." *Children's Literature Association Quarterly* 20, no. 3 (Fall 1995): 129–34.

Harrow, Kenneth. "Ngũgĩ wa Thiong'o's *A Grain of Wheat*: Season of Irony." *Research in African Literatures* 16, no. 2 (Summer 1985): 243–63.

Hooper, Glenn. "History, Historiography and Self in Ngũgĩ's *Petals of Blood.*" *Journal of Commonwealth Literature* 33, no. 1 (1998): 47–62.

Indangasi, Henry. "Ngugi's Ideal Reader and the Postcolonial Reality." *Yearbook of English Studies* 27 (1997): 193–200.

Jabbi, Bu-Buakei. "Conrad's Influence on Betrayal in *A Grain of Wheat.*" *Research in African Literatures* 11, no. 1 (Spring 1980): 50–83.

Jackson, Thomas H. "Orality, Orature, and Ngũgĩ wa Thiong'o." *Research in African Literatures* 22, no. 1 (Spring 1991): 5–15.

Jussawalla, Feroza. "The Language of Struggle: Ngũgĩ wa Thiong'o on the Prisonhouse of Language." *Transition,* no. 54 (1991): 142–54.

Kessler, Kathy. "Rewriting History in Fiction: Elements of Postmodernism in Ngũgĩ wa Thiong'o's Later Novels." *Ariel: A Review of International English Literature* 25 (April 1994): 75–90.

Lindfors, Bernth. "Ngugi wa Thiong'o's Early Journalism." *World Literature Written in English* 20 (Spring 1981): 23–41.

Loflin, Christine. "Ngũgĩ wa Thiong'o's Visions of Africa." *Research in African Literatures* 26, no. 4 (Winter 1995): 76–93.

Lovesey, Oliver. "Chained Letters: African Prison Diaries and 'National Allegory.'" *Research in African Literatures* 26, no. 4 (Winter 1995): 30–45.

Maughan-Brown, David. "Four Sons of One Father: A Comparison of Ngugi's Earliest Novels with Works by Mwangi, Mangua, and Wachira." *Research in African Literatures* 16, no. 2 (Summer 1985): 179–209.

———. "*Matigari* and the Rehabilitation of Religion." *Research in African Literatures* 22, no. 4 (Winter 1991): 173–80.

Mbele, Joseph. "Language in African Literature: An Aside to Ngũgĩ." *Research in African Literatures* 23, no. 1 (Spring 1992): 145–51.

Mbughuni, L. A. "Old and New Drama from East Africa: A Review of the Works of Four Contemporary Dramatists: Rebecca Njau, Ebrahim Hussein, Peninah Muhando, and Ngugi." *African Literature Today* 8 (1976): 85–98.

Ngara, Emmanuel. "The Portrayal of Women in African Literature." *Kunapipi* 11, no. 3 (1989): 34–40.

Nkosi, Lewis. "A Voice from Detention." *West Africa* (20 February 1978): 334–35.

Ogude, James A. "Imagining the Oppressed in Conditions of Marginality and Displacement: Ngugi's Portrayal of Heroes, Workers, and Peasants." *Wasafiri,* no. 28 (Autumn 1998): 3–9.

Palmer, Eustace. "Ngugi's *Petals of Blood.*" *African Literature Today* 10 (1979): 153–66.

Peck, Richard. "Hermits and Saviors, Osagyefos and Healers: Artists and Intellectuals in the Works of Ngũgĩ and Armah." *Research in African Literatures* 20, no. 1 (Spring 1989): 26–49.

Sackey, Edward. "Oral Tradition and the African Novel." *Modern Fiction Studies* 37, no. 3 (Autumn 1991): 389–407.

Sharma, Govind Narain. "Ngũgĩ's *Detained* as a Modern *Consolatio.*" *Research in African Literatures* 19, no. 4 (Winter 1988): 520–28.

———. "Socialism and Civilization: The Revolutionary Traditionalism of Ngugi wa Thiong'o." *Ariel: A Review of International English Literature* 19 (1988): 21–30.

Sicherman, Carol M. "Ngugi wa Thiong'o and the Writing of Kenyan History." *Research in African Literatures* 20, no. 3 (Spring 1989): 347–70.

————. "Revolutionizing the Literature Curriculum at the University of East Africa: Literature and the Soul of the Nation." *Research in African Literatures* 29, no. 3 (Fall 1998): 129–48.

Simatei, Peter. "Versions and Inversions: Mau Mau in Kahiga's *Dedan Kimathi: The Real Story.*" *Research in African Literatures* 30, no. 1 (Spring 1999): 154–61.

Slaymaker, William. "Mirrors and Centers: A Rortyan Reading of Ngũgĩ's Liberation Aesthetics." *Research in African Literatures* 26, no. 4 (Winter 1995): 94–103.

Stratton, Florence. "The Shallow Grave: Archetypes of Female Experience in African Fiction." *Research in African Literatures* 19 (1988): 143–69.

Williams, Katherine. "Decolonizing the Word: Language, Culture, and Self in the Works of Ngũgĩ wa Thiong'o and Gabriel Okara." *Research in African Literatures* 22 (Winter 1991): 53–61.

Williams, Patrick. " 'Like Wounded Birds'? Ngugi and the Intellectuals." *Yearbook of English Studies* 27 (1997): 201–18.

Wise, Christopher. "Resurrecting the Devil: Notes on Ngũgĩ's Theory of the Oral-Aural African Novel." *Research in African Literatures* 28, no. 1 (Spring 1997): 134–40.

Index

The Author

Oliver Lovesey teaches at Okanagan University College, Canada. He has published a number of articles on postcolonial and Victorian literature, and a monograph on George Eliot.

The Editor

Bernth Lindfors is a professor of English and African literatures at the University of Texas at Austin. He has written and edited more than 30 books, including *Black African Literature in English* (1979, 1986, 1989, 1995), *Popular Literatures in Africa* (1991), *Comparative Approaches to African Literatures* (1994), *Long Drums and Canons: Teaching and Researching African Literatures* (1995), *Loaded Vehicles: Studies in African Literary Media* (1996), and (with Reinhard Sander) *Twentieth-Century Caribbean and Black African Writers* (1992, 1993, 1996). From 1970 to 1989 he was editor of *Research in African Literatures*.